AQA
A-level

Psychology
Revision Made Easy

D1614691

95800000052030

HODDER
EDUCATION
AN HACHETTE UK-COMPANY

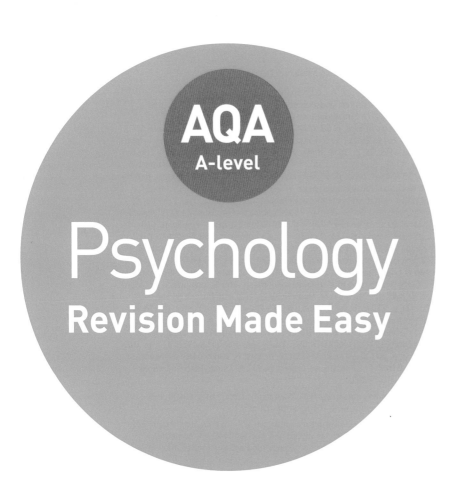

AQA
A-level

Psychology
Revision Made Easy

Jean-Marc Lawton

HODDER
EDUCATION
AN HACHETTE UK COMPANY

The Publishers would like to thank the following for permission to reproduce copyright material.

Photo credits

p. 2 © Kenzo Tribouillard/AFP/Getty Images; **p. 4** © Christopher Dodson/iStockphoto.com; **p. 6** © epa european pressphoto agency b.v./Alamy Stock Photo; **p. 8** © Philip G. Zimbardo, Inc.; **p. 10** © Photo News Service Ltd/TopFoto; **p. 12** © RTimages – Fotolia; **p. 18** © EHStock/E+/Getty Images; **p. 22** © HOWARD JONES/NEWZULU/PA Images; **p. 28** © photogerson – Fotolia; **p. 30** Map data © 2014 Google, reproduced with permission; **p. 32** © Courtesy Everett Collection/REX Shutterstock; **p. 36** © Tom Wang – Fotolia; **p. 38** © Monkey Business – Fotolia; **p. 40** © Rob – Fotolia; **p. 42** © Jeffrey Phelps/Aurora Photos/Corbis; **p. 44** © Monkey Business – Fotolia; **p. 48** © Mike Abrahams/Alamy Stock Photo; **p. 50** © imtmphoto – Fotolia; **p. 55** © epa/Corbis; **p. 57** © Howard Berman/Iconica/Getty Images; **p. 60** © Everett Collection/REX Shutterstock; **p. 62** © Lijuan Guo – Fotolia; **p. 66** © adimas – Fotolia; **p. 70** © Simons, D. J., & Chabris, C. F. (1999). Gorillas in our midst: Sustained inattentional blindness for dynamic events. Perception, 28, 1059–1074. www.dansimons.com or www.theinvisiblegorilla.com; **p. 72** © Papirazzi – Fotolia; **p. 74** © Illustrated London News; **p. 94** © Quasarphoto – Fotolia; **p. 99** © AF archive/Alamy; **p. 100** © luminastock – Fotolia; **p. 120** © michaeljayberlin – Fotolia; **p. 122** © laszlolorik – Fotolia; **p. 124** © michaeljung – Fotolia; **p. 130** © vinnstock – Fotolia; **p. 132** © nyul – Fotolia; **p. 134** © Kalim – Fotolia; **p. 136** © Sashkin – Fotolia; **p. 138** © Syda Productions – Fotolia; **p. 140** © 2005 TopFoto; **p. 142** © The Power of Forever Photography/Getty Images; **p. 144** © ALFRED PASIEKA/SCIENCE PHOTO LIBRARY; **p. 146** © Olga Semicheva – Fotolia; **p. 148** © Illustrated London News; **p. 150** © Laurence Gough – Fotolia; **p. 154** © AFP/Getty Images; **p. 156** © auremar – Fotolia; **p. 160** © lunaundmo – Fotolia; **p. 162** © willypd – Fotolia; **p. 164** © Duane Howell/The Denver Post, MediaNews Group/Getty Images; **p. 166** © SSilver – Fotolia; **p. 168** © gstockstudio – Fotolia; **p. 172** © JackF – Fotolia; **p. 174** © Grafvision – Fotolia; **p. 178** © RioPatuca Images – Fotolia; **p. 180** © Digital Vision/Getty Images; **p. 186** © Friedberg – Fotolia; **p. 188** © Jean-Marc Lawton; **p. 190** © Van D. Bucher/Science Photo Library; **p. 192** Courtesy Han G. Brunner; **p. 194** © michael luckett – Fotolia; **p. 196** © ALBERT BANDURA, STANFORD CENTER ON ADOLESCENCE, STANFORD UNIVERSITY; **p. 198** © igor – Fotolia; **p. 200** © Lopolo – Shutterstock; **p. 204** © AP/Press Association Images; **p. 206** © Mary Evans Picture Library/Alamy; **p. 208** © alphaspirit – Fotolia; **p. 210** © Delphotostock – Fotolia; **p. 212** © Directphoto Collection/Alamy; **p. 214** © nito – Fotolia; **p. 216** © aleciccotelli – Fotolia.

Every effort has been made to trace all copyright holders, but if any have been inadvertently overlooked, the Publishers will be pleased to make the necessary arrangements at the first opportunity.

Although every effort has been made to ensure that website addresses are correct at time of going to press, Hodder Education cannot be held responsible for the content of any website mentioned in this book. It is sometimes possible to find a relocated web page by typing in the address of the home page for a website in the URL window of your browser.

Hachette UK's policy is to use papers that are natural, renewable and recyclable products and made from wood grown in sustainable forests. The logging and manufacturing processes are expected to conform to the environmental regulations of the country of origin.

Orders: please contact Bookpoint Ltd, 130 Park Drive, Milton Park, Abingdon, Oxon OX14 4SE. Telephone: +44 (0)1235 827720. Fax: +44 (0)1235 400454. Email education@bookpoint.co.uk Lines are open from 9 a.m. to 5 p.m., Monday to Saturday, with a 24-hour message answering service. You can also order through our website: www.hoddereducation.co.uk

ISBN: 978 1 4718 4523 9

© Jean-Marc Lawton 2017

First published in 2017 by

Hodder Education,

An Hachette UK Company

Carmelite House

50 Victoria Embankment

London EC4Y 0DZ

www.hoddereducation.co.uk

Impression number   10 9 8 7 6 5 4 3 2 1

Year   2021 2020 2019 2018 2017

Cover photo © Maya Kruchancova – Fotolia

Typeset in India by Aptara, Inc.

Printed in Italy

A catalogue record for this title is available from the British Library.

Contents

How to use this book   1

1 Social influence

Types of conformity   2
Explanations for conformity   4
Variables affecting conformity   6
Conformity to social roles   8
Obedience and the work of Milgram   10
Explanations for obedience   12
Situational variables affecting obedience   14
The dispositional explanation of the authoritarian personality (AP)   16
Explanations of resistance to social influence   18
Minority influence   20
The role of social influence processes in social change   22

2 Memory

The multi-store model (MSM)   24
The working memory model (WMM)   26
Types of long-term memory (LTM)   28
Explanations for forgetting   30
Factors affecting the accuracy of eyewitness testimony (EWT)   32
Improving the accuracy of eyewitness testimony (EWT)   34

3 Attachment

Caregiver–infant interactions in humans   36
Stages of attachment development   38
The role of the father   40
Animal studies of attachment   42
Explanations of attachment   44
Ainsworth's 'Strange Situation'   46
Bowlby's maternal deprivation hypothesis (MDH) (1951)   48
The influence of early attachment on childhood and adult relationships   50

4 Psychopathology

Definitions of abnormality: deviation from social norms   52
Definitions of abnormality: failure to function adequately   54
Definitions of abnormality: deviation from ideal mental health   56
Definitions of abnormality: statistical infrequency   58

Characteristics of phobias, depression and OCD   60
The behavioural approach to explaining and treating phobias   62
The cognitive approach to explaining and treating depression   64
The biological approach to explaining and treating OCD   66

5 Approaches
The behaviourist approach   68
The origins of psychology and the cognitive approach   70
The biological approach   72
The psychodynamic approach   74
The humanistic approach   76
Comparison of approaches   78

6 Biopsychology
The nervous system and neurons   82
The influence of biochemistry on behaviour   84
Localisation of function in the brain   86
Split brain surgery and plasticity and functional recovery of the brain after trauma   88
Ways of studying the brain   90
Biological rhythms   92

7 Research methods
Experimental method and design   94
Non-experimental methods and design   96
Aims, hypotheses, operationalisation of variables, demand characteristics
and pilot studies   98
Sampling and ethical issues   100
Observational design and questionnaire and interview construction   102
The peer review process and implications of research for the economy   104
Reliability and validity   106
Features of science   108
Reporting psychological investigations   110
Quantitative and qualitative data   112
Presentation and display of quantitative data; distributions   114
Inferential testing   118

8 Issues and debates
Gender and culture in psychology   120
Free will and determinism   122
The nature–nurture debate   124

Holism and reductionism 126

Idiographic and nomothetic approaches to psychological investigation 128

Ethical implications of research studies and theory 130

9 Relationships

The evolutionary explanation for partner preferences 132

Factors affecting attraction in romantic relationships 134

Theories of romantic relationships 136

Virtual relationships in social media 138

Parasocial relationships 140

10 Gender

Sex and gender 142

The role of chromosomes and hormones 144

Cognitive explanations for gender development 146

Psychodynamic explanation for gender development 148

Social learning theory as applied to gender development 150

Atypical gender development 152

11 Cognition and development

Piaget's theory of cognitive development 154

Vygotsky's theory of cognitive development 156

Baillargeon's explanation of early infant abilities 158

The development of social cognition 160

The role of the mirror neuron system in social cognition 162

12 Schizophrenia

Classification of schizophrenia 164

Biological explanations for schizophrenia 166

Psychological explanations for schizophrenia 168

Therapies for the treatment of schizophrenia 170

The importance of the interactionist approach in explaining and treating schizophrenia 172

13 Eating behaviour

Explanations for food preferences 174

Neural and hormonal mechanisms involved in the control of eating behaviour 176

Explanations for anorexia nervosa 178

Explanations for obesity 180

14 Stress

The physiology of stress   182

The role of stress in illness   184

Sources and physiological measures of stress   186

Individual differences in stress   188

Managing and coping with stress   190

15 Aggression

Neural and hormonal mechanisms in aggression   192

The ethological and evolutionary explanations for aggression 194

Social psychological explanations for human aggression   196

Institutional aggression in the context of prisons   198

Media influences on aggression   200

16 Forensic psychology

Problems in defining crime   202

Offender profiling   204

Biological explanations for offending behaviour   206

Psychological explanations for offending behaviour   208

Dealing with offending behaviour   210

17 Addiction

Describing addiction and risk factors in the development of addiction   212

Explanations for nicotine addiction   214

Explanations for gambling addiction   216

Reducing addiction   218

The application of theories of behaviour change to addictive behaviour   220

18 Revision and exam skills

Revision   222

Exam skills   224

Question practice: selection questions   226

Question practice: short-answer questions   228

Question practice: application questions   230

Question practice: research methods questions   232

Question practice: research study questions   238

Question practice: essays and longer answer questions   242

How to use this book

This book will help you revise for your AQA A-level Psychology specification. It is designed so that you can use it alongside any appropriate textbook, including *AQA Psychology for A-level 1 and 2*, by Jean-Marc Lawton and Eleanor Willard. We have included page references to appropriate material in these books on each spread.

pp4 – 9

Each spread covers a different topic, outlining the headline factual knowledge you need, as well as providing evaluation material to help you aim for those top marks.

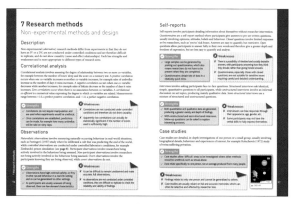

Research methods and techniques are also covered in an interesting way to help you retain and recall the information.

At the end of the book you will find guidance on making sure you are ready to tackle the exams!

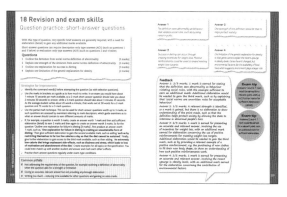

1 Social influence
Types of conformity

Focal study

Asch (1955) investigated whether individuals would conform to an obviously wrong answer. 123 American male student volunteers, having been told that it was a study into visual perception, were tested in groups of between 8 and 10. The participants sat in a line or around a table. A stimulus line was presented with 3 comparison lines, 1 clearly matching the stimulus line while the other 2 did not. Participants had to say out loud which comparison line matched the stimulus. In each group there was in fact only 1 real participant, who answered either last or next to last – the other group members were all *confederates* (pseudo-participants). From 18 trials, confederates gave identical wrong answers on 12 occasions. There was a 32 per cent overall conformity rate to the wrong answers, 75 per cent conforming at least once, 25 per cent never conforming, while 5 per cent conformed all the time. It was also found that most participants conformed publicly, but not privately, a form of *compliance*, in order to avoid rejection.

OTHER STUDIES

- Mori & Arai (2010) replicated Asch's study (though using females as well as males), giving filter goggles to participants, so that one participant perceived a different comparison line to all the others. This meant *demand characteristics* (where participants attempt to guess the aim of a study and act accordingly) could not occur, unlike in Asch's study where the participant might realise the confederates were lying and so just pretended to conform. Females conformed similarly to Asch's participants, but the males a lot less. The study was unethical, as participants thought the goggles were to prevent glare.
- Bogdonoff et al. (1961) measured the stress levels encountered by participants on an Asch-type task, by recording galvanic skin responses – a measurement of electrical conductivity. High stress levels were found when participants gave true answers that went against the majority, but lower levels when individuals complied with obviously wrong answers, implying compliance to be a healthy response.

Description

Conformity occurs when a majority of people influence the beliefs and/or behaviour of a minority. There are 3 types, differing in terms of how much they affect individuals' belief systems.

1. *Compliance* involves public, but not private, agreement with a group's beliefs and behaviour, in order to gain acceptance or avoid disapproval. It is fairly temporary and weak, and only occurs within the presence of the group. For example, an individual claims allegiance to the local football team in order to fit in and be accepted, but in reality has little if any allegiance to the team.

2. *Identification* involves public and private agreement with a group's

Fig 1.1 A religious conversion would be an example of internalisation

- Mann (1969) believed internalisation to be *true conformity*, as it is the only type of majority influence where participants are actually converted to other people's belief systems.
- *Internalisation* relates to *minority influence* (see **page 20**), which allows carefully considered *social change* (see **page 22**) to occur.
- *Compliance* allows individuals to conduct meaningful social interactions by constantly fitting in with and adapting to different groups' social norms.
- *Compliance* relates more to *normative social influence*, where individuals conform to fit in, while *identification* and *internalisation* relate more to *informational social influence*, as individuals genuinely agree with the behaviour they are conforming to.

beliefs and behaviour, because membership of that group is beneficial. A stronger type than compliance, it is still fairly temporary and weak, as it is not retained when an individual leaves the group. For instance, a soldier adopts the beliefs and behaviour of fellow soldiers while in the army, but adopts new beliefs and behaviour on returning to civilian life.

3 *Internalisation* involves public and private agreement and is not dependent on group membership. It is the strongest form of conformity. For instance, beliefs in a religious faith are not dependent on group members being present.

✖ Negative evaluation

✖ There are other reported reasons for why people conform in Asch's study, such as having doubts about individual perceptual ability and the accuracy of individual judgements. Therefore, it may not just be compliance that is occurring.

✖ Most studies of types of conformity, such as Asch's and Mori & Arai's, are unethical and arguably should not be performed, as they involve deceit and therefore a lack of informed consent, as well as possibly causing distress through elevating stress levels.

✖ Asch's study was time-consuming, with only 1 participant being tested at a time. As 123 participants performed 18 trials each, the experiment was conducted 2,214 times.

Practical application

Compliance helps to maintain social order, through majority influence allowing people to unthinkingly know what behaviour and attitudes are expected of them and stick to them. Internalisation meanwhile converts people's belief systems, so that social change occurs through innovative behaviours becoming accepted as mainstream.

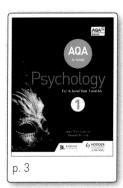
p. 3

1 Social influence
Explanations for conformity

Focal study

Jenness (1932) investigated the effect of group influence on individual judgements, by getting participants to estimate the number of jellybeans in a jar, first as individuals, then in a large group or several small groups, and finally as individuals again. It was found that participants' second individual estimates moved closer to their group estimates than their first individual estimates, with a greater effect seen among females than males. This suggests that ISI occurs in ambiguous and new situations where there is no clear correct answer. This study is more ethical than most conformity studies, as there is no deliberate deceit involved. However, like Asch's study, it was a laboratory-based experiment using an artificial and non-lifelike situation and as such lacks realism. There may also be an element of NSI, with some participants conforming due to a desire for acceptance and not just to be correct.

OTHER STUDIES

- Sherif (1935) used the *autokinetic effect*, a visual illusion, to find participants' second individual estimates – of how far a dot of light in a dark room appeared to move – converged towards a group norm after participants heard the estimates of others. This supports ISI and suggests that participants *internalised* others' judgements and made them their own.

- Bogdonoff *et al.* (1961) measured the stress levels encountered by participants on an Asch-type task, by recording galvanic skin responses – a measurement of electrical conductivity. High stress levels were found when participants gave true answers that went against the majority, but lower levels when individuals complied with obviously wrong answers, which suggests that NSI not only involves compliance, but is also a healthy thing to do.

- Eagli & Carli (1981) found in a meta-analysis of 48 studies that females conform more in public situations, suggesting that females' more nurturing, co-operative nature causes them to have a greater need for social agreement.

Description

Deutsch & Gerard (1955) suggested 2 explanations of conformity, *informational social influence* (ISI) and *normative social influence* (NSI).

Underlying ISI is a need for certainty that brings a sense of control. ISI occurs in ambiguous situations with no clear 'correct' way of behaving, as well as in novel situations not experienced before. In such situations individuals look to the majority for information on how to behave. This involves *social comparison* with others in order to reduce uncertainty. For instance, when eating in a restaurant for the first time you may look to others for which cutlery,

Fig 1.2 How many jellybeans are in the jar?

✔ As well as having research support, both NSI and ISI can be used to explain and understand real-life examples of conformist behaviour, giving them additional support as explanations.

✔ Asch initially criticised Jenness' earlier study as inferior due to having no obvious wrong answer to conform to. However, both studies are equally effective in helping to highlight explanations for conformity: ISI in Jenness' case and NSI in Asch's case.

✔ NSI and ISI should not be seen as opposing explanations; they can be combined together to give an overall explanation of conformity. Different individuals in the same situation may be conforming for reasons of NSI or ISI.

glasses etc. to use. ISI therefore involves stronger types of conformity, such as identification and internalisation, where public and private agreement with a majority occurs.

Underlying NSI is a need to belong, by being accepted and avoiding rejection and ridicule. Individuals agree with others because of their power to reward and punish – for instance, giving in to peer pressure to smoke, even though you may not wish to, in order to be accepted by the group. NSI therefore tends to involve a weaker form of conformity, compliance, where public, but not private, agreement occurs.

✘ ISI can have harmful consequences in crisis situations, where negative emotions and panic can spread quickly. Jones *et al.* (2000) reported that *psychogenic* illnesses, such as mass hysteria, can occur in crisis situations through individuals having little time to think and so looking to others for cues as to how to behave.

✘ NSI can also have harmful consequences. Jordan (1996) reported that due to ridicule, punishment and rejection of non-conforming group members, 12 teenage victims of such bullying killed themselves in 1 year in Japan. NSI can also lead to destructive inter-group violence.

Practical application

To help create group cohesion (unity) in sports teams, ambiguous tasks with no correct answer/ behaviour could be set, so that team members are drawn closer together through ISI.

pp. 4–9

1 Social influence
Variables affecting conformity

Focal study

Asch's variations (1956)

1 With 1 participant and 1 confederate, conformity was very low, rising to 13 per cent with 1 participant and 2 confederates, and up to 32 per cent with 1 participant and 3 confederates. Increasing confederate numbers (up to as high as 15) produced no further increases in conformity.

2 If 1 confederate sided with the real participant by giving the correct answer, conformity dropped from 32 per cent to just 5.5 per cent. More interestingly, if a confederate went against the group but gave a different wrong answer, conformity still dropped, down to 9 per cent. This suggests that the important factor is the reduction in the majority's level of agreement, rather than an individual being given support for their private opinion.

3 When task difficulty was increased, by having comparison lines more similar to each other, conformity to wrong answers increased, demonstrating the effect of task difficulty on conformity.

OTHER STUDIES

- Maslach et al. (1987) found males conform less, as they are more independent and competitive, while females conform more, as they are sensitive to others' needs and like to maintain harmony, thus explaining gender differences in conformity levels.

- Tong et al. (2008) found participants were more likely to conform to wrong answers to maths questions given by confederates when they were in a positive mood rather than in a negative or neutral one, demonstrating the effect of mood on conformity levels.

- Milgram (1961) found that Norwegians conformed more than French participants to obviously wrong answers. Avant & Knudson (1993) believe this occurs as Norway has shared cultural values, a dislike of individualism and fewer ethnic minorities with different cultural norms than France, suggesting a cultural basis for differences in conformity levels.

Description

Asch conducted variations of his study to identify *situational variables*, aspects of the environment that influence levels of conformity. These included:

- *Group size*, which showed that as a majority's size increased, so did the level of conformity, up to a maximum level, after which increases in group size did not lead to any further rise in conformity levels

- *Unanimity*, which showed that conformity rates decreased when majority influence became less unanimous, with group members dissenting against other group members' behaviour

- *Task difficulty*, which showed that greater conformity occurred when task difficulty increased, as the correct answer was less

Fig 1.3 Norwegians are conformist as they share cultural values and norms

- Pike & Laland (2010) found that stickleback fish show increased imitation of 'demonstrator' fish eating at food-rich sites, but that the rate of such conformity declines as the number of demonstrator fish increases, suggesting an evolutionary survival value to conformity.
- Asch's study became a *paradigm* study, the accepted method of investigating conformity. Indeed it is still relevant, as it forms the basis of Mori & Arai's (2010) study (see **page 2**).
- Probably the best way to understand conformity is to see situational and individual variables as acting together to determine overall levels of conformity, rather than them acting on their own.

obvious and so individuals increasingly looked to others for guidance as to the correct answer.

Research has also identified *individual variables*, characteristics of people that influence conformity levels. Important variables here include:

- *Gender*, with females conforming more, possibly due to females being socialised to be more submissive to social influence
- *Mood*, with individuals seen to conform more when in happy moods and when moving to more relaxed emotional states, possibly because they are then more amenable to majority influence
- *Culture*, with some cultures conforming more, as they possess shared values and uniformity, thus making agreement with others easier.

- Higher female conformity may actually result from poor methodology. Eagly & Carli (1981) reported that male researchers find females conform more, possibly because they use experimental materials more familiar to men, thus creating an artificial form of ISI for females to conform to.
- Even if females do conform more, it may not be because women are socialised by society, but instead because evolution has acted upon women to be more co-operative with others.
- There are studies that cast doubt on Asch's findings. Gerard et al. (1968) found conformity rates do rise as more confederates are added (though at an increasingly smaller rate).

Practical application
Advertisers focus on the unanimity of majority influence to sell products. This relates to the 'bandwagon effect', where if individuals believe all members of a group have a product, like a certain mobile phone, then purchase of that phone will allow them to be accepted into the group.

pp. 9–12

1 Social influence
Conformity to social roles

Focal study

Zimbardo (1973) investigated the extent to which people would conform to the roles of guard and prisoner in a simulation of prison life. The participants were 21 students, who were selected for their physical and mental stability and lack of criminal history. A realistic mock prison was set up and the prisoners *dehumanised* (their individual identity was removed) by being made to wear prison uniforms and referred to by numbers instead of names. The uniformed guards' role was to keep order, though physical punishment was banned. Over the course of the experiment, the guards became increasingly abusive and most prisoners increasingly submissive. Four prisoners were released due to their poor mental state. Scheduled to run for 2 weeks, the study was stopped after 6 days when Zimbardo realised the extent of the harm that was occurring. The study illustrated that individuals conform readily to the social roles expected in a situation, even when such roles override individuals' moral beliefs.

OTHER STUDIES

- Haslam & Reicher (2002) replicated Zimbardo's study, aiming to investigate the behaviour of groups that were unequal in terms of power and status. Participants were randomly selected as guards or prisoners, with the guards constructing prison rules and punishments for breaking them. The prisoners increasingly developed a group identity, but the guards did not and were reluctant to impose authority. They were overcome by the prisoners. The participants then set up an equal social system, but this proved unsustainable and attempts to impose a harsher regime met with weak resistance, at which point the study ended. It was concluded that powerlessness and the failure of groups allows cruel domination to occur.

- Snyder (1974) found that *high self-monitors* (people who are able to respond to social cues and adjust their behaviour accordingly) were able to adapt their behaviour to fit the needs of different social situations, while the behaviour of *low self-monitors* (people who are less able to respond to social cues and adjust their behaviour accordingly) was more fixed due to innate personality traits. This suggests that some individuals are more able to conform to social roles than others.

Description

Social roles are the actions that people are expected to display in social situations. They involve the behaviours and attitudes which individuals should adopt as members of different social groups in order to fit in with, and meet the requirements of, those social situations. An individual has first to perceive what role they are expected to play within a given social situation, and then meet the expectation by 'playing the part'. Different social situations have different social roles to adopt – for example, there is an expectation that someone will be outgoing and playful at a party, but reserved and serious at a funeral. People learn social roles from

Fig 1.4 Zimbardo's study showed how people conform readily to social roles

✔ Conformity to different social roles in different social situations may have an evolutionary survival value, as it allows us to understand and adapt to the requirements of different situations and thus fit in. Social order is thereby created and maintained, permitting a safe, predictable world for individuals to interact within.

✔ Research into social roles suggests that behaviour in brutalising institutions, such as prisons, can be improved by the provision of less dehumanising environments.

✔ The fact that social roles are not permanent means people can adapt successfully to changing environments and therefore have the flexibility to meet the needs of a diverse range of social situations.

experience and they become internal mental scripts, which individuals select from in order to behave appropriately in different social settings. Conformity to social roles involves *identification* (see **page 2**), which is stronger than *compliance*, as it involves public and private acceptance of the behaviour and attitudes adopted. Conformity to social roles is not as strong as *internalisation*, which is a more permanent form of conformity, as individuals only conform to specific social roles while in particular social situations. They change their behaviour to suit new social norms when they move to new social situations.

✘ Negative evaluation

✘ Zimbardo hoped his research would lead to beneficial changes in the prison system, but he concluded that, as such, his research was a failure because if anything prison conditions have got worse.

✘ Zimbardo's study was unethical: fully informed consent was not given, there were elements of deceit, the right to withdraw was not made clear and, probably most importantly, high levels of both physical and psychological harm occurred.

✘ There seem to be large individual differences in the ability to identify and adopt required social roles. Therefore, some people are less able to successfully adapt to different environments.

Practical application

The move to all-seater football grounds following the Taylor Report (1992) saw a huge reduction in acts of hooliganism, arguably because the less brutal environments thus created led to less aggressive social roles for supporters to conform to.

pp. 13–16

1 Social influence
Obedience and the work of Milgram

Focal study

Milgram (1963) tested 40 American male volunteers, aged between 20 and 50 years, on their willingness to obey increasingly destructive orders. Believing it a study of memory and learning, volunteers drew lots with a second participant, actually a *confederate* (see **page 2**), to see who would be the 'teacher' and who the 'learner'. This was rigged; the real participant was always the teacher. The learner was strapped into a chair in an adjacent room with electrodes attached to him. It was explained by a confederate researcher wearing a laboratory coat (that gave him legitimate authority) that every time the learner got a question wrong the teacher should shock him by pressing a switch on a (fake) shock machine. If the teacher refused, the researcher ordered him to carry on with a series of verbal 'prods' (such as 'the experiment requires you continue'). The shocks went up in 15-volt increments to 450 volts, which was given 3 times per teacher. Initially happy to take part, the learner then began to protest and at 300 volts refused to answer more questions. At 315 volts he screamed loudly and was not heard from again. 100 per cent of participants obeyed up to 300 volts and 62.5 per cent went to 450 volts, even though some wept, some argued, and 3 had seizures. It was concluded that obeying authority figures is usual in a hierarchically arranged society, even when orders violate moral codes.

Description

Obedience is defined as *'complying with the demands of an authority figure'*. Milgram, from a New York Jewish family that fled Europe before the Holocaust, and a student of Asch's, was interested in understanding how 10 million Jews and Gypsies were exterminated on the orders of the Nazis during the Holocaust. He set out to test the 'Germans are different' hypothesis, which argued that the Holocaust occurred because Germans

OTHER STUDIES

- Sheridan & King (1972), by using a puppy receiving real electric shocks, tested the idea that Milgram's participants obeyed because they knew the procedure was false. 53 per cent of male participants and 100 per cent of female participants obeyed to the maximum voltage, suggesting that Milgram's results were valid and that females are more obedient.

- Burger (2009) developed an ethically acceptable variation of Milgram's study, with participants explicitly given the right to withdraw. Using males and females, an obedience rate of 70 per cent was found, suggesting that Milgram's study can be conducted ethically and that obedience rates have not changed in the 50 years since Milgram's study.

- Hofling et al. (1966) tested obedience in the real world, getting a pretend doctor to order real nurses to give an apparent overdose to a patient. 21 out of 22 obeyed, suggesting that obedience to destructive orders from a legitimate authority does occur in the real world.

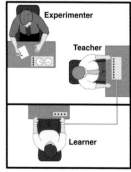

'I observed a mature and initially poised businessman enter the laboratory smiling and confident. Within 20 minutes he was reduced to a twitching, stuttering wreck, who was rapidly approaching nervous collapse. He constantly pulled on his ear lobe, and twisted his hands. At one point he pushed his fist into his forehead and muttered "Oh God, let's stop it". And yet he continued to respond to every word of the experimenter, and obeyed to the end.'

Fig 1.5 The Milgram experiment set up

✔ Milgram's is a *paradigm study* (the accepted method of researching obedience), which has allowed comparison of obedience rates in different countries, between genders, ages and occupations.

✔ Valuable knowledge about obedience was gained; 74 per cent of Milgram's participants said they learned something useful about themselves. Only 2 per cent regretted being involved.

✔ Over 50 years later, Milgram's study continues to fascinate new generations of psychology students, illustrating its long-lasting impact.

blindly obey authority figures. Milgram showed that people are more obedient than they realise, getting participants to apparently carry out painful acts against an unobjectionable stranger purely because a researcher ordered them to. Many objected to the researcher's commands, but obeyed them to the end, showing that individuals do not necessarily agree with orders that they obediently carry out.

✗ Negative evaluation

✗ Milgram's study is unethical. It involves: (1) deceit through confederates believing the shocks were real and that the study involved learning and memory; (2) a lack of informed consent, as deceit was used; (3) no right of withdrawal; (4) psychological harm. Milgram argued that participants could withdraw, as 37.5 per cent of them did; also that the harm was only short-term, was reduced by debriefing and made justifiable by the valuable findings.

✗ Orne & Holland (1968) believed that Milgram's study lacked *internal validity*, as participants knew the shocks were fake. However, 80 per cent of participants had 'no doubts' about the authenticity of the study.

✗ Rank & Jacobsen (1977) argued that Hofling *et al.*'s study lacks external validity. Their more realistic replication, which allowed nurses to consult each other and used Valium, a familiar drug, saw only an 11 per cent obedience rate.

Practical application

The knowledge gained from Milgram's study is used to teach people to recognise and resist attempts to get them to obey destructive orders. Trainee aeroplane pilots undergo simulations where captains give wrongful orders so that they learn how to resist such potentially destructive commands.

pp. 17–25

1 Social influence
Explanations for obedience

Focal study

Milgram (1974) reported on several variations of his study that were designed to identify important variables associated with obedience. In a *remote authority* variation, where the confederate researcher was not in the same room as the real participant, but gave his orders over a telephone, obedience declined from the 62.5 per cent seen in the original study to 20.5 per cent. This suggests that participants were in the *autonomous state* (the opposite end of the *agentic state*) and saw themselves as responsible for their actions. In his original 1963 study, Milgram argued that many participants showed moral strain, for example 3 had seizures, but continued to obey, which suggests they were in an agentic state and felt they had to keep obeying the higher-ranked authority figure. Some participants showed no harm themselves, ignored the learner's distress and concentrated on 'doing their duty', thus seemingly recognising the legitimate authority of the researcher.

Description

Situational explanations focus on environmental factors associated with obedience.

The *agentic state* (part of the *agency theory*) is one such explanation, which sees humans as socialised from an early age to learn that obedience is necessary to maintain social order. This involves individuals seeing themselves as agents of an authority figure and thus giving up and transferring personal responsibility onto that authority figure. (The opposite state in the agency theory is the *autonomous state*, where individuals see themselves as personally responsible for their actions.) The agentic state occurs in hierarchical social systems (where people are in ranks),

OTHER STUDIES

- Tarnow (2000) found that a major contributory factor to 80 per cent of aeroplane accidents was co-pilots feeling that they could not challenge wrong decisions by the captain, due to the perceived power and legitimacy of his authority. This suggests that the perception of legitimate authority helps explain obedient behaviour.

- Hamilton (1978), in a replication of Milgram's study, found that when participants were told they were responsible for what happened, their obedience reduced. This suggests that an increase in personal responsibility and the autonomous state leads to a reduction in obedience.

- The Centre of Risk (2000) reported on how 18-year-old Wayne Jowett, on remission for leukaemia, died when a doctor wrongly ordered a toxic drug to be injected into his spine and a junior doctor obeyed, even though he knew the order to be wrong. This illustrates the strength of the legitimacy of authority.

Fig 1.6 Wayne Jowett died after a junior doctor unquestioningly obeyed the wrongful orders of a more senior colleague

1 Social influence

- ✓ The socialisation process – whereby people learn to obey legitimate authority figures with higher perceived status – can have a beneficial effect, as it enables hierarchical groups to function effectively. This allows meaningful social life within and between groups to occur.
- ✓ Milgram's variations allowed explanations for obedience to be highlighted, thereby identifying the reasons why people obey and allowing a deeper understanding of the phenomenon.

with people obeying those of perceived higher ranks.

The *legitimacy of authority* is another situational explanation, where individuals accept the power and status of authority figures to give orders, which should be obeyed, as such figures are seen as being 'in charge'. This links to the agency theory, as individuals are again seen as being socialised to accept that obedience to authority helps maintain social order. Individuals learn from experience examples of social roles relating to 'master and servant' relationships, such as parent–child, worker–boss etc., which involve accepting that we have a 'duty' to obey those higher in a social hierarchy.

❌ Negative evaluation

- ✗ The agentic state involves individuals giving up some of their *free will* (their conscious control over their thoughts and actions) and therefore their behaviour becomes determined by unconscious forces outside their control. Milgram commented that when his students watched a film of his study they said they would never follow such orders and yet a few months later some of them enlisted in the army to serve in the Vietnam War and follow orders to kill people.
- ✗ Being in the agentic state and following the orders of a legitimate authority involves being *deindividuated*, that is losing self-awareness, which can result in individuals performing actions with negative consequences that go against their moral code.
- ✗ As well as situational explanations, there are *dispositional* explanations, such as gender and culture, which focus on personality characteristics that influence obedience.

Practical application

Due to cases such as that of Wayne Jowett (see **page 12**), staff in institutions like hospitals are now trained to follow official procedures and to have the confidence to challenge wrongful orders from legitimate authority figures, so that similar tragic events do not occur again.

AQA
A-level

Psychology
For A-level Year 1 and AS

1

HODDER

pp. 26–8

1 Social influence
Situational variables affecting obedience

Focal study

Bickman (1974) investigated the effect uniforms have on obedience. In his study, a researcher, dressed either in civilian clothes, as a milkman, or as a security guard, ordered people in the street to pick up rubbish that they had not dropped, loan a coin to a stranger, or to move away from a bus stop. Overall, he found 14 per cent of participants obeyed when the researcher dressed as a milkman, 19 per cent when he dressed in civilian clothes and 38 per cent when he dressed as a security guard. This supports the idea that people obey those in uniform, as it gives them an increased sense of legitimate authority. In a variation of the study, Bickman found that people still obeyed the researcher when dressed as a security guard, even if he walked away after giving the order. This further illustrates the power of uniforms in increasing a sense of legitimate authority.

Description

Situational variables form an *external* explanation of obedience, where aspects of the environment are seen as affecting obedience. Milgram's variations (see Other studies) identified several important situational variables. One such variable is *proximity*, which concerns how aware individuals are of the consequences of obedient behaviour. The closer the proximity individuals have to the consequences of obedient behaviour that has a negative outcome, the less able they are to separate themselves from such consequences and the more likely it is that obedience rates will be lower. For example, most people find it easier to obey an order to press a button that releases a missile that kills people hundreds of miles

OTHER STUDIES

- Milgram (1974) reported that in a variation of his study, when the teacher and learner were in the same room so that the teacher could see the learner's distress, obedience declined from the 62.5 per cent seen in the original study to 40 per cent. When the teacher had to force the learner's hand onto a pretend shock-plate, obedience declined further to 30 per cent. This illustrates the effect of proximity on obedience levels.

- Milgram (1974) reported that another variation, performed in a run-down office, saw obedience fall from 62.5 per cent down to 47.5 per cent when performed in high-status Yale University. This illustrates how location can affect the degree of legitimacy that an authority figure has to deliver orders.

- In Milgram's (1963) study the confederate researcher wore a laboratory coat, which gave him a sense of increased legitimacy of authority and is assumed to have contributed to the high overall obedience rate.

Fig 1.7 Uniforms give a sense of legitimacy to authority

- ✔ Bickman's 1974 study occurred in a real-life setting and so is high in *ecological validity*. Participants did not even know they were in a study, which implies their actions were not artificial.
- ✔ Milgram's variations turn each study into an experiment (something the original study is not) as they create independent variables (IVs) through comparison with the findings from his standard procedure. For example, when the learner is in the same room as the teacher, it creates an IV of whether the learner was visually present or not.
- ✔ Milgram's variations isolate individual situational variables, allowing us to see their specific effects on obedience levels.

away, than obey an order to shoot someone, as the proximity from the consequences of such behaviour would be much closer when shooting someone up close. Another such variable is *location*, with people likely to be more obedient in environments/situations that add to the level of perceived legitimacy that an authority figure issuing orders has. For example, obedience will be higher in institutional rather than non-institutional settings, as with a teacher in a school. An additional variable is *uniforms*, as the wearing of uniforms gives an impression of increased legitimacy to an authority figure issuing orders, as with an army officer.

- ✘ Orne & Holland (1968) argued that Milgram's studies lacked *internal validity*, because participants knew the shocks were fake. However, 80 per cent said they had 'no doubts' about the authenticity of the study.
- ✘ Other situational variables exist too, like *entrapment*, where participants were increasingly 'sucked into' the study by being told to give shocks of ever-increasing voltages. As the voltage of the shocks they gave increased, not obeying became increasingly difficult.
- ✘ Participants may also have obeyed due to *dehumanisation* (degrading people by lessening their human qualities). Milgram (1963) reported that some participants made comments like 'that guy in there was so stupid he deserved to be shocked'.

Practical application
The knowledge gained from studying situational variables has helped psychologists to form methods and strategies for resisting obedience (and conformity), such as the provision of social support.

pp. 29–30

1 Social influence
The dispositional explanation of the authoritaria personality (AP)

Focal study

Adorno *et al.* (1950) designed a questionnaire to measure levels of AP. Nine personality dimensions were assessed: *conventionalism, authoritarian submission, authoritarian aggression, superstition, power* and *toughness, stereotyping, destructiveness* and *cynicism, anti-intraception,* and *sexuality*. The questionnaire was given to 2,000 Americans, with 30 questions in total, such as *'Obedience and respect for authority are the most important virtues children should learn'*. The degree to which individuals agreed with such statements was measured, so that individuals' attitudes towards religious and ethnic minorities, as well as political, economic and moral views, could be determined. A suh-sample of 1 in 10 participants, comprising the most and least prejudiced, with an equal number of males and females, was compared in order to identify factors that gave rise to an AP. These proved to be: a strong belief in absolute obedience, submitting to authority figures, and a mistrust of minorities – supporting the idea that certain personality characteristics are associated with high obedience.

Description

The *dispositional* explanation is an *internal* explanation, as it centres on the idea that certain internal personality characteristics are associated with high levels of obedience (as opposed to the situational explanation, which believes *external* situational factors determine obedience levels). The *authoritarian personality* (AP) was proposed by Fromm (1941) as an attempt to categorise individuals who held right-wing, conservative views. He saw such individuals as having a belief in unquestioning obedience, submission to authority and domination of minorities. Adorno *et al.* (1950) additionally saw such individuals as having insecurities, formed in childhood through having domineering, authoritarian (controlling)

OTHER STUDIES

- Zillmer *et al.* (1995) examined the personality characteristics of 16 Nazi war criminals (comprising both high-ranking officers and lower-ranking soldiers), who were tried at the Nuremberg trials after the Second World War, to ascertain whether a 'Nazi personality' existed – similar to Fromm's idea of the AP. The Nazis scored high on 3 of the 9 F-scale dimensions, but not on all 9 as expected, giving limited support for the concept of an AP.

- Elms & Milgram (1966) found that highly obedient participants in Milgram's study scored significantly higher for authoritarianism on the F-scale than participants who disobeyed and refused to deliver shocks. These findings give stronger support for the idea of an AP that makes people more unquestioningly obedient.

- Altemeyer (1988) found that participants who scored high on the F-scale, who were ordered to give themselves shocks, gave stronger shocks than those who scored low on the F-scale, providing additional support to the existence of an AP type.

✔ Supporting research for the AP shows that dispositional factors (personality) affect obedience levels, as well as situational factors. However, for the best understanding of obedience behaviour, dispositional and situational factors should be considered together.

✔ Milgram found situational factors were stronger than dispositional ones, which led him to conclude that the 'Germans are different' hypothesis was wrong (that Germans have personality traits that make them highly obedient to destructive orders – see **page 10**). However, research into the AP suggests that some people might be more naturally obedient than others, though whether this can be generalised to all people of a certain culture is debatable.

parents, which led them to be hostile to non-conventional people and to have a belief in the need for power and toughness that made them very obedient to authority figures. In order to measure an individual's level of AP, Adorno created the F-scale questionnaire (the 'F' stands for fascist). It has 30 questions that assess 9 personality dimensions. More recently, Jost *et al.* (2003) suggested a more cognitive explanation of AP. They saw it as being motivated by thought processes that underpin a desire to reduce the anxieties and fears that social change brings – obedience is seen to help prevent such disruptive social change.

✗ Negative evaluation

✗ Hyman & Sheatsley (1954) found that lower educational level was a better explanation of high F-scale scores than an authoritarian personality. Cultural and social norms have also been shown to be better predictors of prejudice than personality variables.

✗ Authoritarian individuals do not always score high on F-scale dimensions, while domineering parents do not always produce children with an AP. Nor can the AP explain why individuals may be prejudiced against some minorities, but not others. This lowers support for the concept.

✗ The theory is also politically biased, as it has a negative viewpoint of individuals who hold right-wing, conservative views.

Practical application

If the concept of the AP being a negative personality type formed in childhood is valid, then promoting less domineering and controlling parenting styles should result in fewer people developing the personality type. This in turn should result in the creation of more individuals able to resist orders with potentially negative consequences.

pp. 30–2

1 Social influence

Explanations of resistance to social influence

Focal study

Avtgis (1998) conducted a meta-analysis of studies involving LoC and conformity, in which the average effect size for internal and external LoC was measured. Earlier research had indicated that those scoring high on internal LoC are less easily persuadable, less socially influenced and less conformist than those who score high on external LoC. After subjecting the data to statistical analysis, it was found that these predictions were generally true, with participants who displayed an internal LoC being less easily influenced and therefore more able to resist conformity. These results support the idea that differences in conformist behaviour are related to differences in measures of LoC, which suggests that differences in LoC are linked to differences in the ability to resist social influence.

Description

The consequences of conforming and obeying, although often positive for society, can sometimes be negative. Therefore, it is important that psychologists, as well as understanding why people conform and obey, also know how such social influences can be resisted. Effective strategies for resistance can then be formulated.

One important explanation of resistance is that of *social support*, which involves the perception of assistance and solidarity being available from others. If dissenters (people who go against the attitudes and behaviour of the group) are present in a social group, they break up the *unanimity* of the group, making it easier for individuals to resist social influence to conform and obey. This works even if a dissenter displays a different

OTHER STUDIES

- Asch (1956) (see **page 6**) found that if a confederate dissenter answered correctly from the start of his study, conformity dropped from the usual 32 per cent to 5.5 per cent, but if the confederate only dissented later in the study conformity only dropped to 8.5 per cent. This suggests social support received earlier is more effective than that received later.

- Milgram (1974) in a variation of his study found that when 2 confederate teachers refused to obey and left the study, only 10 per cent of participants gave the maximum shocks, which suggests that *disobedient models* are a powerful source of social support, as they reduce the unanimity of a situation. This makes it easier for an individual to act independently.

- Shute (1975) found that students with an internal LoC, exposed to peers expressing pro-drug attitudes, conformed less to such pro-drug attitudes than students with an external LoC. This supports the idea that having an internal LoC increases resistance to social influence.

Fig 1.8 Whistle-blowers who report illegal activities within institutions tend to have a high internal LoC

✅ **Positive evaluation**

✔ Many studies into social support – such as Asch's variations that concentrated specifically on the role of dissent – are experiments, which isolate and rigorously test individual variables. This demonstrates such variables' specific effects – in Asch's studies, on the ability to resist social influences of conformity and obedience.

✔ The extensive knowledge gained from research into conformity and obedience can be used to formulate and teach effective strategies to help individuals to resist social pressures to conform and obey in situations with potentially negative consequences. Even just being taught about studies like Asch's and Milgram's can help people recognise and therefore resist similar attempts to manipulate their social behaviour.

attitude or behaviour to one preferred by a given individual who also privately disagrees with the group.

Another important explanation is that of *locus of control* (LoC), which involves the extent to which things happen as a result of an individual's choices and decisions. Internal LoC involves the belief that things happen due to internally controlled factors, such as effort, while external LoC involves the belief that things happen as a result of fate and other uncontrollable external forces. Rotter (1966) argued that a high internal LoC made individuals more resistant to social influence, as such individuals see themselves as having a free choice over whether to conform or obey.

❌ **Negative evaluation**

✘ Most research into LoC involves correlations, which do not show causality. Therefore, the direction of the relationship is not known (for example, resisting social influence may create a higher internal LoC, rather than a high internal LoC, making people able to resist social influence). Other non-measured variables may be involved too.

✘ Asch (1956) found that even if a dissenter gave a different wrong answer to other confederates, conformity dropped from 32 per cent to 9 per cent, which suggests it is the reduction in the majority's agreement, rather than the social support given by the dissenter, which is the important factor in resisting social influence.

Practical application

Chui (2004) reports that 'whistle-blowers' (people within institutions who report illegal activities) have a high internal LoC. Therefore, it would be useful for institutions to appoint such people to investigate possible instances of corporate fraud, like paying bribes, money laundering and covering up institutional abuses, such as avoidable hospital deaths.

pp. 33–40

1 Social influence
Minority influence

OTHER STUDIES

- Nemeth (1986) had groups of three participants and one confederate, who were asked to consider how much compensation to pay to an accident victim. When confederates consistently argued for a low amount, they had no effect on the majority, but when they compromised and offered a slightly higher amount, the majority changed their opinion and lowered their original amount. This suggests flexibility is more important than consistency in minority influence.

- Mugny & Papastamou (1982) found that minorities who refused to budge on opinions about controlling pollution, were not persuasive, but flexible minorities were. This supports the idea that flexibility is more influential than consistency.

- Smith *et al.* (1996) found that if a minority could get a majority to consider an issue in terms of the arguments for and against the issue, then the minority became more influential. This suggests that *systematic processing* (thinking deeply about something) is also an important factor in minority influence.

Description

Minority influence is a type of social influence that motivates individuals to reject established majority group norms. This is achieved through *conversion*, where individuals become gradually won over to a minority viewpoint. Conversion requires a permanent change in an individual's belief system and a new belief/behaviour being accepted both privately and publicly. This involves *internalisation* (see **page 3**) and as such is a strong, true form of conformity. Conversion generally occurs through *informational social influence*, where a minority exposes the majority to new information and ideas. This is a gradual process, where individuals

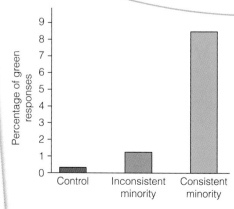

Fig 1.9 Bar chart showing conformity to inconsistent and consistent minority influence

✔ Moscovici *et al.*'s findings that consistent minorities have greater social influence on majorities than inconsistent minorities have been shown to be valid, as they have support from other studies. For example, Meyers *et al.* (2000) found that minority groups successful in affecting minorities were more consistent than inconsistent minority groups.

✔ Minority influence has an important role to play in social influence. Without minority influence, important social change, innovation and the introduction of new ideas and practices cannot occur (see **page 22**).

rethink their belief systems in regard to such new information and ideas. It is known as *social cryptoamnesia*, where initial converts are few, but then there are more and more converts as the minority gets bigger, acquiring more status, power and acceptability. Minority influence is most persuasive if the minority has a behavioural style that is: (1) *consistent*, as this suggests the minority has confidence in its beliefs; (2) *committed*, as this shows the minority may have resisted social pressures, ridicule and abuse against their beliefs; (3) *flexible*, as this suggests the minority can be moderate, co-operative and reasonable enough to show some compromise.

✘ Moscovici *et al.*'s study lacks external validity, as asking participants to identify the colour of slides is artificial and not true to life. Moscovici *et al.* also only used females as participants in their study, so findings cannot be generalised to males.

✘ Studies into minority influence that use confederates pretending to be minorities are unethical. They involve deceit, which means it is not possible for participants to give informed consent. Participants may also experience mild stress in such studies.

✘ Studies into minority influence also often fail to identify important variables like group size, status and the minority group's degree of organisation.

Practical application

Because minority influence needs careful consideration and changes in beliefs and behaviour occur over time, new, innovative practices can be road-tested for suitability. This means that any unforeseen dangers of a new practice should emerge before it becomes a mainstream practice, for example, the adoption of euthanasia (voluntary ending of life) as an accepted practice.

pp. 41–4

1 Social influence
The role of social influence processes in social change

Focal study

Martin *et al.* (2007) investigated whether opinions given by minority or majority group influence are more resistant to conflicting opinions. Forty-eight participants, who were initially supportive of voluntary euthanasia, received 2 messages. The first was the *pro-attitudinal message*, which gave 6 arguments **against** voluntary euthanasia and was supported by either minority or majority group influence. The second was the *counter-attitudinal message*, which gave 6 arguments **for** voluntary euthanasia. Attitudes were then measured. When the pro-attitudinal message was supported by minority influence, attitudes were more resistant to change. This suggests that minority influence creates *systematic processing* (consideration) of its viewpoints, leading to attitudes resistant to counter-persuasion. Therefore, the opinions of minorities are subjected to higher-level processing than those of majorities. The findings also suggest that minority influence leads to social change through systematic processing, causing changes to belief systems that lead to changes in viewpoints and behaviour.

Description

Social change is the process by which society changes beliefs, attitudes and behaviour to create new social norms (expected ways of behaviour and thinking).

Minority influence is the main force for social change, with minority viewpoints slowly winning the majority over to accept new social norms. Minority influence acts slowly, involving *systematic processing* (thought processes) that changes belief systems. It is therefore resistant to change.

Majority influence is more immediate and unthinking. Its main role is to help maintain social order by getting people to conform to social norms which have already been established through minority influence.

OTHER STUDIES

- Martin & Hewstone (1999) found that minority influence leads to more creative and novel outcomes than majority influence, which supports the idea that minority, rather than majority, influence is a greater force for innovation and change.

- Burgoon (1995) reported that it is the unexpected and unusual behaviours exhibited by minority groups that are alerting and attention-grabbing, and which lead to deep-level analysis of such behaviours and ideas. This suggests that it is the breaking of social norms by minorities that leads to systematic processing and ultimately to social change.

- Nemeth (2009) reported that it is the 'dissent' of minorities to accepted social norms that 'opens' individuals' minds to search for information and consider other choices, which ultimately makes them more creative, better informed and better able to make decisions. This demonstrates how the resistance of minorities to conform to and obey social norms acts as a starting point for social change to occur.

Fig 1.10 Would an argument against voluntary euthanasia be more resistant to change if supported by a minority or a majority group?

During the process of social change comes a moment of critical mass, whereby the minority viewpoint becomes that of the mainstream and the majority begin to conform to the new viewpoint through *compliance* (see **page 2**). This involves only public (not private) agreement, with individuals still holding their original beliefs. More permanent social change requires conformity through *identification*, where belief systems are changed.

Obedience serves like majority influence to help oversee and maintain existing social orders. Individuals who show high levels of resistance to social influence are more likely to become agents for social change by modelling the attitudes and behaviour necessary for such change to occur.

❌ Negative evaluation

✘ Clark & Maas (1990) found no minority influence effect upon a majority group larger than 4 people, which suggests that minority influence is restricted in its ability to convert and incur social change.

✘ Many experiments into the role of social influence processes in social change lack external validity, as they often involve artificial tasks that lack relevance to real-life situations. This lowers the validity of conclusions drawn from the findings.

✘ Experiments into the role of social influence processes in social change often result in ethical issues, especially deceit, meaning that informed consent cannot be gained.

Practical application

A practical application of research into social change is that in business and industry companies should not place only 'yes men' (people who conform and obey readily) into management, as they stifle innovation. Minorities of dissenters should also be included, as they will promote an atmosphere of innovative change.

pp. 45–8

2 Memory

The multi-store model (MSM)

Focal study

Baddeley (1966) examined encoding in STM and LTM by giving 75 participants either: *acoustically similar* words (rhyming words) like 'caught' and 'taut', *acoustically dissimilar* words (non-rhyming words) like 'foul' and 'deep', *semantically similar* words (words with similar meanings) like 'big' and 'huge', or *semantically dissimilar* words (words with non-similar meanings) like 'pen' and 'ring'. With STM, acoustically dissimilar words were better recalled (80 per cent) than acoustically similar words (10 per cent), indicating acoustic encoding to be dominant. Semantically dissimilar words (71 per cent) were recalled slightly better than semantically similar ones (64 per cent), suggesting semantic coding does occur in STM but isn't dominant. With LTM, participants followed the same procedure, but with a 20-minute gap between presentation and recall. There was no difference between acoustically similar and dissimilar words, but more semantically dissimilar words (85 per cent) were recalled than semantically similar ones (55 per cent), suggesting semantic encoding is dominant in LTM.

OTHER STUDIES

- Crowder (1993) found that memories in the SR only retain information in the iconic store for a few milliseconds, but retain information for up to 3 seconds within the echoic store. This supports the idea that sensory information is coded into different stores, while additionally suggesting that sensory memories have different durations.

- Peterson & Peterson (1959) read participants nonsense trigrams (words of 3 random letters, e.g. XPJ), then asked them to count backwards from a large digit between 3 and 18 seconds later to prevent recall. 90 per cent of trigrams were recalled after 3 seconds, but only 5 per cent after 18 seconds, suggesting STM duration is between 18 and 20 seconds.

- Bahrick *et al.* (1975) found that participants who had left school in the last 15 years recalled 90 per cent of faces and names of schoolmates from photos, while those who had left 48 years previously recalled 80 per cent of names and 70 per cent of faces. This implies LTM duration to be very long-lasting.

Description

The multi-store model (MSM) explains how data (pieces of information) move between 3 storage systems, each system differing in terms of:

- *capacity* – how much information is stored
- *duration* – how long information is stored
- *encoding* – the form in which information is stored.

The *sensory register* (SR) holds huge amounts of unprocessed sensory information received by sensory organs for a short duration. Information that is paid attention to goes for further processing in *short-term memory* (STM) and non-attended information is immediately lost. The SR has separate stores for sensory inputs, e.g. *iconic*

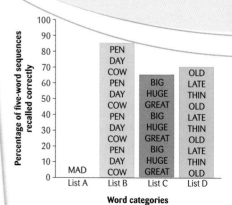

Fig 2.1 Baddeley's (1966) acoustic/semantic study findings, where List A = acoustically similar words, List B = acoustically dissimilar words, List C = semantically similar words and List D = semantically dissimilar words

✔ The MSM was the first cognitive explanation of memory and inspired interest and research, leading to later theories like the working memory model that gave an even greater understanding of memory.

✔ The brief duration of SR and STM has an evolutionary value, as we only need to focus on sensory information with an immediate survival value. LTMs are retained for longer as they may have an ongoing survival value.

✔ The theory is supported by amnesia cases (loss of memory). Patients lose either their STM or their LTM ability, but not both, supporting the idea that STM and LTM are separate memory stores located in different brain areas.

store for visual and *echoic store* for auditory information.

STM is a temporary memory system holding information in use. The dominant encoding type here is *acoustic*, with other sensory codes also used. Capacity is limited to 5–9 items, extended by *chunking*, where the size of the units of information is increased. Duration is limited to around 20 seconds, though rehearsal retains data within the STM loop, until eventually it becomes more permanent within *long-term memory* (LTM). The dominant encoding type in LTM is *semantic*, though other encoding types also occur, e.g. *visual* and *acoustic*. Potential capacity is assumed to be unlimited, with duration potentially lifelong. Information in LTM does not have to be continually rehearsed to be retained.

✖ Negative evaluation

✖ The MSM is oversimplified as seeing STM and LTM as single stores. Research suggests there are several types of STM, such as separate stores for visual and auditory information, as well as different types of LTM, such as *procedural*, *episodic* and *semantic* LTM (see **page 28**).

✖ Cohen (1990) thinks memory capacity is not measurable only by the amount of information, but by the nature of the information to be recalled. Some things are easier to recall regardless of the amount of information being recalled. MSM does not consider this.

✖ MSM focuses too much on memory structure rather than on processes.

Practical application

Research into the MSM has allowed psychologists to create strategies for improving memory performance, such as chunking, where STM capacity is increased by grouping separate pieces of information into larger units with a collective meaning. This can be useful for students when revising.

pp. 52–62

2 Memory
The working memory model (WMM)

Focal study

Alkhalifa (2009) examined the existence of the EB, by presenting 48 students with numerical information on a screen, either in sequential fashion (e.g. 1, 2, 3, 4) or in parallel fashion (where information was presented in different parts of the screen simultaneously). The numbers used were of sufficient complexity to override the capacities of both the PL and the VSS. Participants were set problem-solving questions based on the numbers presented. Those using sequentially presented material were superior. This suggests a limitation exists on information passing from perception to learning, as parallel processing was a hindrance to learning. As sequential processing was superior, it indicates that the capacity of the working memory (WM) is larger than that determined by the capacity of the PL and the VSS, implying the existence of a limited-capacity EB, which acts as a temporary 'general store' of integrated material.

OTHER STUDIES

- Trojani & Grossi (1995) reported the case study of 'SC', who had brain damage affecting the functioning of his PL, but not his VSS. This suggests the PL and VSS are separate systems associated with different brain areas.
- Gathercole & Baddeley (1993) found that participants had difficulty simultaneously tracking a moving point of light and describing the angles on a hollow letter 'F', as both tasks involved using the VSS. However, they had little difficulty tracking the light and performing a simultaneous verbal task, as those tasks used the VSS and the PL, indicating the VSS and PL to be separate systems.
- Alkhalifa (2009) reported a case study of a patient with severely impaired LTM, who had a STM capacity of 25 prose items, far exceeding the capacity of both the VSS and the PL. This supports the idea of an EB, which holds items in working memory until they are recalled.

Description

Replacing the single STM of the MSM (see **page 24**), the working memory model (WMM) proposes a 4-component working memory based on the form of processing each carries out.

The limited-capacity *central executive* (CE) acts as a filter, dealing with all sensory information and determining which information is attended to, and then allocating this to 'slave systems', temporary stores dealing with different types of sensory information.

The *phonological loop* (PL) is a slave system dealing with auditory information. It is similar to the rehearsal system of the MSM, with a limited capacity determined by the amount of information spoken in about 2 seconds.

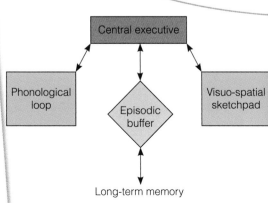

Fig 2.2 The working memory model

Positive evaluation

✔ PET scans show different brain areas are activated when individuals perform verbal and visual tasks. This supports the idea of the PL and the VSS being separate systems based within the biology of the brain.

✔ The PL is associated with the evolution of human vocal language, as the development of the PL produced an increase in the short-term ability to remember vocalisations. This helped the learning of more complex language abilities, like grammar (the rules of language) and semantics (the meanings of things).

✔ The WMM is a superior explanation of STM to the MSM, as it explains STM as having several storage systems and so is better able to explain how STM actually operates.

It divides into the *primary acoustic store* (PAS), which stores words in the order they were heard, and the *articulatory process* (AP), which permits sub-vocal repetition of information stored in the PL.

Another slave system is the *visuo-spatial sketchpad* (VSS), a temporary store for visual and spatial items and the relationships between them. It divides into the *visual cache* (VC), which stores visual material concerning form and colour, and the *inner scribe* (IS), which stores information about spatial relationships (where objects are in relationships to each other).

A slave system added to the model later on is the *episodic buffer* (EB), which is a temporary store of integrated information from the CE, PL, VSS and LTM.

Negative evaluation

✗ Studies of the PL and VSS often use a *dual task technique* (doing 2 tasks at once), but the tasks performed are often ones that do not relate to everyday life (like tracking a moving dot of light) and so are artificial and thus lacking in external validity.

✗ Although the CE is seen as the most important component of the WMM (as it oversees the operation of working memory), little is known about how it works – for example, how it decides what we pay attention to.

Practical application

Children with **attention deficit hyperactivity disorder** (ADHD) often have impairments in working memory. Alloway (2006) recommends: using brief, simple instructions (so they are not forgotten); giving instructions as individual, frequently repeated steps; and getting children to periodically repeat instructions so that they stay focused.

pp. 63–8

2 Memory
Types of long-term memory (LTM)

Focal study

Tulving (1989) investigated differences in the processing of episodic and semantic memory. Six participants performed 8 successive trials involving 4 SMs and 4 EMs. During a trial, participants attempted to retrieve a self-selected memory. EMs involved personally experienced events, like a holiday, while SMs involved knowledge acquired through learning, such as from reading a book. Radioactive gold was injected into the participant 60 seconds after retrieval began and their brain was scanned 8 seconds later (after the gold had arrived in the brain). In 3 participants there was greater activation in the frontal lobes of the brain during EM retrieval and in the posterior region of the cortex during SM retrieval (3 participants produced inconclusive data). This suggests SMs and EMs involve different brain areas and are therefore separate forms of LTM.

Description

Research indicates several types of long-term memory (LTM), each with a separate function and associated with different brain areas. LTM sub-divides into *explicit* (easy to express in words), which requires conscious thought to be recalled, and *implicit* (difficult to express in words), which does not require conscious thought to be recalled.

One type of explicit LTM is *episodic memory* (EM), which gives an autobiographical record of personal experiences, like when your birthday is. Strength of EM relates to strength of emotions and the degree of processing at coding. EM helps us distinguish between real events and imagination.

A second type of explicit LTM is *semantic memory* (SM), which contains knowledge

OTHER STUDIES

- Herlitz *et al.* (1997) assessed explicit LTM abilities in 1,000 Swedish participants and found that females consistently performed better than males on tasks requiring episodic LTM, although there were no differences in SM ability. This suggests there are gender differences in EM ability, possibly because females tend to have better verbal ability.

- Finke *et al.* (2012) reported the case study of 'PM', a professional cellist who suffered severe amnesia due to damage in several brain areas through illness. His episodic and semantic LTM was so badly affected that he could not remember musical facts, but his ability to read and play music, including new pieces, was unaffected. This suggests different types of LTM are located in different brain areas.

- Van Gorp *et al.* (1999) found that abstinence from cocaine by heavy users led to a rapid increase in procedural memory ability. As abstinence from cocaine stimulates dopamine production, it suggests dopamine levels are linked to procedural LTM.

Fig 2.3 Recalling how to surf is an example of procedural LTM

✔ Episodic LTMs may differ from semantic LTMs in terms of different types of thinking and emotion, as EMs are associated with conscious awareness of events and emotional feelings related to them, while SMs are more associated with non-emotional, objective analysis of phenomena.

✔ The frontal lobe brain area's association with episodic LTMs is supported by case studies of amnesiacs with impaired episodic memories having damaged frontal lobes.

✔ Procedural memories may take longer to learn than explicit LTMs, as they often involve motor functions and spatial abilities, while explicit memories tend to involve higher-level thought processes.

learned. Strength of SM also relates to the degree of processing at coding, with SMs generally longer lasting than EMs. SMs link to EMs, as new knowledge (SMs) is generally learned from specific experiences (EMs). Over time, such memories become less episodic and more semantic.

Procedural memory (PM) is a type of implicit LTM, allowing us to perform learned tasks with little conscious thought, for example surfing. Many PMs concern motor skills, like walking, and are learned early in life. PMs are also involved in language, helping individuals to speak and use grammar without thinking how to. As PMs do not need conscious thought, we can simultaneously perform other cognitive tasks requiring attention.

✘ Negative evaluation

✘ The extent to which episodic and semantic LTM systems are different is unclear. Although different brain areas are involved, there is also a lot of overlap between the 2 systems, with semantic LTMs often emerging from episodic LTMs. Therefore, it is not known whether or not the gradual transformation of an EM into a SM involves a change in memory systems.

✘ As only 3 out of Tulving's 6 participants showed differences in the processing of semantic and episodic LTMs, the findings cannot be generalised. Also, as 2 of the participants were Tulving and his wife, the findings may be prone to researcher bias.

Practical application

Psychologists at Vanderbilt University have programmed EM into a robot, so that it can recall past experiences to help solve problems. Attempts are now being made to give it an episodic buffer (see **page 27**) so it can combine information from different sensory memory channels like a human does.

pp. 69–75

2 Memory
Explanations for forgetting

Focal study

Schmidt *et al.* (2000) investigated the influence of retroactive interference on the memory of street names learned in childhood. 211 Dutch participants aged 11 to 79 years were given a map of Molenberg, where they had gone to school, with 48 street names replaced with numbers. Participants had to recall as many names as possible. Other relevant details were also collected, such as how many times they had moved house, where they had lived and for how long, how often they visited Molenberg etc. The amount of retroactive interference was assessed by how many times participants had moved to other neighbourhoods (and therefore learned new sets of street names). A positive correlation was found between the number of times participants had moved neighbourhoods outside of Molenberg and the number of street names forgotten. This suggests retroactive interference, as learning new sets of street names makes recalling old sets difficult.

OTHER STUDIES

- Peterson & Peterson (1959) gave participants meaningless words of 3 letters and got them to count backwards aloud to prevent rehearsal. After 18 seconds only 5 per cent of participants showed correct recall. This illustrates how memories fade over time, and suggests that forgetting may be due to information no longer being in storage, as well as to retrieval problems.

- Darley *et al.* (1973) found that participants who had hidden money while they were high on marijuana could not recall where they had put it, but they could when they were high again. This supports the idea that forgetting occurs when internal context of retrieval differs from that of coding, as stated by state-dependent learning.

- Abernethy (1940) found that students recalled information best when in the room they had learned the material in with their usual teacher, rather than in an unfamiliar room with an unfamiliar teacher. This supports the idea of forgetting occurring when external context of retrieval differs from that of coding, as stated by context-dependent failure.

Description

Forgetting is the failure to retrieve memories, with information either no longer in, or unable to be retrieved from, storage. *Interference theory* sees material becoming confused with, or disrupted by, other information during coding, leading to inaccurate recall. *Proactive interference*, which works forwards in time, occurs where information previously stored interferes with attempts to recall new information. For example, the memory of your old phone number disrupts attempts to recall your new phone number. *Retroactive interference*, which works backwards in time, occurs when coding of new information disrupts previously stored information. For example, the memory of your new password prevents recall

Fig 2.4 Street map of Molenberg in Holland

- ✔ Schmidt *et al.*'s (2000) street name study is especially useful, as it involves a real-life scenario and therefore has high external validity.
- ✔ Schmidt *et al.*'s methodology can also quite easily be adapted to assess the effect of proactive, as well as retroactive, interference.
- ✔ Cue-dependent theory is regarded as the best explanation of forgetting in LTM, due to the huge amount of supportive research the explanation has, which shows the importance of retrieval cues in facilitating accurate recall.

of your old password. *Cue-dependent forgetting* sees recall as dependent upon *retrieval cues* (prompts that facilitate recall). Forgetting occurs if the retrieval cue under which a memory is stored cannot be accessed. *Context-dependent failure* occurs with *external* retrieval cues, where forgetting occurs as the external environment is different at recall from how it was at coding. For example, you may perform worse in an exam sat in an unfamiliar room than in the room where you learned the material. *State-dependent failure* occurs with *internal* retrieval cues, where forgetting occurs because an individual's internal environment is dissimilar to that when the information was coded. For example, a person may fail when sober to recall information that was learned when drunk.

✘ Negative evaluation

- ✘ There are a number of extraneous variables in Schmidt *et al.*'s (2000) study. For example, participants who played a lot in the streets of Molenberg as children, or who walked to school, may have learned street names to a greater extent and therefore would have had better recall than those who did not play in the streets or went to school by car.
- ✘ Interference theory only explains forgetting when 2 sets of information are similar, like simultaneously learning 2 languages at school. This does not happen that often and so cannot explain the majority of forgetting.
- ✘ Although studies show interference to be a real effect, they do not identify the cognitive processes at work, which means the explanation is incomplete.

Practical application

One practical application of the interference explanation of forgetting is that, wherever possible, in order to cut down on retrieval failures, students should sit an exam in the room where they learned the material, so that the context of retrieval is the same as that of coding.

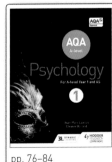

pp. 76–84

2 Memory

Factors affecting the accuracy of eyewitness testimony (EWT)

Focal study

Loftus & Pickrell (2003) investigated whether false memories could be created through the use of post-event information. 120 participants who had visited Disneyland as children were placed into 4 groups. They were asked to evaluate some advertising copy about Disneyland and answer questions about their visit there. Group 1 read fake copy featuring no cartoon characters; Group 2 read the fake copy featuring no cartoon characters but there was a large figure of Bugs Bunny (a Warner Brothers character) in their room; Group 3 read the fake copy which now featured Bugs Bunny; Group 4 read the fake copy featuring Bugs Bunny and also had the large figure in the room. 30 per cent of participants in Group 3 and 40 per cent of participants in Group 4 recalled meeting Bugs Bunny at Disneyland – some even recalled having their photo taken with him. This suggests that post-event information can be misleading so that false memories are created.

OTHER STUDIES

- Ginet & Verkampt (2007) found that participants made moderately anxious by being told that fake electrodes on their bodies produced electric shocks in response to incorrect answers had better recall of a traffic accident viewed on video than participants with low anxiety through being told the electrodes simply monitored bodily activity. This supports the inverted-U hypothesis.

- Loftus & Palmer (1974) found that participants' estimates of car speeds viewed on a video were affected by which verb they were given in a question asking 'How fast were the cars going when they *contacted/hit/bumped/collided/ smashed* each other?' This illustrates how misleading information in the form of leading questions can affect EWT.

- Koehler *et al.* (2002) found that participants were less able to recall stressful words than non-stressful words, supporting the concept of repression. However, Hadley & MacKay (2006) found that stressful words were better recalled, as they are more memorable, which suggests the case for repression is not proven.

Description

Eyewitness testimony (EWT) concerns the accuracy of recall of those present at an event when it occurred. It is especially important in courts of law.

Bartlett (1932) detailed how *schemas*, ways of perceiving the world formed from experience, affect EWT, as memories are not accurate 'snapshots' but reconstructions of what we believe happened in an event based on previous experience, stereotypes, mood etc.

Misleading information can affect EWT, first through *leading questions*, which suggest a certain answer to a witness, and also through *post-event discussion*, where misleading information is

Fig 2.5 This image of Bugs Bunny was used in the study by Loftus & Pickrell to produce a fake memory

✔ Loftus & Pickrell's (2003) Bugs Bunny study can be regarded as superior to the more famous Loftus & Palmer (1974) study, as it uses memory of a real-life event, visiting Disneyland as a child, and therefore has higher external validity.

✔ Research into EWT has led to changes in court procedures. The Devlin report (1976) led to convictions based on uncorroborated EWT (where there is only one independent EWT) being disallowed.

✔ Loftus has performed many studies over many years which have produced a wealth of information that has increased our understanding of how false memories can be created.

added to a memory after an event has been witnessed.

The witnessing of real-life events can often involve *anxiety*, which can severely affect the quality of recall. The *Yerkes–Dodson inverted-U hypothesis* explains how low and high levels of anxiety are both associated with poor recall in terms of detail and accuracy of events witnessed, while moderate anxiety is associated with good recall.

Anxiety can also affect the quality of recall through *repression*, where traumatic events become hidden in the unconscious mind so that a witness is unaware of them and cannot recall them. Repression, however, is a controversial idea and few psychologists see it as a valid concept.

❌ **Negative evaluation**

✘ Many studies of the effects of anxiety on EWT are laboratory based and therefore not generalisable. Real-life studies often find different results, e.g. Yuille & Cutshall (1986) found that high anxiety produced excellent recall of a real armed robbery, thereby refuting the inverted-U hypothesis.

✘ Loftus & Palmer's findings may be due to demand characteristics, not leading questions, as participants may have given answers they thought the researchers wanted, rather than their actual recollections.

✘ Participants do not expect to be misled by researchers, so inaccurate recall in studies may be due to participants believing researchers' misleading statements to be true.

Practical application

One practical application of research into EWT is in advertising, where advertisers use post-event information (usually through fake nostalgic images) to try and create false positive memories of products, so that we will buy them.

pp. 86–91

2 Memory

Improving the accuracy of eyewitness testimony (EWT)

Focal study

Meissner & Fraser (2010) performed a meta-analysis of studies of the CI, including the ECI and the MCI, to assess their relative effectiveness. They reviewed 57 studies involving comparison of the CI with a control technique, such as the SPI, that had been published in peer reviewed journals. 32 per cent of the studies used the CI, 23 per cent the ECI and 45 per cent the MCI. The CI was found to produce more accurate detail than non-CI techniques, though there was a small increase in inaccurate details with the CI. The MCI produced more inaccurate details than the CI or the ECI and also produced slightly more false memories. This suggests that CIs are superior, as they produce more accurate, detailed information than non-CI techniques. The CI technique is therefore an effective means of conducting interviews, though some inaccurate detail is noticeable.

Description

One strategy for improving EWT is the *cognitive interview* (CI). Replacing the *standard police interview* (SPI), which depended on free recall of events, it is an interview procedure facilitating accurate, detailed recall, based on Tulving's (1974) idea that several retrieval paths to memory exist. The CI also makes use of Tulving & Thomson's *encoding specificity theory* (1973), which suggests the use of as many retrieval cues as possible to improve recall. The CI has 4 components:

1 *change of narrative order* – events being recalled in different chronological orders, e.g. from end to beginning

2 *change of perspective* – events being recalled from different perspectives, e.g. from the offender's point of view

OTHER STUDIES

- Verkampt & Ginet (2010) interviewed children after a painting session, and found that the CI and 4 types of MCI were superior to the SPI in producing accurate detail and that versions of the MCI that removed the 'change of narrative' component were most superior. This suggests that specific versions of the MCI are most appropriate for certain types of witnesses.

- Holliday (2003) gave children either a SPI or a MCI, specially designed for children, after showing them a video of a child's birthday party. She found that the MCI produced more accurate detail than the SPI, demonstrating the effectiveness of MCIs with children.

- Milne & Bull (2002) found the 'report everything' and 'context reinstatement' components of the CI to be the key techniques in gaining accurate, detailed recall, which implies that some components of the CI are more effective than others.

Fig 2.6 The modified cognitive interview is often used to allow police officers to interview children

✔ The CI has potential uses within other organisations, not just the police, where accurate memory is necessary – for example, in the army, where debriefing of soldiers after active combat incidents is used to gain valid recollections.

✔ Fisher & Geiselman (1988) have continued to develop the CI using information gained from watching 'good' and 'poor' interviewers. This has led to more open-ended questions and fitting the order of questioning to the witness's order of experience, increasing accuracy of recall from 40 per cent to 60 per cent.

✔ Variations of the CI have proven to be effective with specific groups of people in generating accurate witness recall of incidents.

3 *mental reinstatement of context* – making use of environmental context, e.g. weather and emotional context (feelings) of the crime scene

4 *report everything* – all information is recalled, even trivial or muddled content.

Fisher *et al.* (1987) produced the *enhanced cognitive interview* (ECI) to overcome problems caused by inappropriate sequencing of questions. Extra features include: (a) *minimisation of distraction*, (b) *reduction of anxiety*, (c) *getting witnesses to speak slowly*, (d) *asking open-ended questions*. The *modified cognitive interview* (MCI) is a shortened version of the CI technique, which is often preferred by police forces as it takes less operational time. MCIs usually omit the 'change narrative order' and 'change perspective' components.

✗ Many police forces have problems using the CI, as it is too time-consuming for practical use. This has led to poorer or rushed versions of the technique being used, which can be less effective. The production of confabulations (false memories) is also problematic for police usage.

✗ A limitation of CIs is that they are not generally effective as a method of memory enhancement for recognition of suspects from identity parades or photographs.

✗ Police forces use widely differing versions of the SPI, making objective comparisons difficult to achieve.

Practical application

MCIs can be used with children. Omitting the 'change perspective' component is useful here, as children are often too young to see things from others' point of view. Other groups of witnesses, like those with learning difficulties, can also be interviewed effectively with specifically designed forms of the MCI.

pp. 92–8

3 Attachment

Caregiver–infant interactions in humans

Focal study

Papousek *et al.* (1991) investigated whether 'caregiverese' (see **page 37**) is universal. They did this by performing a cross-cultural study involving mothers and infants in 3 diverse countries. It was found that mothers in America, China and Germany all exhibited the same behaviour of using a rising tone to indicate to their infants that it was their turn in an interaction between the pair. This supports the idea that caregiverese is an innate, biological device to help promote the formation and maintenance of attachments.

OTHER STUDIES

- Condon & Sander (1974) slowed down infants' movements by analysing frame-by-frame video recordings of their actions to find that they moved in sequence with adults' speech to create a type of turn-taking 'conversation'. This supports the idea of interactional synchrony.

- Melzoff & Moore (1977) reported that 2- to 3-week-old infants tend to imitate adults' specific facial expressions and hand movements. This supports the notion that infant mimicry is an innate ability that helps to form attachments, especially as it was later observed in infants of less than 3 days old.

- Klaus & Kennell (1976) performed a comparison of mothers who had lengthy periods of physical contact with their babies that lasted several hours a day with mothers who only had physical contact with their babies during feeding in the 3 days after birth. They found that mothers with the greater physical contact cuddled their infants more and made greater eye contact with them. The effects were still noticeable a year later, which suggests greater physical contact creates stronger and closer attachment formation.

Description

Interactions between a caregiver and an infant serve to develop and maintain the attachment bond between them. Though an infant cannot talk at this stage of development, meaningful and complex communication between the infant and caregiver does occur in several ways.

- *Interactional synchrony* concerns how infants move their bodies in time with the rhythm of their caregivers' vocal language to create a type of 'turn-taking', as seen in 2-way spoken conversations. This helps to reinforce and maintain the attachment bond between infants and caregivers.

- *Reciprocity* concerns the interactions between caregivers and infants that result in mutual behaviour, where both

Fig 3.1 Interactions between caregivers and infants help to develop and maintain attachment bonds

✔ Klaus & Kennell's (1976) findings that infants who have greater physical contact with their mothers go on to develop stronger and closer attachments is backed up by Chateau & Wiberg (1984), who found the same results with middle-class Swedish mothers.

✔ The study of infant–caregiver interactions has seen the development of innovative research methods, such as analysing video recordings of interactions frame-by-frame as performed by Condon & Sander (1974). This has allowed psychologists to gain an understanding of such interactions and their role in helping form attachments.

✔ Non-verbal forms of communication between infants and caregivers have an evolutionary survival value, as they help a child to be nurtured and protected. Infants can express their needs and have them met. The attachment bond such communications help to create also serves to keep close proximity between infant and caregiver.

individuals motivate responses from each other. This also serves to reinforce and maintain the attachment bond.

- *Bodily contact* concerns the physical interactions between caregivers and infants that help to form the attachment bond, especially in the period immediately after birth.

- *Mimicking* concerns infants' apparent innate ability to imitate their caregivers' facial expressions. This is seen as a biological device to assist in the formation of attachments.

- *Caregiverese* concerns how adults who interact with infants often use a modified form of vocal language that is high-pitched, slow, repetitive and song-like. This assists communication between caregivers and infants and again helps strengthen and maintain attachment bonds.

✘ Interactional synchrony is not found in all cultures. Le Vine et al. (1994) reported that Kenyan mothers have little such interactions with their infants, but form a high amount of secure attachments (see **page 46**). This goes against the idea that interactional synchrony is necessary for healthy attachment development.

✘ Caregiverese is often used by adults with all infants, not just the ones they have an attachment with. Therefore, although it seems to assist communication between adults and children, it is possible that it does not specifically help form attachments.

✘ Infants cannot speak, so interpreting their behaviour is problematic, making it difficult to draw conclusions about infant–caregiver interactions.

Practical application

A practical application that comes from Klaus & Kennell's study is that hospitals now place mothers and babies in the same room after birth (rather than in different rooms, which used to be the case) to encourage the formation of attachments.

pp. 102–4

3 Attachment
Stages of attachment development

Focal study

Schaffer & Emerson (1964) investigated whether there was a common pattern of attachment formation. Sixty newborn infants were studied each month in their own homes, with their mothers, for 12 months. They were studied again at 18 months of age. Interviews were conducted with mothers, and questions were asked about whom infants smiled at, whom they responded to, and who and what caused them distress. Observations were also made on the monthly visits. Most infants began showing separation protest (see **page 48**) from their main caregiver at between 6 and 8 months of age, with stranger anxiety following a month later. Mothers of strongly attached infants responded more quickly to their needs and gave more opportunities for interactions. Most infants developed multiple attachments – at 18 months, 87 per cent had at least 2 attachments and 31 per cent had 5 or more. Infants behaved similarly to different attachment figures. 39 per cent of prime attachments were not to the main caregiver. This suggests there is a common pattern of attachment formation and that attachments are more easily made with those showing sensitive responsiveness. Multiple attachments are the norm and of similar quality.

Description

The development of infants' attachments occurs in 4 universal, distinct stages.

1   The first stage, the *pre-attachment phase*, lasts from birth to 3 months of age. From 6 weeks of age infants become attracted to other humans, preferring them to objects and events. This preference is demonstrated by infants smiling at people's faces.

2   The second stage, the *indiscriminate attachment phase*, lasts from 3 to 7 or 8 months of age. Infants start to discriminate between familiar and unfamiliar people, smiling more at people they know. They still allow strangers to handle and look after them though.

OTHER STUDIES

- Carpenter (1975) gave infants unfamiliar and familiar voices and faces. Sometimes the face and the voice were of the same person and sometimes not. It was found that 2-week-old babies looked at a face longer when it was their mother's accompanied by her voice and showed distress when it was her face accompanied by a different voice. This suggests that infants can recognise and are attracted to their mothers from an early age, which contradicts Schaffer & Emerson's (1964) finding that infants were initially attracted to anyone who interacted with them.

- Lamb *et al.* (1982) studied the relationships and attachments that infants had to people like fathers, grandparents and siblings, and found that different attachments served different purposes but were of equal strength. This supports Schaffer & Emerson's finding that multiple attachments are of similar quality.

- Rutter (1981) found that multiple attachments were the norm, supporting Schaffer & Emerson's similar findings.

Fig 3.2 Most children develop multiple attachments to other people, such as grandparents

- ✔ Children with multiple attachments have an advantage, as they are more able to form and conduct social relationships. This is because they have more experience of doing so than children without multiple attachments. They are further advantaged in that if they lose an attachment figure they have several others to turn to.

- ✔ The common pattern of attachment development implies that it is biologically controlled and has evolved. Developing the ability to prefer those who are sensitive to your needs and being wary of those who are unfamiliar would have a survival value.

- ✔ Schaffer & Emerson's study was conducted under real-life conditions, so the conclusions drawn can be seen to have external validity.

3   The third stage, the *discriminate attachment phase*, lasts from 7 to 8 months onwards. Infants develop specific attachments, staying close to preferred people, showing distress and anxiety when separated from them. They avoid unfamiliar people and protest when strangers handle them.

4   The final stage is the *multiple attachment phase*, occurring from 9 months onwards. Infants develop strong, emotional bonds with other major caregivers, like grandparents, and non-caregivers, like siblings. Fear of strangers weakens, but the prime attachment to the mother figure is still the strongest.

✖ **Negative evaluation**

- ✖ Schaffer & Emerson's findings came from observations made by the researchers and the children's mothers, which may have been affected by bias and inaccuracies. This would lower the validity of conclusions drawn from the study.

- ✖ There were quite large individual differences in when attachments formed in Schaffer & Emerson's study, which casts doubt about whether the process of attachment development is under biological control.

- ✖ Research findings that multiple attachments are of equal quality goes against Bowlby's idea of *monotropy* (see **page 45**) that sees infants as having one prime attachment, superior and stronger to other secondary attachments.

Practical application

The main practical application drawn from research into attachment formation is that to develop strong, secure attachments caregivers should show sensitive responsiveness, recognising and responding appropriately to their infants' needs.

pp. 104–6

3 Attachment
The role of the father

Focal study

Lucassen *et al.* (2011) performed a meta-analysis of 22 studies to investigate the association between the sensitivity of childcare provided by fathers and the security of attachment with their children. The review consisted of studies that used observational measures to measure interaction between fathers and children as well as the Strange Situation procedure (see **page 46**). High levels of paternal sensitivity were found to be associated with higher infant–father attachment security. This suggests that, with fathers as well as with mothers, showing sensitive responsiveness to children's needs leads to more secure attachments with them. Interestingly, fathers' sensitive play combined with stimulation was not more strongly associated with attachment security than sensitive interactions without the stimulation of play, which implies that a father's role as playmate is not that important in developing strong, secure attachments.

OTHER STUDIES

- Hrdy (1999) found that fathers were less able than mothers to detect low levels of infant distress, which supports the idea that males are less suitable attachment figures. However, Lamb (1987) found that when men become main caregivers they quickly develop sensitivity to children's needs, which implies that sensitivity is not limited to just women.

- Bernier & Miljkovitch (2009) found that single-parent fathers develop similar attachments with their children to those that they had with their own fathers. However, this was not found in married fathers, so continuity of attachment seems to occur more where fathers are sole caregivers.

- Belsky *et al.* (2009) found that fathers with high levels of marital intimacy had more secure attachments with their children. This supports the idea that the emotional closeness of relationships between fathers and partners is reflected in the quality of relationships that fathers have with their children.

- Brown *et al.* (2010) found that high levels of supportive co-parenting (sharing childcare duties) was related to more secure attachment types between fathers and children, but not between mothers and children. This suggests that supportive co-parenting is important for fathers in developing positive relationships with their children.

Description

Traditionally fathers have been seen as minor attachment figures, providing resources, but little childcare. Females were seen as 'natural' caregivers and males were considered to be biologically unsuited to such a role. Some people see fathers not as caregivers, but as a source of exciting, unpredictable, physical play. However, in Britain, in heterosexual partnerships, 10 per cent of main child caregivers are male, while 9 per cent (186,000) of single parents are also male (2013 figures). Research shows that fathers can develop sensitive responsiveness (perceiving and providing appropriate care) when assuming a main caring role. Several important factors have been identified in the relationship between fathers and children:

Fig 3.3 Do children attach to fathers just as playmates, or can the father fulfil a greater role?

✔ Positive evaluation

✔ Children who have secure attachments with their fathers have good peer relationships, fewer problem behaviours and are more able to control their emotions. This illustrates the positive influence fathers can have on children's development.

✔ Fathers are important for mothers as well as children. Fathers who help with childcare allow mothers to have some time for themselves, which helps reduce stress, increases self-esteem and enables mothers to interact positively with their children.

✔ Children without fathers often do less well at school and show high levels of risk-taking and aggression. This suggests that fathers can help prevent negative developmental outcomes.

- *Degree of sensitivity* – fathers who are sensitive to their children's needs develop more secure attachments with them.
- *Type of attachment with father's own parents* – single-parent fathers tend to develop similar attachment types with their children to those that they had with their own parents.
- *Marital intimacy* – the amount of intimacy (emotional closeness) a father has with his partner is positively correlated with the security of attachment he develops with his children.
- *Supportive co-parenting* – fathers who assist their partners in providing childcare develop stronger, more secure attachments with their children.

✘ Negative evaluation

✘ Much research evidence concerning father–infant attachments is correlational and does not show causality. For example, there is a relationship between fathers who interact a lot with their children and those children developing secure attachments. But, it might be that more sensitive fathers interact more with their children.

✘ Early interaction with their children is important for fathers in developing positive relationships with them, but few employers encourage male workers to take the paternal leave they are legally entitled to.

✘ Although research shows that men make good main caregivers, society has a long way to catch up. Few nursery and primary school teachers are male and many airlines will not even let men sit next to children.

Practical application

One practical application is in parenting classes. Skills which increase male sensitivity to children's needs can be taught in such classes so that fathers develop more secure relationships with their children. Research evidence could also be used to help break down society's suspicions about men who care for children.

pp. 107–9

3 Attachment
Animal studies of attachment

Focal study

Lorenz (1935) investigated the mechanisms behind imprinting, whereby newborn animals follow the first moving thing they meet. Lorenz split a clutch of goose eggs into 2 batches, 1 of which hatched naturally by the mother and the other hatched in an incubator. Lorenz made sure he was the first moving object the goslings met. He marked each one, so he knew which were naturally hatched and which were incubator hatched. He then placed them all under a box, releasing them simultaneously in the presence of both the mother and himself. Straight after birth, the naturally hatched goslings had followed their mother, while the incubator hatched goslings followed Lorenz. When released from the upturned box, the same behaviour was seen, and these attachments proved to be irreversible. Imprinting only occurred in a 'critical time period' between 4 and 25 hours after hatching. This suggests that imprinting is a form of attachment that helps young creatures keep close proximity to the first moving object they encounter.

Description

A lot of the early research into attachment theory was performed on animals. Indeed most of the theories that were put forward to explain attachment came out of research performed on animals. One of the earliest explanations of attachment behaviour was that of the *learning theory*. This saw attachments as being based on feeding and formed from experience with environmental interactions. Support for behaviourist explanations, such as this, came mostly from animal studies. The major theorist into attachment behaviour was John Bowlby. Although he was originally influenced by Freudian psychodynamic thinking, his classic *monotropic theory of attachment*

OTHER STUDIES

- Harlow (1959) gave baby rhesus monkeys, separated at birth from their mothers, a choice between a harsh wire surrogate mother that provided milk and a soft towelling mother that provided no food. The monkeys preferred the soft towelling mother, using it as a safe base to explore from. This suggests that attachment is based more on emotional security than on feeding.

- Sluckin (1966) performed a variation of Lorenz's study on ducklings. He found that imprinting would still occur after ducklings had been isolated for 5 days – beyond the established critical time period. This suggests that the critical period is actually a 'sensitive' (best) period, beyond which imprinting, though more difficult, can still be achieved.

- Harlow et al. (1965) found that newborn monkeys raised in total isolation showed signs of psychological disturbance. The females made very poor mothers, some even killing their babies. This suggests social interactions are essential for normal development.

Fig 3.4 Whooping cranes and their imprinted micro-light aircraft parents

✔ The shocking results of Harlow *et al.*'s (1965) study were found to be reversible by Harlow & Suomi (1972). They placed isolated monkeys with an opposite sex younger 'therapist' monkey, gradually increasing contact time. By 3 years of age they had totally recovered.

✔ The use of animal research enabled psychologists to study attachment behaviour in ways that would not have been practically or ethically possible with human participants.

✔ The results of animal studies enabled psychologists to realise that attachment theories based on feeding were wrong. They led to the much better considered theories of Bowlby that saw attachment as a biological device centred on its survival value.

(see **page 45**), which explains how attachments are formed and maintained, and his *maternal deprivation hypothesis* (see **page 48**), which explains what happens when attachments are broken, were formed from animal studies. The work of Konrad Lorenz centred on the idea of *imprinting* that saw animals following the first large moving object they encountered. Bowlby came to see attachment as a human form of imprinting. Harry Harlow's work with rhesus monkeys was also important. Harlow showed, in studies involving separating baby monkeys from their mothers, that behaviourist explanations were wrong and that attachment appeared to be based more on emotional security than feeding.

❌ Negative evaluation

❌ The problem with animal studies is *generalisation*: what is true for animals is not necessarily true for humans. Imprinting only occurs in nidifugous birds (ones that leave the nest early), so imprinting behaviour is not representative of most bird species (non-nidifugous species), let alone humans.

❌ There are ethical issues of harm with animal studies, like those of Harlow where many of the monkeys died. Harlow even invented a 'rape rack', a device to which female monkeys were tied and forcibly mated.

❌ Lorenz's membership of the Nazi party has led to accusations that his belief in genetically inherited characteristics contaminated his work with researcher bias.

Practical application

Imprinting research has helped reintroduce migratory birds to areas where they have become extinct. Whooping cranes are imprinted onto micro-light aircraft and taught the traditional migratory flight paths. Farmers also use imprinting by putting an orphaned lamb wearing the skin of a dead lamb with the dead lamb's mother so that she will accept it.

pp. 109–14

3 Attachment
Explanations of attachment

Focal study

Fox (1977) investigated learning theory's central belief that attachments occur due to feeding from the main caregiver. The participants were 122 children who were born and raised on Israeli kibbutzim (collective farms). Due to their parents' working commitments, the majority of the children's caregiving, including feeding, was provided by *metapelets* (specialist child caregivers). Care was provided by the metapelets in specialist children's centres, with some children returning to their parents in the evenings and others only at weekends. Separation and reunion behaviours with both metapelets and mothers were observed and recorded. It was found that although children protested equally to either mother or metapelet separation when left with a stranger, generally children were more attached to their mothers. Some children showed little if any attachment to their metapelets. As metapelets did most of the feeding, these findings go against the learning theory.

Description

Explanations of attachments give reasons as to why and how attachments form.

Learning theory is a behaviourist explanation that sees attachments as developing through conditioning processes, where an infant learns to associate a caregiver with feeding. With *classical conditioning* the stimulus of food, which produces a natural response of pleasure, is paired with the stimulus of a caregiver, until the caregiver alone produces the pleasure response. With *operant conditioning* caregivers are a source of *negative reinforcement* (escaping something unpleasant), as they become associated with removing the unpleasant sensation of hunger.

OTHER STUDIES

- Dollard & Miller (1950) calculated that babies are fed over 2,000 times by their mothers in the first year of life, thus presenting ample opportunities for attachments to form via association, in line with learning theory.

- Schaffer & Emerson (1964) (see **page 38**) found that in 39 per cent of cases, the mother, who was usually the main caregiver and feeder, was not a baby's main attachment figure. This goes against learning theory, as it suggests that attachments are often made not for reasons of food.

- Rutter (1981) found that infants display a whole range of attachment behaviours towards a variety of attachment figures, not just mothers. Indeed there is no particular attachment behaviour used specifically and exclusively for mothers. This lowers support for Bowlby's theory of monotropy (that infants form one prime attachment to a mother-figure).

Fig 3.5 Learning theory sees attachments as forming due to an association being developed between mother and feeding

Positive evaluation

✔ Although not generally supported by research evidence, learning theory did stimulate a lot of interest in attachment theory and research into it eventually led to Bowlby's more favoured theory.

✔ There is plenty of evidence to support many aspects of Bowlby's theory, for instance the *continuity hypothesis*, where later relationships are seen to reflect early attachment types. Research has shown that the quality of early attachment patterns is indeed reflected in later romantic relationships.

✔ Bowlby's theory puts attachment behaviour into an evolutionary perspective, showing how attachments have developed through natural selection. Those who demonstrated such behaviour had an adaptive advantage to survive to maturity, reproduce and pass on the genes for attachment behaviour to their children. Thus the behaviour became more widespread throughout the population.

Bowlby's *monotropic theory* is an evolutionary explanation of attachment. It sees infants as having an innate tendency to form a bond with one prime attachment figure, which brings with it a survival value through keeping close proximity to that attachment figure. Infants have *social releasers* (innate social behaviours), such as crying, smiling, vocalising and following behaviours, which stimulate adult caregiving. These behaviours become focused on the adult giving the most sensitive care. Bowlby believed there was a *critical period*, a specific time period within which this attachment must form, else it never would. Bowlby saw the monotropic attachment (to one person) as forming an *internal working model*, a blueprint for all future relationships.

Negative evaluation

✘ Schaffer (1971) argued that learning theory puts things the wrong way round: babies do not 'live to eat', but 'eat to live'. Therefore they are active seekers of stimulation, not passive recipients of nutrition.

✘ Learning theory, via conditioning, explains the acquisition of simple behaviours, but not more complex behaviours like attachment, which has an intense emotional component.

✘ Bowlby sees attachments as forming due to mere exposure of infants to caregivers. However, Schaffer & Emerson's (1964) study showed that attachments form with those adults who display the most *sensitive responsiveness*, identifying and responding appropriately to an infant's needs. This suggests that attachment formation is a more dynamic process than Bowlby claimed.

Practical application

A practical application of Bowlby's theory is that parents should receive parenting classes that emphasise the importance of sensitive responsiveness in developing secure attachments – important not just immediately, but also in developing successful romantic relationships in later life.

3 Attachment
Ainsworth's 'Strange Situation'

Focal study

Ainsworth *et al.* (1978) tested 106 young infants between 9 and 18 months old under conditions of mild stress and novelty, to assess *stranger anxiety*, *separation anxiety* and the *secure base concept*. The Strange Situation procedure involved an 81 square foot (about 7.5 square metre) novel environment divided into 16 squares, which was used to track movements and consisted of 8 episodes involving mothers and strangers in various scenarios of arrival and departure. Five categories were recorded: *proximity and contact-seeking behaviours*, *contact-maintaining behaviours*, *proximity and interaction-avoiding behaviours*, *contact and interaction-resisting behaviours* and *search behaviours*. Every 5 seconds the category of behaviour was recorded and assessed on a scale of 1–7. 15 per cent of infants were *insecure-avoidant* attachment type, 15 per cent were *insecure-resistant* and 70 per cent were *securely attached*. Ainsworth concluded that *sensitive responsiveness* was the key factor, as sensitive caregivers are accepting, co-operative and accessible, attending appropriately to their infant's needs. Sensitive mothers tend to have securely attached infants.

OTHER STUDIES

- Van Ijzendoorn & Kroonenberg (1988) performed a meta-analysis of 32 Strange Situation studies from 8 countries. They found Type A = 21 per cent, Type B = 67 per cent and Type C = 12 per cent, so generally the results were similar to Ainsworth's. However, there were some differences in attachment types in some cultures, reflecting differences in childrearing practices. Greater intra-cultural differences were found that reflected socio-economic differences within a culture. Overall, Type B was dominant in all cultures, which suggests some degree of biological origin to attachment types.
- Main & Solomon (1986) found a fourth attachment type, *insecure-disorganised* (Type D), a rare type where children display a confusing mix of approach and avoidance behaviours. Ainsworth agreed with the existence of this type.
- McMahon-True *et al.* (2001) found no existence of Type A in the Dogon people of Mali, due to their natural childrearing practices. This suggests the Strange Situation is not suitable for all cultures.

Description

Following on from her earlier work with mothers and babies in Uganda and Baltimore, Ainsworth created the *Strange Situation*, a controlled observation of a mother and stranger leaving and returning to a room where an infant is playing. Three types of attachment were observed:

1 *Securely attached* (Type B), where children are willing to explore, have high stranger anxiety, are easy to soothe and are enthusiastic at their caregiver's return. Caregivers are sensitive to their infants' needs.

2 *Insecure-avoidant* (Type A), where children are willing to explore, have low stranger anxiety, are indifferent to separation and avoid contact at the

Mother   Stranger

Fig 3.6 The Strange Situation is a procedure for measuring the strength and type of infants' attachments to their mothers

- ✔ The Strange Situation became a *paradigm* study, the accepted method of assessing attachment behaviour, and has been used in countless studies.
- ✔ The Strange Situation is accused of being unethical, as it subjects infants to stress. But it is modelled on everyday experiences where mothers do leave children for brief periods in different settings and with strangers, for example babysitters.
- ✔ Van Ijzendoorn & Schuengel (1999) see Ainsworth's studies as important, as her central finding of parental sensitivity being linked to the quality of attachment has been widely replicated by others using larger samples. This is true also in cross-cultural studies.

return of their caregiver.
Caregivers ignore their infants.

3   *Insecure-resistant* (Type C), where children are unwilling to explore, have high stranger anxiety, are distressed at separation and seek and reject contact at the return of caregivers. Caregivers show simultaneous opposite feelings and behaviour towards their infants.

Differences have been found in patterns of attachment types in replications of the Strange Situation in other cultures, such as that by Van Ijzendoorn & Kroonenberg (1988), though generally results were similar to what Ainsworth found. Indeed intra-cultural differences (differences between sub-cultural groupings within a culture) were often greater than inter-cultural differences (differences between different cultures).

✖ **Negative evaluation**

- ✖ Improper use of the Strange Situation has serious implications. Yeo (2003) reported how judgements are made about whether Aboriginal children should be in care, based on what white Australian culture deems appropriate parenting, leading to 25 per cent of children in care being Aborigines.
- ✖ The Strange Situation is not a valid measure of attachment, as the technique only measures attachment type to one attachment figure. Main & Weston (1981) found that children acted differently in the Strange Situation depending on which parent they were with.
- ✖ As attachment types vary cross-culturally and the Strange Situation is not applicable to all cultures, attachment theory is *culture bound* and appropriate mainly to Western cultures.

Practical application

The Strange Situation is used to make informed decisions about child placements in such instances as fostering – for example, to assess what children's attachment needs are when being placed in care and to determine whether or not children should be removed from their home environment.

pp. 119–28

3 Attachment

Bowlby's maternal deprivation hypothesis (MDH) (1951)

Focal study

Rutter et al. (1998) investigated whether sensitive care could overturn the effects of privation suffered in Romanian orphanages. Three groups of children were studied: orphans adopted before 6 months of age, orphans adopted between 6 months and 2 years of age, and orphans adopted after 2 years of age. A control group of 52 British adopted children were also assessed (to see if negative effects were due to separation from caregivers or institutional conditions). The children's level of cognitive functioning was measured. It was found that 50 per cent of Romanian orphans were cognitively retarded and underweight at initial assessment, while the children in the control group were not. At 4 years of age the orphans showed great improvements in physical and cognitive development, especially those adopted before 6 months of age, who did as well as the British adopted children. This suggests that negative effects of institutionalisation can be overcome with sensitive care.

OTHER STUDIES

- Robertson & Robertson (1971) found that children did show the short-term separation effects predicted by Bowlby's PDD model, but that such effects were preventable if alternative sensitive care and a normal home routine were provided. This suggests that Bowlby is wrong, as attachment disruption effects are not inevitable.

- Hetherington & Stanley-Hagan (1999) found that 25 per cent of children had long-term adjustment problems after parental divorce but most eventually adapted. This suggests that the effects of long-term separation are reversible.

- Schaffer (1996) found that nearly all children are negatively affected by divorce in the short term, which suggests that the effects of long-term deprivation are universal.

- Freud & Dann (1951) reported on 6 orphans, rescued from a Nazi concentration camp, suffering from privation. They had little language, refused to be separated and displayed hostility to adults. They gradually formed attachments with their caregivers, developing rapidly both physically and intellectually. Follow-up studies suggested their recovery was full and permanent.

Description

Bowlby's maternal deprivation hypothesis (MDH) argues that if attachments are broken, even in the short term, serious, permanent damage will occur to children's emotional, social and cognitive development. The MDH is examined by assessing the effects on children of various forms of disruption.

- *Separation* consists of short-term attachment disruption, like being left with a babysitter. The distress is characterised by Bowlby's PDD model (protest, despair, detachment). However, later research shows that such effects are avoidable if alternative, sensitive care is provided.

- *Deprivation* consists of long-term attachment disruption, such as through divorce. Effects are more

Fig 3.7 Professor Rutter's studies of Romanian orphans have aimed to see if the effects of institutionalisation can be overcome through loving care by adoptive parents

✔ It would seem logical that long-term separation would have greater negative effects on children's development than short-term separation, and research evidence backs this up.

✔ Robertson & Robertson's work detailing the effects of children undergoing short-term separations led to radical changes in hospital care. Regular visiting by family members was introduced, and work shifts were arranged so that children had consistent contact with familiar nurses in order for alternative attachments to form and negative separation effects to be avoided.

✔ Morison & Elwood (2005) found similar results to Rutter with a group of Romanian orphans adopted in Canada, which suggests Rutter's findings are reliable.

severe and longer lasting, but most children recover over time.

● *Privation* involves never forming attachments, with severe developmental retardation occurring. However, such effects are generally reversible in the long term if sensitive care is provided.

● *Institutionalisation* concerns childcare, such as that provided by children's homes. The effects resemble those of deprivation and privation. *Romanian orphanage studies* have shown that such negative effects can again be overcome by the provision of sensitive, nurturing care.

Overall, Bowlby's MDH can be seen to be valid in terms of the negative effects it details as a result of attachment disruption. However, contrary to Bowlby's beliefs, most negative effects seem to be avoidable or reversible.

✗ Negative evaluation

✗ Most evidence linking short-term separation to negative outcomes is correlational and does not show causality. Other factors may be involved; indeed Kagan *et al.* (1978) found no direct causal link between separation and later emotional and behavioural difficulties.

✗ Divorce can be beneficial to children, as it removes the negative environment of marital conflict and allows parents to have more time to give sensitive care to their children, meaning development actually improves in the long term rather than worsens.

✗ As the Romanian orphans were not studied during their time within the Romanian orphanages, it is not possible to state which aspects of their privation were most damaging to their development.

Practical application

A practical application of research into long-term deprivation is that some American states legally require divorcing parents to attend educational classes that teach them to understand and avoid the difficulties associated with disrupted attachments.

pp. 129–37

3 Attachment
The influence of early attachment on childhood and adult relationships

Focal study

Hazan & Shaver (1987) assessed possible links between childhood attachment and adult romantic relationships. 620 heterosexual participants responded to a 'love quiz' in a newspaper, selecting which of 3 descriptions – a secure, an insecure-resistant or an insecure-avoidant attachment type – reflected their feelings of adult romance. Participants also completed a checklist relating to childhood relationships with parents. The percentages of adults in the different attachment types matched those in Ainsworth's Strange Situation. Those identified with childhood secure attachments had positive perceptions of adult relationships and longer-lasting relationships. Those with insecure-resistant attachments doubted the existence of romantic love and its essentialness to happiness. Those with insecure-avoidant attachments had more self-doubts and, as in those with insecure attachments, increased loneliness. It was concluded that childhood attachment types are positively correlated with childhood attachment experiences.

Description

Bowlby's *continuity hypothesis* sees children's attachment types reflected in later relationships. This is based on the *internal working model*, which perceives an infant's main attachment relationship as forming a blueprint for future relationships. Attachment style is seen as providing children with beliefs about themselves and others and about the nature of relationships. According to this model, attachment types predict adult relationships, so that those with secure attachments in childhood go on to have intimate, secure adult relationships, while those with insecure attachments do not. Hazan & Shaver (1987) additionally proposed that early attachment patterns affect *romantic relationships*, *caregiving* and *sexuality* in adulthood.

OTHER STUDIES

- McCarthy (1999) assessed women with childhood insecure attachments. He found that women with insecure-avoidant attachments had less successful adult romantic relations, while those with insecure-resistant attachments had problems forming non-romantic adult friendships. This supports Bowlby's idea of an internal working model.

- Brennan & Shaver (1995) found that participants with insecure-avoidant attachments would have sex without strong feelings of love or being in a long-lasting relationship. Hazan & Shaver (1994) found that such individuals were more likely to have one-night stands and casual sex outside of established relationships and also preferred purely sexual contact to emotional contact. These studies support the concept of the internal working model.

- Kirkpatrick & Davis (1994) studied 300 dating couples for 3 years and found that participants with secure childhood attachments were more likely to have secure, satisfying relations. This supports Bowlby's continuity hypothesis.

Fig 3.8 Research suggests that individuals who form secure infant attachments go on to enjoy loving, long-lasting adult relationships

✔ Wood *et al.* (2003) reported that insecurely attached individuals are not doomed to have poor relationships, as the quality of relationship results from the interaction of partners' attachment styles. Insecurely attached people can have positive relationships if paired with securely attached partners.

✔ Hazan & Shaver's research provided a means of assessing the continuity between early attachment styles and the quality of later adult romantic relationships, which has been used by many other researchers to conduct further research.

✔ Much of the evidence in this area is correlational and therefore does not show causality. Important non-measured factors may also exert an influence.

Research indicates that continuity between early attachment styles and the quality of childhood relationships exists. Evidence also suggests that children who form attachments to each other in early life do not form romantic, sexual relationships with each other in adulthood. The idea of continuity between adults' attachment types and their children's is supported, possibly indicating a social learning effect. The quality of later adult relationships is related to early attachment styles, though it is not inevitable that those with insecure attachments as children will be condemned to unsuccessful relationships as adults. Individuals with insecure attachments as children can develop secure adult relationships if they are in relationships with those with secure attachments.

✖ An alternative viewpoint is the *temperament hypothesis*, which sees the quality of adult relationships as being determined biologically by innate personality. If true, then attempts to develop better relationships by changing attachment styles would not work.

✖ The internal working model is not universally supported. Zimmerman *et al.* (2000) reported that early attachment style did not predict the quality of later relationships. Life events, such as divorce, had a greater effect.

✖ The Strange Situation only measures attachment type with one person. Therefore, measurements using this technique in adults might only relate to a current relationship and not all adult relationships of an individual.

Practical application

The main practical application of research into this area is in relationship counselling. Attention needs to be paid to attachment styles of partners, in order for the best strategies to be formed to successfully guide individuals through times of relationship stress.

AQA
A-level

Psychology

For A-level Year 1 and AS

1

pp. 138–43

4 Psychopathology
Definitions of abnormality: deviation from social norms

Description

The *deviation from social norms* definition of abnormality implies that there is a 'correct' and an 'incorrect' way of behaving and that any deviation from the 'correct' way is abnormal. The social norms, to which there is an expectation for individuals to adhere, are therefore a set of unwritten rules of what is acceptable behaviour, which have been constructed by society. There is an argument that these norms are set by the ruling elite within a society and are more a means of policing people and maintaining social order than an objective definition of what is normal and abnormal. The deviation from social norms definition permits a distinction between what is seen as desirable and undesirable behaviour, classifying those exhibiting undesirable behaviour as *socially deviant*. This gives society, through its controlling institutions, like the health service, the right to intervene in people's lives in order to protect the rest of society and to 'treat' social deviants so that they can become 'normal' again and be returned to mainstream society. The definition can be seen as beneficial to abnormal individuals because deviants, such as those classed as sexually deviant, may be unable to recognise that their behaviour is maladaptive and therefore be unable to seek help by themselves. The deviation from social norms definition can also be seen to add a social dimension to the concept of abnormality, as it perceives the main purpose of mental health care as being to exclude from society individuals who are seen as behaving in unacceptable ways.

There are several types of social norms to which adherence is expected:

- *Situational/contextual norms,* where certain behaviours are expected/ not expected in certain situations. For example, it is acceptable for females to wear a bikini on the beach but not in the supermarket.
- *Developmental/age norms,* where certain behaviours are expected at different times in one's lifespan. For example, temper tantrums are perfectly acceptable for a 2-year-old to exhibit but not for a 40-year-old.
- *Cultural norms,* where certain behaviours are acceptable/unacceptable in different cultural settings, like homosexuality being accepted in Western cultures, but not in African ones.

✔ The social norms definition gives a clear indication of what is and what is not perceived as normal and this allows the relevant agencies, such as mental health practitioners, to know when they have a responsibility to intervene in people's lives. This is beneficial because it means individuals will get the clinical help that they probably would not have sought themselves if left to their own devices.

✔ The definition can be seen to establish norms of normality that apply in different circumstances, therefore giving a degree of flexibility that no other definition has. *Situational norms*, where the definition considers the social dimensions of behaviour, are where a behaviour seen as abnormal in one setting may be regarded as normal in another. For example, being naked in town is seen as abnormal, but not in a nudist colony. *Developmental norms* establish what behaviours are normal/abnormal at different ages. Playing hopscotch as a child is seen as normal, but not in adulthood. There are also *cultural norms* and *gender norms*, where normality changes across cultures and between genders, again showing the flexibility the definition offers.

❌ **Limitations**

✗ Szasz (1960) argued that the definition is used to justify discriminating against sections of society as a form of social control. Some countries, such as China, categorise political opponents as being abnormal and then forcibly treat them in mental institutions.

✗ There are individuals who adhere so strictly to social norms that they can be considered *conforming neurotics*. Such individuals fear rejection and ridicule so much that they conform rigidly to society's norms and worry excessively about them. This is a form of abnormality, yet the individuals are not classified as abnormal by the deviation from social norms definition.

✗ Social norms are not real in an objective sense, but are subjective, as they are based on the opinions of a society's elite and are then used to police those seen as challenging social order. Also, social norms refer to moral standards that change over time, like homosexuality once being classed as a mental disorder. A truly objective definition would not have such variations. Additionally, those who deviate from social norms may simply be individualistic or eccentric, rather than abnormal.

Practical application

For positive social change to occur, it is often necessary for social norms to be broken. This is a form of *minority influence*, where a *minority slowly* wins a majority over by going against mainstream social norms and changing people's belief systems. This is to be encouraged in organisations that require the formation of innovative ideas and practices.

pp. 147–8

4 Psychopathology
Definitions of abnormality: failure to function adequately

Description

The failure to function adequately definition of abnormality sees mental disorders as resulting from an inability to cope with day-to-day living. Behaviour is perceived as abnormal when individuals become so distressed with the pressures of everyday life that their behaviour becomes dysfunctional, for example, when an individual's ability to work properly is affected or when individuals cannot conduct normal interpersonal relationships. Due to an inability to cope with life, harmful behaviours are indulged in, like heavy drinking or drug taking. Such behaviours are themselves dysfunctional, but also contribute to further declines in personal functioning, leading to a diagnosis of abnormality.

Rosenhan & Seligman (1989) proposed that personal dysfunction has 7 features and that the more of these features an individual has, the more they are classed as abnormal:

1 *Personal distress*, which is seen as a key feature of abnormality and involves such things as depression and anxiety disorders

2 *Maladaptive behaviour*, which consists of exhibiting behaviour that prevents people from realising their life goals, both socially and at work

3 *Unpredictability*, which consists of exhibiting unexpected behaviours characterised by a loss of control, like mutilating oneself after a relationship is terminated

4 *Irrationality*, which consists of exhibiting behaviours non-explicable in any rational way, like heavy drinking in response to work pressures

5 *Observer discomfort*, which entails the exhibition of behaviours that cause discomfort to others, like behaving in an aggressive manner

6 *Violation of moral standards*, which consists of exhibiting behaviours that go against society's ethical standards, like being naked in a public place

7 *Unconventionality*, which entails the exhibition of non-standard behaviours, like dressing in the clothes of the opposite gender.

An overall assessment of how well individuals can cope with life is made by clinicians using the *Global Assessment of Functioning scale* (GAF), which rates levels of social, occupational and psychological functioning. In general, this is a definition used by clinicians that focuses on individuals' perceptions of their own mental health and is judged through criteria such as 'can hold down a job', 'is able to dress themself' etc.

- ✔ Most people who seek clinical help do so because they see themselves as suffering from psychological problems that interfere with their ability to function normally, both socially and at work. Therefore, sufferers' perceptions of their problems match the criteria of the definition, giving it support.
- ✔ The GAF scale, used by clinicians to calculate an individual's overall level of functioning, is scored on a continuous scale. It therefore allows clinicians to see the degree to which individuals are abnormal and helps them to decide who needs what degree of psychiatric help.
- ✔ The definition permits judgement by knowledgeable others, as to whether individuals are functioning properly, because it focuses on observable and therefore measurable behaviour. This also allows the formation of a practical 'checklist' of factors that individuals can use to assess their own level of abnormality.
- ✔ As the definition recognises the importance of the role of the personal experience of individuals, it permits mental disorders to be regarded from the personal perspective of the individuals suffering from the disorders, therefore giving a greater depth of understanding to the definition.

✖ Limitations

- ✖ Although an individual's behaviour may be distressing to others and perceived as an inability to function adequately, it may bring no distress to the individual and be perceived by them as perfectly functional. For example, Stephen Gough is known as the 'naked rambler' for his long-distance walks that he conducts in the nude. He has been jailed many times for his behaviour, which he sees as perfectly normal and which causes him no distress.

- ✖ Mental disorders are not always accompanied by personal dysfunction; indeed the opposite may be true. Harold Shipman, a Lancashire doctor, displayed an outwardly normal disposition, while over a 23-year period as a doctor he murdered at least 215 of his patients before killing himself in prison.

- ✖ Some of the features comprising 'adequate functioning' are subjective and difficult to define and measure objectively. This also applies to individual differences between people; what is normal behaviour for introverts, like wearing non-flamboyant clothes, would be completely different for extroverts. The definition fails to incorporate this.

Fig 4.1 Harold Shipman

Practical application

A great practical application of the definition is that it permits a large element of self-diagnosis by individuals. Using a checklist of factors to assess their own level of abnormality, individuals are then able to seek clinical help through self-recognition that this is necessary. Most people receiving clinical help sought it themselves in the first instance.

pp. 148–9

4 Psychopathology

Definitions of abnormality: deviation from ideal mental health

Description

The deviation from ideal mental health definition of abnormality concentrates on identifying the characteristics and abilities people should possess in order to be considered normal. A lack of or impoverishment of these characteristics and abilities constitutes a diagnosis of abnormality. The definition therefore has a perception of mental disorder as being similar to that of physical health, in that an absence of wellbeing means that an individual is ill. Jahoda (1958) devised the concept of ideal mental health and identified set characteristics that individuals need to exhibit to be seen as normal. The more of these criteria an individual fails to realise, and the further away they are from meeting individual criteria, then the more abnormal they are considered to be. Similar to the deviation from social norms definition and the failure to function adequately definition, the deviation from ideal mental health definition also concentrates on behaviours and characteristics that are seen as desirable, rather than undesirable.

There are 6 characteristics of ideal mental health:

1 *Positive attitude towards oneself*, which involves having self-respect and a positive self-concept where individuals regard themselves favourably

2 *Self-actualisation*, where individuals should experience personal growth and development. Self-actualisation involves 'becoming everything one is capable of becoming'

3 *Autonomy*, which concerns individuals being independent, self-reliant and able to make personal decisions

4 *Resistance to stress*, where individuals should be in possession of effective coping strategies in response to stress and should be able to cope with everyday anxiety-provoking situations

5 *Accurate perception of reality*, where individuals should be able to perceive the world in a non-distorted manner and possess an objective and realistic perception of the world

6 *Environmental mastery*, which concerns individuals being skilled in all aspects of their lives, both socially and occupationally and being able to meet the requirements of all situations they experience. Additionally, individuals should possess the flexibility to be able to adapt to changing life circumstances, both socially and occupationally.

✔ Strengths

✔ As the definition gives identification to specific types of dysfunction, it permits targeting of exact areas for mental health practitioners to work on when treating a person's abnormal condition. This can prove beneficial when treating different types of disorders – for example, focusing on the specific problem areas of a person with depression.

✔ A positive aspect to this definition is that it stresses positive accomplishments, rather than failures and distress, and therefore promotes a positive approach to mental disorders by focusing on what qualities are appropriate, rather than which ones are inappropriate.

✔ The definition can be seen to take a *holistic* approach, one that is interested in developing the whole person, rather than a *reductionist* approach that just focuses on individual areas of a person's behaviour.

✔ A positive aspect of the definition is that, as it identifies areas where personal weaknesses exist, it can be seen to be promoting self-growth by giving opportunities to improve on these areas.

✖ Limitations

✖ According to these criteria, most – if not all – people would be abnormal most of the time. Therefore, the criteria are over-demanding. For example, few people experience continual personal growth, indeed the opposite may be periodically common. Self-actualisation is seen as something that very few people achieve, so does this mean the majority of us are abnormal? The criteria may actually be *ideals* of mental health: how we would like to be, rather than how we actually are.

✖ The characteristics used to assess mental health are *culturally relative* and should not be used to judge people from other cultures and sub-cultures. For instance, some mental disorders only exist in certain cultures, such as *Koro*, found only in south-east Asia, China and Africa, which is a disorder concerning the belief that a man's penis is fatally retracting into his body. Therefore, Western cultural views of abnormality, like the deviation from ideal mental health definition, are not culture-free.

✖ Many of the criteria are subjective, being vague in description and rather hard to measure in any objective way. Measuring physical indicators of health is generally easy, for example by using blood tests and scans, but diagnosis of mental health is much trickier and relies largely upon the self-reports of patients, which may not be reliable if they have a mental disorder.

Practical application
A practical application of the definition is that it permits identification of what is needed specifically to achieve normality. This therefore allows mental health practitioners to create personal targets for patients to work towards so that they can achieve better mental health.

Fig 4.2 The deviation from ideal mental health definition may be more about the ideal self than the actual self

pp. 150–1

4 Psychopathology

Definitions of abnormality: statistical infrequency

Description

The statistical infrequency definition of abnormality sees behaviours that are statistically rare as being abnormal. Data are collected about various behaviours and personal characteristics, so that their distributions throughout the general population can be calculated and plotted. This then allows the formation of *normal distributions* for these behaviours and characteristics. Normal distribution concerns the idea that for any given behaviour or characteristic there will be a spread of scores that forms a bell-shaped curve. Most people's scores occur on or around the mean and a decreasing amount of scores occur on either side of the mean, further away from the norm. This means there will be a symmetrical distribution of scores (as many scores below the mean as above the mean). Any scores that fall outside of normal distribution, which is usually seen as being 2 standard deviation points away from the mean (about 5 per cent of a population, which is 1 in 20 people), are regarded as abnormal in this definition. So taking intelligence, for example, data are collected on an individual's IQ scores (seen as being a valid measurement of intelligence, though this is disputed by many psychologists) and then used to plot the distribution of IQ scores on and around the mean. The mean score for IQ is supposed to be 100 IQ points and most individuals will be seen to score on or around this amount of measured intelligence. Decreasing amounts of people will have IQ scores that are further away from the norm (either above or below it) and therefore the data form the classic bell-shaped (also known as the Gaussian) curve. Two standard deviation points below the norm brings us to a score of 70 IQ points and 2 standard deviation points above the norm brings us to 130 IQ points. In terms of the definition, the 5 per cent of people in total who score below and above these levels are classed as abnormal, as they fall outside the normal distribution.

The statistical infrequency definition does nothing more than create the statistical criteria upon which behaviours and personal characteristics can be deemed to be normal or abnormal; it makes no judgements about quality of life or the nature of mental disorders.

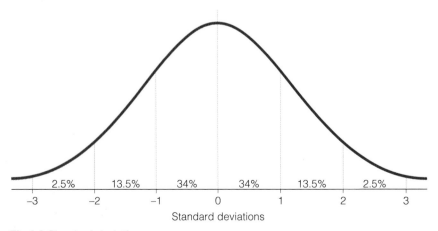

Fig 4.3 Standard deviation

✔ The definition makes no value judgements about what is or is not abnormal. So, for example, homosexuality, once defined as a mental disorder under earlier versions of diagnostic criteria, would not be seen under this definition as 'morally wrong' or 'unacceptable' – instead it would be viewed merely as less statistically frequent than heterosexuality.

✔ There are definite examples of situations where statistically determined criteria can be used to decide abnormality – for example, with mental retardation, where individuals will suffer with severe learning difficulties and thus need assistance with day-to-day living.

✔ The definition is a very objective one, as it relies on real, unbiased data. Once data about a behaviour or personal characteristic have been collected, the information becomes a very non-subjective and value-free means of deciding who is abnormal and who is not.

✔ The definition also permits an overall view of which particular behaviours and characteristics are infrequent within the population and so can help us determine which behaviours and characteristics can be regarded as abnormal.

✘ Limitations

✘ A major weakness of the definition is that not all statistically infrequent behaviours are actually abnormal. Many statistically rare behaviours and characteristics are desirable rather than undesirable ones. For example, being highly intelligent (determined by normal distribution, as being above around 130 IQ points) is indeed statistically rare, but would be regarded as desirable.

✘ Although the definition claims to be objective in not using value judgements, but instead statistical data, to determine what deviations in behaviour and characteristics are to be considered abnormal, a judgement is made about where exactly to draw the line. Indeed some mental disorders, like depression, vary greatly between individuals in terms of severity, but the definition does not account for this.

✘ Not all abnormal behaviours are statistically infrequent. Some statistically frequent and therefore 'normal' behaviours are actually abnormal. For instance, about 10 per cent of people are chronically depressed at some point in their lives, which would be so common as not to be seen as statistically rare and hence abnormal.

Practical application

A practical application of the definition is that as it is based purely on objective data, with no subjective judgements made about what is and what is not abnormal, it gives mental health practitioners a clear indication of when an individual needs clinical help. It can therefore be used as objective evidence to decide when an individual needs treatment.

pp. 151–3

4 Psychopathology
Characteristics of phobias, depression and OCD

Phobias

Everyone experiences anxiety – it is a natural response to potentially dangerous stimuli. Phobias, however, are anxiety disorders characterised by extreme irrational fears that go beyond any real risk. These can be very enduring, lasting for many years. Around 10 per cent of people will suffer from a phobia at some point in their lives, with females having twice the incidence of phobias as males. Most phobias emerge in childhood, but lessen in strength during adulthood. Sufferers generally have insight into their phobias and know that their fears and reactions are irrational, but they cannot consciously control them. Phobias divide into:

- *simple phobias*, involving fears of specific things, like coulrophobia (fear of clowns). Simple phobias further divide into sub-types of *animal phobias*, *injury phobias*, *situational phobias* and *natural environment phobias*
- *social phobias*, involving being over-anxious in social situations, like giving public speeches
- *agoraphobia*, involving fear of leaving home or a safe place.

Characteristics of phobias

Behavioural

- *Avoidance responses* – efforts are made to avoid anxiety-producing situations.
- *Disruption of functioning* – severe disability to everyday working and social functioning occurs.

Emotional

- *Persistent, excessive fear* – high levels of anxiety are produced by phobic stimuli.
- *Fear from exposure to phobic stimulus* – production of immediate fear response to phobic stimulus.

Cognitive

- *Recognition of exaggerated anxiety* – phobics are consciously aware that their anxiety levels are over-stated.

Fig 4.4 Coulrophobia is a fear of clowns

Depression

About 20 per cent of people will suffer from depression, with women twice as vulnerable as men, especially in adolescence, a time where many people experience body dissatisfaction and low self-esteem. Depression is a mood disorder characterised by feelings of despondency and hopelessness, generally occurring in cycles. The average age of onset is in one's 20s and 10 per cent of people with severe depression commit suicide. There are 2 main types: *unipolar depression*, which is where a constant low mood is experienced, and *bipolar depression*, where sufferers swing between elevated (high) and despondent (low) moods. Depression is also broken down into *endogenous depression*, which is related to internal biochemical factors, and *exogenous depression*, which is related to stressful experiences. At least 5 *symptoms* (clinical characteristics) must be apparent every day for 2 weeks for depression to be diagnosed.

Characteristics of depression

Behavioural

- *Loss of energy* – sufferers experience reduced energy levels.
- *Social impairment* – reduced levels of interaction with friends and family occur.

Emotional

- *Loss of enthusiasm* – sufferers experience a lessened interest in, and pleasure of, everyday activities.

- *Sense of worthlessness* – persistent feelings of reduced worth and inappropriate sensations of guilt are experienced.

Cognitive

- *Reduced concentration* – difficulties with paying and maintaining attention, as well as slowed-down thinking and indecisiveness, can be experienced.
- *Poor memory* – difficulties with retrieval of memories can occur.

OCD

About 2 per cent of people have obsessive–compulsive disorder (OCD), an anxiety disorder characterised by persistent, recurrent, unpleasant thoughts and repetitive, ritualistic behaviours. Obsessions are the things that sufferers think about, while compulsions are the behaviours they indulge in as a result of the obsessions. Obsessions generally comprise forbidden or inappropriate ideas and visual images that are not based in reality, like being convinced that germs lurk everywhere, and these lead to feelings of extreme anxiety. Common obsessions include contamination, fear of losing control, perfectionism, sex and religion. Female obsessions tend to be more about contamination, while male ones can concern sex and religion more. Compulsions consist of intense, uncontrollable urges to perform repetitive tasks in order to reduce the anxiety caused by obsessive ideas, such as constantly washing yourself to get rid of the germs. There is a realisation that the obsessions and compulsions are inappropriate, but they cannot be consciously controlled. OCD symptoms often overlap with those of autism and Tourette's syndrome.

Characteristics of OCD

Behavioural

- *Hinders everyday functioning* – obsessive ideas create such high levels of anxiety that the ability to perform everyday actions is severely hindered.

- *Social impairment* – anxiety levels are so high that they limit the ability to conduct meaningful interpersonal relationships.

Emotional

- *Extreme anxiety* – persistent inappropriate ideas and visual images create excessive levels of anxiety.

Cognitive

- *Attentional bias* – perception tends to focus primarily on anxiety-generating stimuli.
- *Recurrent and persistent thoughts* – constantly repeated, obsessive, intrusive thoughts and ideas are experienced.

Practical application

Characteristics of mental disorders like phobias, depression and OCD allow clinicians to create 'checklists' that permit them to diagnose which particular disorder an individual may be suffering from. Such characteristics are written up into diagnostic criteria, such as the **International Classification of Diseases** (ICD) and the **Diagnostic and Statistical Manual of Mental Disorders** (DSM).

pp. 154–61

61

4 Psychopathology
The behavioural approach to explaining and treating phobias

Focal study

Brosnan & Thorpe (2006) investigated whether a fear of computers could be treated with SD. In Study 1, computer-anxious participants were given a 10-week programme of SD; while in Study 2, one group of computer-anxious participants were given a similar programme of SD and another group of computer-anxious participants received no treatment. In both studies there was also a control group of non-computer-anxious participants. In Study 1, anxiety levels in the computer-anxious participants declined to levels similar to the control group, while coping strategies noticeably improved. In Study 2, reduction in anxiety in the computer-anxious participants was 3 times greater than in the non-treated group over the course of a year. At the end of 1 year the computer-anxious participants' anxiety levels matched those of the control group, while the non-treated group remained significantly more anxious. This suggests that SD is effective in reducing technophobia (fear of technology).

OTHER STUDIES

- Watson & Rayner (1920) got a boy to hold a rat that he was not afraid of, while simultaneously scaring him by banging a bar behind his head. This was repeated over a period until the boy, when presented with the rat, would show fear. This illustrates how phobias can be learned through classical conditioning.

- Di Gallo (1996) showed that phobias of cars, developed through traumatic car accidents, were maintained by sufferers making avoidance responses, such as remaining at home rather than making car journeys to see friends. This illustrates how phobias are maintained by negative reinforcements associated with operant conditioning.

- King et al. (1998) reported that case studies showed that children acquired strong phobias through traumatic experiences, demonstrating the role of classical conditioning in the development of phobias, where a fear response becomes associated with an originally neutral stimulus.

Description

The behavioural explanation sees phobias as learned through experience via the process of association. The *two-process model* sees phobias as being learned through *classical conditioning*, with the maintenance of phobias occurring through *operant conditioning*.

- Classical conditioning sees a neutral stimulus becoming associated with a fear response so that the neutral stimulus produces the fear response on its own. For example, if a person gets mugged at night, then the neutral stimulus of night-time could become paired with a fear response, so that a person develops a phobia of the dark.

- With operant conditioning, a behaviour that is rewarding reinforces

Fig 4.5 Systematic desensitisation involves a step-by-step approach to a feared object or situation

the behaviour (makes it likely to occur again). So when an *avoidance response* is made to reduce the chances of contact with a phobic stimulus, it is *negatively reinforcing* – it reduces the fear response and thus the phobia is maintained, as the sufferer repeatedly makes reinforcing avoidance responses.

Systematic desensitisation (SD) is a behavioural therapy for treating phobias and involves a sufferer learning relaxation techniques, which are then used to repeatedly reduce anxiety, as the sufferer goes through a progressive hierarchy of exposure to the phobic stimulus – for example, a step-by-step approach to holding a spider to reduce a fear of the beasties.

pp. 163–71

4 Psychopathology
The cognitive approach to explaining and treating depression

Focal study

Beevers et al. (2010) investigated whether brain areas associated with cognitive control were affected by emotional stimuli in participants with depression. Thirteen females with low levels of depression were compared with 14 females with high levels of depression. Participants were given 3 facial stimuli cues: happy, sad and neutral (as well as a control geometric-shape cue). A single cue was presented on a screen along with 1 of 2 target stimuli (either * or **). Time taken to recognise which target stimulus was presented was measured. Participants simultaneously had their brains scanned. Lower levels of activation were found in the high depression group in brain areas requiring cognitive control over emotional stimuli (when processing happy and sad faces) but no differences were found between the two groups in brain areas not requiring such cognitive control (neutral faces and geometric shapes). This supports the cognitive explanation that people with higher levels of depression have problems activating brain areas associated with cognitive control of emotional information.

OTHER STUDIES

- Boury et al. (2001) used the Beck depression inventory to monitor participants' negative thoughts and found that people with depression misinterpret facts and experiences in a negative way and feel hopeless about the future. This supports Beck's cognitive theory.

- Koster et al. (2005) showed participants a screen with positive, negative or neutral words on it. Then a square appeared on the screen and participants were asked to press a button to show where it was. He found that depressed participants took longer to disengage from depressive words than non-depressed participants. This supports the cognitive theory that depressives over-focus on negative stimuli.

- McIntosh & Fischer (2000) investigated whether the negative triad contains the proposed 3 distinct types of negative thought. They found no separation of negative thought, but instead a one-dimensional negative perception of self. This suggests that a negative triad of separate types of negative thought does not exist.

Description

The *cognitive approach* sees depression as occurring as a result of maladaptive (irrational) thought processes. Beck (1987) saw people becoming depressed through *negative schemas* (tendencies to perceive the world negatively), consisting of:

- *ineptness schemas* that make people with depression expect to fail

- *self-blame schemas* that make people with depression feel responsible for all misfortunes

- *negative self-evaluation schemas* that constantly remind people with depression of their worthlessness

and fuelled by *cognitive biases* (tendencies to think in particular ways) that make individuals misperceive reality in a negative way.

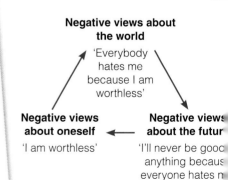

Fig 4.6 Beck's negative triad

✔ The explanation is supported by the existence of a wealth of research evidence supporting the idea of cognitive vulnerability being linked to the onset of depression, with people with depression tending to selectively attend to negative stimuli.

✔ Cognitive therapies for depression have proven to be very effective compared to therapies based on other explanations, which suggests the explanation may have a higher validity than other explanations.

✔ The explanation acknowledges that non-cognitive aspects, like genes, development and early experiences, can lead to negative thinking patterns, which then leads to the onset of depression. This gives the theory greater explanatory power.

Negative schemas and cognitive biases maintain the *negative triad*, three pessimistic thought patterns concerning the *self*, the *world* and the *future*.

Ellis' *ABC model* sees depression occurring through an *activating agent* (where an event occurs), a *belief* held about the event and a *consequence* involving a response to the event. Cognitive treatments are based on modifying maladaptive thought processes to alter behavioural and emotional states – for example, *rational emotive behaviour therapy* (REBT), which seeks to make irrational and negative thinking more rational and positive. Therapists help patients realise how irrational their thinking is and encourage them to practise more optimistic thinking by *reframing*, which involves reinterpretation of the ABC in a more positive and logical way.

❌ **Negative evaluation**

✗ The cognitive approach has difficulties in explaining and treating the manic component of bipolar depression, lessening support for the theory as an overall explanation for depression.

✗ Most of the evidence concerning negative thought patterns and depression is correlational and does not therefore show that negative thinking causes depression. Beck believed it was a bi-directional relationship where depressed thoughts cause depression and vice versa.

✗ The treatment aetiology fallacy argues that the fact that cognitive therapies are effective in treating depression does not necessarily give support to the cognitive explanation on which they are based.

Practical application

Another effective cognitive therapy for treating depression is the treatment of negative automatic thoughts (TNAT), which, like REBT, works by restructuring maladaptive ways of thinking into more adaptive, rational ways of thinking.

pp. 172–83

4 Psychopathology
The biological approach to explaining and treating OCD

Focal study

Koran *et al.* (2000) investigated whether treating non-responsive forms of OCD with simultaneous drug treatments was more effective than single-drug treatments. Ten patients who had not responded to 10 weeks of treatment with the SRI antidepressant fluoxetine were the participants. All participants had been diagnosed with OCD for at least a year. Treatment with fluoxetine continued but increasing levels of another atypical antipsychotic drug, olanzapine, were also given for an additional period of 8 weeks. Nine participants completed the treatment and it was found that mean OCD symptom scores dropped by 16 per cent, with 1 patient showing a 68 per cent improvement and 2 others 30 and 29 per cent improvements. This suggests that giving simultaneous drug therapies can be more effective than single-drug treatment with resistant forms of OCD. However, 6 participants did experience significant weight increase, illustrating the possible side effects of such treatments.

Description

The biological approach sees obsessive–compulsive disorder (OCD) as occurring by physiological means through genetic transmission and faulty brain mechanisms.

The genetic explanation focuses on the degree to which OCD is inherited. Findings from twin and gene mapping studies indicate a genetic link, with particular genes seen as increasing vulnerability to the disorder. There is a possibility of varying rates of genetic influence upon different sub-types of OCD.

Some forms of OCD are linked to breakdowns in immune system functioning, like streptococcal throat infections, Lyme's disease and influenza. This indicates that OCD may also develop

OTHER STUDIES

- Hu (2006) compared serotonin activity levels between sufferers and non-sufferers of OCD and found that serotonin levels were significantly lower in OCD sufferers. This gives support to the idea that the neurotransmitter is involved in the development of the disorder.

- Fallon & Nields (1994) reported that 40 per cent of people contracting Lyme's disease incur neural damage resulting in psychiatric conditions like OCD, supporting the idea that OCD may develop from damage to brain mechanisms.

- Stewart *et al.* (2007) used gene mapping on sufferers and non-sufferers of OCD, to find a link to chromosome 14 marker D14S588, indicating a possible genetic link to the condition.

- Julien (2007) reviewed studies of the effectiveness of SSRI antidepressants in treating OCD and reported that although symptoms do not fully disappear, between 50 and 80 per cent of patients show improvements that allow them to live a fairly normal lifestyle. This supports the effectiveness of the treatment.

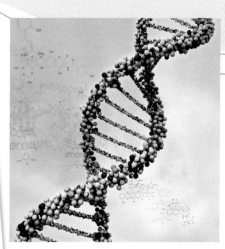

Fig 4.7 Gene mapping studies allow researchers to test the genetic explanation

✔ Evidence suggests that genetic factors are more at work in the expression of certain types of OCD, especially those involving obsessions about contamination, aggression and religion, and compulsions involving washing, ordering and arranging. This implies that some types of OCD are more genetic in nature than others.

✔ Drug treatments for OCD are effective, as they reduce symptom levels, are relatively cheap, do not require a therapist to administer them and are a familiar means of treatment.

✔ Gene mapping studies have been useful in indicating that a single 'OCD' gene does not exist, but that instead there are a number of genes that appear to contribute to increased vulnerability to the disorder.

from damage to brain mechanisms, with children more at risk from such factors than adults. PET scans have shown relatively low levels of serotonin activity in the brains of OCD sufferers. As drugs that increase serotonin activity reduce the symptoms of OCD, this suggests that the neurotransmitter may play a key role in determining the condition. Research also indicates faulty functioning of the orbital frontal cortex brain area, which results in sufferers having difficulties in ignoring impulses, so they turn into obsessions, resulting in compulsive behaviour.

The main biological treatment is drugs, with antidepressants that heighten serotonin activity most favoured.

✘ **Negative evaluation**

✘ Although research suggests a genetic component to OCD, there must also be an environmental influence because otherwise twin studies would show a concordance rate of 100 per cent in MZ twins, which they do not.

✘ Not all OCD patients respond positively to drugs that increase serotonin activity, which lowers support for the idea that the neurotransmitter is involved in all cases of the disorder.

✘ A limitation of treating OCD with drug therapies is that they can result in a wide range of unpleasant side effects, including loss of sex drive or sexual ability, irritability, sleep pattern disturbance, headaches and lack of appetite.

Practical application

Aside from drug therapies, another biological treatment of OCD is that of psychosurgery, but only for severe cases of the disorder which are non-responsive to other treatments. A more recent and less invasive treatment is deep-brain stimulation, which uses magnetic pulses to block out obsessional thoughts.

pp. 184–94

5 Approaches
The behaviourist approach

Focal study

Pavlov (1903), investigating the role of salivation in digestion, became interested in how dogs learned to salivate before food was presented to them. The dogs had learned to predict the arrival of food by making associations, such as the kitchen door being opened, with being fed. The stimulus of food (unconditioned stimulus – UCS) naturally produced the response of salivation (unconditioned response – UCR), but Pavlov also rang a bell (conditioned stimulus – CS) when presenting the food, something that does not naturally produce the response of salivation. After doing this an average of 7 times, a dog would then salivate just to the sound of the bell (conditioned response – CR) with no presentation of food. This suggests that the dogs had learned to associate the bell with the presentation of food. Pavlov called this kind of learning classical conditioning.

OTHER STUDIES

- Skinner (1948) found that rats, placed in a Skinner box, would move around and sometimes accidentally knock a lever, triggering the release of a food pellet. Gradually the rats came to associate pressing the lever with getting rewarded with food, and eventually they did this immediately and consistently upon being put in the box. This suggests the food pellet was acting as a positive reinforcement, strengthening the behaviour and increasing the chances that it would occur again in similar circumstances.

- Bandura et al. (1961) found that children who observed an adult model behave aggressively by beating a 'Bobo doll' were more aggressive when allowed to play with toys than children who observed a non-aggressive adult model or no model at all. Boys tended to imitate a model more if the model was male, while girls tended to imitate a model more if the model was female. This suggests that behaviour can be learned through observation and imitation of a role model, especially when an individual identifies with a model.

Description

The behaviourist approach sees humans born as *tabula rasa* ('blank slates') with all behaviour learned from experience and no genetic influences. The approach only focuses on observable behaviours, as they are seen as scientifically measurable. Therefore, there is no place in behaviourism for the study of hidden mental processes. Behaviourism believes it is valid to study animals, as they share similar principles of learning with humans. There are 3 main forms of learning:

1 *Classical conditioning*, investigated by *Pavlov*, concerns reflex actions, where a stimulus becomes associated with a response and as such occurs when a response produced naturally by a specific stimulus becomes associated with another stimulus not normally associated with that response.

2 *Operant conditioning*, investigated by *Skinner*, concerns voluntary behaviour, with learning occurring via reinforcement of

Before learning
Food (UCS) → *Salivation* (UCR)

During learning
Food (UCS) + *Bell* (CS) → *Salivation* (UCR)

After learning
Bell (CS) → *Salivation* (CR)

Fig 5.1 Classical conditioning as produced by Pavlov's dogs

- ✔ The behaviourist approach is supported by a wealth of research evidence that demonstrates that humans do indeed learn through classical and operant conditioning and social learning. The approach is also supported by people's everyday experiences of how they learn new behaviours.
- ✔ Behaviourism is seen as having scientific rigour, as the approach is based on the use of strictly controlled laboratory experiments and an emphasis on objective measurements of observable behaviour.
- ✔ Social learning theory acknowledges the role of thought processes in determining whether behaviour will be imitated or not.

behaviour. This may be through *positive reinforcement*, where a behaviour becomes likely to occur again because it had a pleasant outcome, or through *negative reinforcement*, where a behaviour becomes likely to occur again because it resulted in avoidance of something unpleasant happening.

3 *Social learning theory*, investigated by *Bandura*, involves behaviour being learned through observation and imitation of models whose behaviours are seen to be reinforced. *Identification* concerns when an individual is influenced by another because they are likeable or similar to them. *Vicarious reinforcement* concerns the rewards an observer sees another receiving for their behaviour. The types of consideration (thinking) that occur before an observed behaviour is imitated are known as *mediational processes*.

❌ Negative evaluation

- ✗ Critics see behaviourism as being far too rooted in the results from animal research. Animals do not necessarily learn in the same way as humans, which creates problems of generalising research findings from animals to humans.
- ✗ Behaviourism sees behaviour as deterministic, whereby experience programmes us to act unthinkingly in certain ways. There is no role for free will, whereby individuals consciously decide on their behaviour.
- ✗ Behaviourism tends to ignore the important role that nature plays in determining behaviour. The approach sees all behaviour as learned, therefore neglecting the influence of factors such as genetics and evolution in shaping behaviour.

Practical application

One practical application of the approach is behavioural treatments for mental disorders. An example of this is **systematic desensitisation** (see **page 63**), which is used to treat phobias by using relaxation strategies to break down irrational fears in a step-by-step approach.

Lights

Loudspeaker

Food dispenser

Electrified grid

Response lever

Fig 5.2 Skinner's box for rats

pp. 206–17

5 Approaches
The origins of psychology and the cognitive approach

Focal study

Simons & Chabris (1999) investigated to what extent people are aware of information present in their visual field. 228 participants watched films of 2 teams of 3 players, one team dressed in white T-shirts and the other in black T-shirts, passing a basketball to team members. Participants were specifically asked to count the number of passes made by the white team. After doing this, participants were asked if they had noticed anything unusual. 54 per cent failed to notice a man in a gorilla suit or a woman with an umbrella who were prominent in the films. This suggests that humans are only aware of information in their visual field that they select to pay attention to. The study also illustrates how scientific means of investigation can be used to explore the role of mental processes in behaviour.

Description

Wundt (1875) established the first psychology laboratory in Leipzig, Germany, using *introspection* as his research tool, whereby researchers examined their own conscious thoughts, feelings and sensations in a controlled environment. However, findings proved not to be replicable, as they were based on only one person's subjective viewpoint. Introspection was soon abandoned, but it was from this starting point that psychology developed to use increasingly scientific methods. Although not all aspects of modern psychology are totally scientific, nor are all psychologists scientists, the majority of the subject and its practitioners are seen as scientifically based.

Neisser (1959) is credited with starting *cognitive psychology*. Although a more modern approach, cognitive psychology has links with introspection, as both see behaviour as being understood by reference to the mental processes

OTHER STUDIES

- Postman & Bruner (1947) showed participants a photo of a black man and a white man arguing, with the white man brandishing a knife. When asked to recall the photo, many participants wrongly recalled the black man having the knife. This illustrates how schema affect mental processes such as perception, as the stereotype of black people being aggressive and carrying weapons was a common view held at the time.

- Hemond *et al.* (2007) gave participants pictures of faces and objects to look at while simultaneously scanning their brains with an fMRI scanner. It was found that the *fusiform gyrus* brain area was activated significantly more during face recognition than during object recognition, which suggests this brain area is associated with processing faces. This demonstrates how the cognitive and biological approaches can be combined together to investigate mental processes.

Fig 5.3 Simons & Chabris found that many observers did not notice a man in a gorilla suit. Figure provided by Daniel Simons.

underpinning it. The approach has 4 assumptions:

1 *Scientific study* – mental processes should be investigated through scientifically based studies.

2 *Mind as a computer* – the mind can be seen as similar to a computer in having an input of sensory information, which is then processed to produce an output in the form of behaviour.

3 *Importance of mental processes* – the role of stimulus and response in behaviour can only be truly understood by reference to the mental processes occurring between them.

4 *The role of schemas* – behaviour is affected by schemas, mental representations of the world formed from experience, which affect how individuals perceive the world. Ultimately an individual will perceive what they expect to perceive based on previous experience.

Practical application

Findings from research into mental processes have produced practical applications, such as devising strategies for people with impairments to their working memory to help them focus better on tasks at hand. Examples include breaking instructions down into individual steps and getting sufferers to periodically repeat these instructions.

pp. 198, 218–23

5 Approaches
The biological approach

Focal study

Grootheest *et al.* (2005) investigated the extent to which obsessive–compulsive disorder (OCD) is an inherited condition. A meta-analysis of 28 twin studies, ranging from 1929 to the modern era (though the vast majority were carried out since 1965 under modern diagnostic criteria), was conducted. It comprised 10,034 twin pairs. It was found that OCD seemed to have a genetic component ranging from 45 to 65 per cent in children and from 27 to 47 per cent in adults. This strongly suggests that OCD has a genetic basis, especially childhood forms of the disorder. The use of twin studies demonstrates how biology, in this instance in the form of genetics, can have a dominant influence on behaviour.

Description

The *biological approach* sees behaviour as based within the physiology of the body, with *genes, evolution, brain structures* and *biochemistry* being the main influences. The chromosomes inherited from our parents form our *genotype* (our basic genetic make-up) and this interacts with environmental factors to form our *phenotype* (our actual behaviour and characteristics shown). The gradual process of behavioural change that occurs due to the *evolutionary* process of *natural selection* is genetically transmitted and so is also included within the biological approach. *Brain structures* are also seen as important in determining and monitoring behaviour, with different brain areas associated with different types of behavioural functioning. Specific *biological structures* within the

OTHER STUDIES

- Kessler *et al.* (2003) used PET and MRI scans to find that people with schizophrenia had elevated levels of the neurotransmitter dopamine in the basal forebrain and substantia nigra/ventral tegemental brain areas, which illustrates how biochemistry can affect behaviour, on this occasion in the form of a mental disorder.

- Dudley *et al.* (2008) found that ants in salt-poor environments preferred salty solutions to sweet ones, which suggests that this is an adaptive response to maintain evolutionary fitness (salt being essential to survival). This was supported by carnivorous ants not showing the salt preference, as they get ample salt from their prey, and therefore showed how evolution can shape behaviour.

- Siegel & Victoroff (2009) found that defensive and predatory forms of aggression appear to be controlled by the limbic system in the brain, with the cerebral cortex brain area playing an important role in moderating levels of aggression. This illustrates how brain areas are related to specific forms of behaviour in line with the biological approach.

Fig 5.4 Research with identical twins is useful for investigating the basis of certain behaviours

✔ The biological approach uses scientific methods of investigation that incorporate measures which are mainly objective (not a researcher's personal opinions). Examples include brain scanning, like MRI and PET scans, and measurements of biochemistry, like dopamine levels.

✔ It is possible to combine the biological and cognitive approaches together, as in cognitive neuroscience, to give a fuller understanding of human behaviour. Cognitive neuroscience uses biological techniques, like brain scanning, to try and identify in which particular brain areas specific mental processes are located and managed.

✔ The biological approach is supported by a wealth of research evidence that suggests much human behaviour has large biological elements.

body connect together to determine behaviour, such as the 2 parts of the nervous system, the *central nervous system* (CNS) (consisting of the brain and spinal cord), which transmits information to and from the environment, and the *peripheral nervous system* (PNS) (the accompanying system running throughout the body that acts with the CNS), which transmits information concerning the limbs and torso. *Neurons* are the individual nerve cells that transmit information within the nervous system, with each individual possessing billions of them.

The *biochemistry* of the body consists of chemical messengers within the body. *Hormones* are chemical messengers that travel in blood and other bodily fluids, while *neurotransmitters* are chemicals that travel within the brain in cerebral fluid.

❌ **Negative evaluation**

✗ Critics argue that explanations based on the biological approach are too simplistic and do not acknowledge the complexity of a lot of human behaviour. This means that such explanations are *reductionist* (explaining a complex phenomenon in terms of its basic parts) in nature, often failing to appreciate the important role of environment in determining behaviour. Social factors, like childhood experiences and the influence of family and friends, are ignored.

✗ The biological approach is better at explaining behaviours which are mainly biologically determined, like Alzheimer's disease, than those which are not so biologically determined, like emotional experiences.

✗ Biological therapies often treat the effects of, rather than the causes of, mental disorders. This lowers support for the argument that such disorders are biologically determined.

Practical application

The biological approach has led to many effective treatments for mental disorders, such as drug treatments for depression and schizophrenia, which are by far the most common treatments. There is also electroconvulsive therapy (ECT), which is used to treat severe cases of depression and treatment-resistant schizophrenia.

pp. 199–205

5 Approaches
The psychodynamic approach

Focal study

Freud (1909) performed a case study on a 5-year-old boy, 'Hans', the details of which were reported to him by the boy's father. Hans had a phobia of horses. The key features of the analysis were (1) that Hans' interest in his own and the horse's penis showed he was in the phallic stage (where the libido is centred on the genitals), (2) Hans enjoyed having his mother to himself, indicative of him having an *Oedipus complex* (where a boy desires his mother and hates his father) and (3) Hans had a *castration complex* as he feared his father would castrate him as a rival for his mother's affections. Freud saw this as supporting his psychodynamic approach, especially for the existence of the phallic stage and the concept of an Oedipus complex.

Description

The *psychodynamic approach* sees conscious behaviour occurring through the influence of the unconscious mind, formed during childhood as an individual develops through a series of psychosexual stages. This occurs through instincts and drives that motivate the development of personality and behaviour. Personality has three parts: the *id,* which develops from birth to 18 months and seeks selfish pleasure (based on the pleasure principle), the *ego,* which develops from 18 months to 3 years of age and tries to balance the unrealistic demands of the id and the super-ego (based on the reality principle), and the *super-ego,* which develops from 3 to 6 years of age, which seeks to be morally correct (based on the morality principle). Individuals also progress

OTHER STUDIES

- Williams (1994) found that 38 per cent of women diagnosed in childhood as having suffered sexual abuse had no recall of the abuse and of those who did recall it, 16 per cent had at one time not been able to recall it. This supports the Freudian concept of repression.

- Wiszewska *et al.* (2007) found that women who had been well treated by and had close relationships with their fathers were attracted to men who resembled their fathers. This supports the Freudian concept of the Electra complex, where girls fall in love with their fathers.

- Snortum *et al.* (1969) found that 46 males exempted from military service for being homosexual had more controlling mothers and detached fathers than a control group of heterosexual men. This supports the Freudian idea of men who fail to resolve their Oedipus complex becoming homosexual.

Fig 5.5 Sigmund Freud, founder of the psychodynamic approach

- ✔ The approach highlights the importance of childhood experiences to overall and later development, illustrating the value of carefully nurturing children to become competent and balanced adults.

- ✔ Freud created a great interest in the human mind and psychology itself, stimulating further research and the development of the subject. He can be credited as probably the first person to investigate our hidden mental world.

- ✔ Freud can also be credited as having popularised the use of the case study research method in psychology. The study method is especially useful when investigating unique or rare examples of individuals.

through a series of *psychosexual stages* where the *libido* (positive life force) is focused on different erogenous zones. The first is the *oral stage*, with the libido centred on the mouth, second is the *anal stage* with libido focused on defecation, third comes the *phallic stage*, with libido centred on the genitals, and finally the *latency* and *genital stages* before adulthood is reached. Defence mechanisms are used by the unconscious mind to reduce anxiety, for instance *repression* – where unresolved traumas encountered during development are repressed into the unconscious mind where they affect adult behaviour; *denial* – where external events are blocked from awareness; and *displacement* – where emotions are focused on a neutral target.

❌ **Negative evaluation**

- ✘ Freud's theory was based upon very few case studies, which presents problems of generalisation, as the findings from single participants cannot be said to be representative of the population as a whole.

- ✘ Hans had developed his phobia of horses after seeing one fall over in the street, therefore his phobia may be explicable through behaviourism as due to classical conditioning rather than having a psychodynamic explanation.

- ✘ The psychodynamic approach is not scientific, as it cannot be falsified since many of the approaches' ideas and concepts cannot be subjected to experimental research. For example, the idea of an unconscious mind is merely hypothetical and cannot be proven.

Practical application

The main practical application of the approach is in psychotherapy, where a trained psychoanalyst uses various techniques to access an individual's unconscious mind in order to give them insight into their problems so that they are more able to come to terms with them.

AQA

AQA A-level

Psychology 2

Jean-Marc Lawton
Eleanor Willard

DYNAMIC   HODDER

pp. 2–10

5 Approaches
The humanistic approach

Focal study

Elliot & Freire (2008) conducted a meta-analysis of research studies covering 60 years of humanistic therapies. 191 studies were reviewed, involving data from more than 14,000 participants. It was found that humanistic therapies led to a positive improvement in the condition of clients and there was a post-therapy benefit, as such improvements were maintained over a period of at least 1 year. Indeed, improvements were generally even more noticeable after 1 year, supporting the humanistic idea that the levels of self-determination and enhancement gained by clients in therapy lead to them continuing to develop on their own after finishing therapy. Additionally, data from 60 studies where there was a control group receiving no therapy were compared with those receiving humanistic therapies, with the latter being found to be significantly superior. Finally, 109 studies comparing humanistic with other therapies were reviewed, with humanistic therapies found to be equally effective to other therapies.

OTHER STUDIES

- Sheffield *et al.* (1995) measured levels of self-actualisation and psychological health in 185 students and found that there was a positive correlation between an individual's level of self-actualisation and level of psychological health. This supports the idea of movements towards self-actualisation having a positive effect.

- Stiles *et al.* (2006) compared participants receiving humanistic therapies with those receiving cognitive behavioural therapy and psychodynamic therapies. It was found that all three groups of participants showed equal levels of improvement, which suggests humanistic therapies are as effective as other therapies, giving support to the approach they are based upon.

- Tay & Diener (2011) used a questionnaire to generate data about self-actualisation from 60,865 participants from 123 countries. It was found that universal human needs appear to exist, regardless of cultural differences, providing support for the idea of a hierarchy of needs towards self-actualisation.

Description

Humanism emphasises *holism* (studying the whole person). This means that individual aspects of a person should not be examined in isolation, but all aspects of someone should be considered to understand them. There is also an emphasis on the uniqueness of individuals and a movement away from generalising findings to groups of people and sub-dividing the population into those with shared characteristics, such as age and gender. *Free will* is the assumption that individuals have personal control over thoughts and behaviour, with an important aspect being that individuals are seen as responsible for behaviour. Humanists do not see it as desirable to use scientific methods, as humans are

Practical application

A useful practical application of the humanistic approach is in counselling psychology through self-help groups, such as Alcoholics Anonymous and Weight Watchers, which meet in an atmosphere of mutual acceptance to promote self-growth among members. The approach is also used in holistic forms of education that focus upon promoting self-growth and human goodness.

✔ The humanistic idea that humans are all unique is supported by research that finds within-group differences to be greater than between-group differences. For example, gender research shows differences between men (or women) as a group are greater than the difference between men and women.

✔ The humanistic approach promotes self-growth and personal improvement and acknowledges that individuals can change as a result of environmental experience, a viewpoint that is supported by research.

✔ Humanistic psychology tends to use qualitative data, which give genuine insight and a more holistic view of behaviour, which highlights individualism and idiographic methods of study.

not scientifically objective but instead subjective in the ways that they think and act. The subjective experiences of individuals are central to understanding such individuals. Maslow's hierarchy of needs sees everyone as having an innate drive to achieve *self-actualisation,* fully realising their potential. This is more attainable with *positive self-regard* (a positive view of oneself) and an integrated sense of self, which is seen as having three parts: *self-concept* (the way you see yourself), *ideal-self* (who you want to be) and *real-self* (who you actually are). *Congruence* occurs when ideal-self matches self-concept and real-self. *Conditions of worth* are requirements an individual feels they need to be loved.

✘ Many humanistic concepts are somewhat vague and as a consequence difficult to objectively define and measure, though humanistic psychologists do not see this as a problem, as they do not see the value of objective measurements in understanding human behaviour.

✘ The approach neglects the important contribution that biology plays in determining behaviour. For example, the influence of genetics, biochemistry and evolution in shaping behaviour.

✘ Humanism is accused of being culturally biased, as its concentration upon the individual and personal growth reflects the cultural norms of Western, individualistic cultures and therefore does not fit more collectivist cultures.

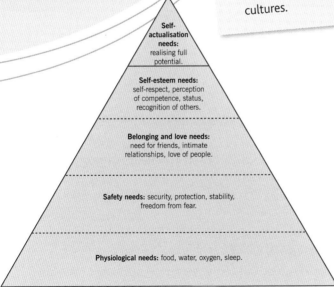

Self-actualisation needs: realising full potential.

Self-esteem needs: self-respect, perception of competence, status, recognition of others.

Belonging and love needs: need for friends, intimate relationships, love of people.

Safety needs: security, protection, stability, freedom from fear.

Physiological needs: food, water, oxygen, sleep.

Fig 5.6 Maslow's hierarchy of needs

AQA A-level

Psychology 2

Jean-Marc Lawton
Eleanor Willard

pp.11–18

5 Approaches
Comparison of approaches

Description

Differing psychological approaches can be compared and contrasted on a series of criteria that highlight the similarities and differences between them. The debates for comparison are: free will and determinism, nature–nurture, holism and reductionism, idiographic and nomothetic approaches, science versus non-science, and extrapolation from animals. The diagrams provided show the *approximate* position of each approach along the debate continuum, to show how the approaches compare.

Free will versus determinism

Free will is the ability to behave as one consciously wishes to. *Determinism* sees behaviour as controlled by factors outside of conscious control.

- Determinism: the *biological approach* sees behaviours generated from physiological sources and therefore outside of conscious control. The *behaviourist* approach sees behaviour as due to learned stimuli and responses and therefore controlled by experience. The *psychodynamic approach* sees behaviour as controlled by the unconscious mind over which individuals have no conscious control.
- Free will: the *humanistic approach* sees individuals as having full control over their thoughts and behaviour. The *cognitive approach* sees individuals as having the conscious ability to change ways of thinking (though how information is processed is *determined* by past experience).

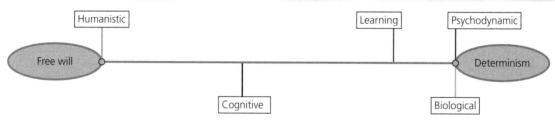

Fig 5.7 Free will and determinism continuum

NATURE VERSUS NATURE

Nature sees behaviour as determined by internal innate factors. *Nurture* sees behaviour as determined through external environmental factors.

- Nature: the *biological approach* sees behaviour as rooted in genetics (though the idea of *phenotype* acknowledges environmental influence).
- Nurture: the *behaviourist approach* sees all behaviour as learned through experience, with no innate input.

The *cognitive approach* acknowledges *nature* through innate thought mechanisms, but also acknowledges *nurture* through environmental influences shaping mental processes.

The *psychodynamic approach* believes in *nature* due to the existence of innate drives, but recognises that *nurture* affects how parents raise children. *Humanism* sees *nature* present in innate drives to improve oneself, with *nurture* also present in the environment helping this process.

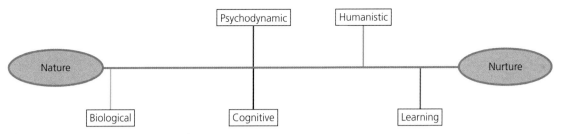

Fig 5.8 Nature–nurture debate continuum

Holism versus reductionism

Holism sees a person as a whole rather than the sum of their constituent parts. *Reductionism* sees behaviour as explicable through reference to the simplest mechanisms at work.

- Holism: the *psychodynamic approach* generally regards an individual as a whole (though seeing drives as underpinning behaviour is somewhat *reductionist*) and does not use scientific methods, so rejects experimental reductionism. *Humanism* regards individuals as wholes and also rejects experimental reductionism.
- Reductionism: the *biological approach* reduces behaviour to physiological causes and uses the reductionist experimental method. The *behaviourist approach* reduces behaviour to stimuli and responses and also relies upon the experimental method. The *cognitive approach* reduces mental processes to basic components to understand them and again uses the experimental method.

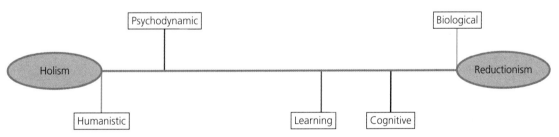

Fig 5.9 Holism and reductionism continuum

5 Approaches
Continued

Idiographic explanations focus on the uniqueness of an individual. *Nomothetic* explanations concentrate on what individuals share in common.

- Idiographic: *humanism* sees individuals as unique, with no scope for generalising to others. The *psychodynamic approach* focuses on the unique childhood of each individual and favours the individualistic case study method (though is nomothetic in generalising from innate drives).
- Nomothetic: the *biological approach* sees humans as having a shared physiology, while the *behaviourist approach* seeks to establish general laws of behaviour that apply to everyone. The *cognitive approach* sees underlying mental processes as being generalisable to all humans and that people are similar in processing information like a computer.

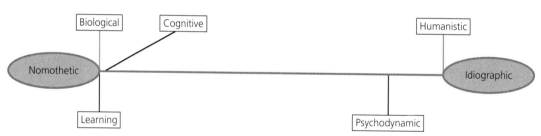

Fig 5.10 Idiographic and nomothetic continuum

Science versus non-science

Science focuses on objective measurements conducted under controlled laboratory conditions. *Non-science* concentrates on methods of study other than those conducted under objective, laboratory conditions.

- Scientific: the *biological approach* is very scientific in experimentally measuring physiological output. The *behaviourist approach* is also very scientific in focusing on measuring observable behaviour (though *social learning* is not directly observable, so is less scientific). The *cognitive approach* uses controlled laboratory experiments, though as mental processes are not directly observable it is not as scientific as the *biological* and *behaviourist* approaches.
- Non-scientific: the *psychodynamic approach* is very subjective in its research methods and provides no scientific evidence of concepts such as the unconscious mind. *Humanism* rejects scientific analysis of behaviour and sees measuring behaviour scientifically as inappropriate in understanding individuals.

Fig 5.11 Scientific methods continuum

EXTRAPOLATION FROM ANIMALS

Extrapolation from animals concerns generalising the findings from animal studies to an explanation of human behaviour.

- Extrapolation: the *biological approach* generalises from animal studies, as animals are seen as physiologically similar to humans. The *behaviourist approach* also generalises, as it sees learning mechanisms as similar for animals and humans.
- Non-extrapolation: the *cognitive approach* does not generalise from animals, as animals do not use human forms of language to think (though some studies of perception are generalised from animals). The *psychodynamic approach* focuses solely on humans, with no animal experimentation or comparisons. *Humanism* sees animal experimentation as scientific and therefore inappropriate in understanding human behaviour.

Fig 5.12 Extrapolation continuum

Practical application

One practical application of psychological approaches is combined treatments for mental disorders. Separate treatments taken from different psychological approaches are combined. For instance, drug treatments (from the biological approach) are often given to depressives first, to reduce symptoms, and then cognitive behavioural therapy (from the cognitive approach) is administered to create a more effective treatment.

pp. 19–24

6 Biopsychology
The nervous system and neurons

The divisions of the nervous system

The nervous system divides into the *central nervous system* (CNS) and the peripheral nervous system (PNS). It provides the biological basis to an individual's psychological experiences.

The CNS

The CNS comprises the *brain* and *spinal cord* and is concerned with maintaining life functions and psychological processes.
- There are many different brain areas with differing functions. Some brain areas are seen as primitive and involved in basic functioning to maintain life, while other areas are more complex and involved with higher level functioning such as thinking and decision making.
- The function of the spinal cord is to facilitate the transfer of information to and from the brain to the PNS.

The PNS

The PNS conveys information to and from the CNS and in essence is the messaging service for the limbs and torso. It sub-divides into 2 divisions: the *somatic nervous system* (SNS) and the *autonomic nervous system* (ANS).
- The SNS mainly transmits and receives information from the senses, such as auditory information from the ears. It also directs muscles to react and move.
- The ANS helps to transmit and receive information from bodily organs, such as the stomach, and divides into 2 further sub-systems: the *sympathetic nervous system*, which generally helps to increase bodily activities, and the *parasympathetic nervous system*, which generally conserves bodily activities by maintaining or decreasing activity.

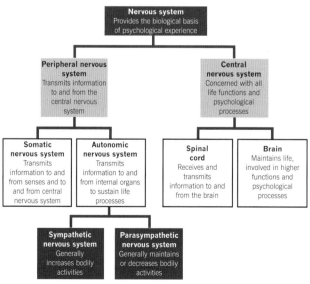

Fig 6.1 Divisions of the nervous system, with an indication of the function of each division

The structure and function of sensory, relay and motor neurons

Neurons are cells that transmit nerve impulses around the nervous system, acting as a kind of bodily communication system. There are about 100 billion neurons in the brain and 1 billion in the spinal cord. There are 3 main types of neurons: *sensory*, *relay* and *motor*, each having a different specialised role to play. The structure of all neurons is generally the same, though there are structural differences in size relating to their function – for instance, motor neurons tend to be longer than other neurons. In all neurons the *dendrite/receptor cell* receives the signal, which then travels through the neuron to the *pre-synaptic terminal*.

- *Sensory neurons* inform the brain about a person's external and internal environment by processing sensory information received by the sensory organs. As sensory neurons only transmit information, they are known as *unipolar* neurons, while *relay* and *motor* neurons are *bipolar*, as they send and receive information.
- *Relay neurons* transmit information from one area of the CNS to another. Relay neurons also connect motor and sensory neurons together.
- *Motor neurons* transmit information from the CNS to help the functioning of bodily organs (including glands – important for the endocrine system) and muscles.

The process of synaptic transmission

Synaptic transmission is the process by which nerve impulses are carried across *synapses* (small gaps between neurons). The nerve impulses transmitted through neurons are electrical in nature and are transmitted across synapses by chemicals called *neurotransmitters*. Initially a nerve impulse travels down a neuron and initiates release of neurotransmitters (brain chemicals) at the *pre-synaptic terminal*. The neurotransmitters are then released into the synaptic fluid within the synapse. The adjoining neuron takes up the neurotransmitters from the synaptic fluid and converts them to an electrical impulse, which travels down the neuron to the next pre-synaptic terminal, and so on.

Not all signals prompt activation in the same way. How this occurs is dependent on the *action potential* of the post-synaptic neuron and the type of information received.

- *Excitatory potentials* act like the accelerator pedal in a car, as they make it more likely to cause the post-synaptic neuron to fire. When this occurs it is known as an *excitatory synapse*.
- *Inhibitory potentials* act like the brake on a car, as they make it less likely for the neuron to fire, and when this occurs and the signal is stopped at the post-synaptic neuron it is known as an *inhibitory synapse*.

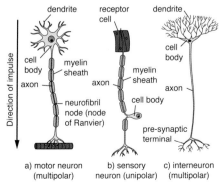

Fig 6.2 The anatomical differences between neurons

a) motor neuron (multipolar)   b) sensory neuron (unipolar)   c) interneuron (multipolar)

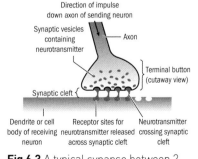

Fig 6.3 A typical synapse between 2 neurons. The nerve impulse travels from the pre-synaptic neuron, across the synaptic cleft, to the post-synaptic neuron

pp. 226–30

6 Biopsychology
The influence of biochemistry on behaviour

The function of the endocrine system

The nervous system receives and sends information around the body using electrical and chemical means (see **page 82**). Another bodily messaging system is the *endocrine system*, a series of glands found throughout the body that release chemicals known as *hormones* via blood and other bodily fluids. This allows information to be sent to the organs of the body in order to affect their behaviour, rather like neurons do in the nervous system.

There are a number of specialist glands in the endocrine system. Each of these, when stimulated, releases particular hormones that produce specific behavioural effects. The *pituitary gland* is located behind the bridge of the nose and to the base of the brain just below the hypothalamus brain area (to which it is attached via nerve fibres). It is a pea-sized structure known as the 'master gland', due to its important role within the endocrine system in regulating the functions of other glands – such as the *ovaries* in females, the *testes* in males and the *thyroid* and *adrenal* glands – and the hormones they secrete.

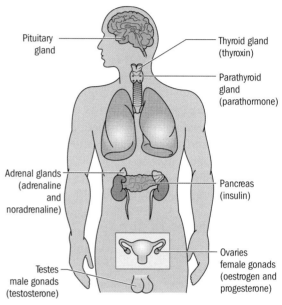

Pituitary gland

Thyroid gland (thyroxin)

Parathyroid gland (parathormone)

Adrenal glands (adrenaline and noradrenaline)

Pancreas (insulin)

Ovaries female gonads (oestrogen and progesterone)

Testes male gonads (testosterone)

Fig 6.4 The endocrine system, showing the major glands in the human body

The pituitary gland

The pituitary gland has 2 lobes (parts): a front part known as the *anterior pituitary* and a back part known as the *posterior pituitary*. The anterior pituitary releases several important hormones: growth hormone, gonadotrophins (puberty hormones), thyroid-stimulating hormone and adrenocorticotrophic hormone (ACTH), which stimulates the adrenal stress hormone cortisol. The posterior pituitary releases the fluid-balance hormone ADH (anti-diuretic hormone).

To activate the pituitary gland the hypothalamus signals to it to either stimulate or inhibit hormone production. The anterior lobe releases hormones on receiving releasing or inhibiting hormones from the hypothalamus. These hypothalamic hormones inform the anterior lobe whether to release more of a specific hormone or cease its release. The hormones of the pituitary gland send signals to other endocrine glands to stimulate or inhibit their own hormone production. For instance, the anterior pituitary lobe will release ACTH to stimulate cortisol production from the adrenal glands (situated near the kidneys) when an individual is stressed. The adrenal glands are an important component of the *fight-or-flight response* (see opposite) as they facilitate the release of *adrenaline*.

Another important hormone that increasingly interests psychologists is *oxytocin*, which is released from the posterior lobe of the pituitary gland and is secreted during pleasurable activities like playing, cuddling or having sex. Oxytocin is especially important for females, as it causes contractions during labour and also causes the release of milk during breastfeeding. It is important in both males and females in creating bonds between individuals.

The **fight-or-flight response** is generated from the **sympathetic nervous system** branch of the **autonomic nervous system** (ANS) (see **page 82**). It is an innate reflex action (that is, one that requires no conscious thought) that has an evolutionary survival value in helping protect an individual confronted by potentially dangerous situations. The response is activated in times of stress when something is perceived to be a threat to safety, and helps an individual to react more quickly than usual, as well as optimising functioning so the body is able to effectively fight or run away from the threat.

The response can be broken down into separate steps:

1. The *hypothalamus* brain area perceives a threatening stressor and sends a signal to the *adrenal glands*.
2. The *adrenal medulla* within the adrenal glands triggers the release of the hormone *adrenaline* into the endocrine system and the neurotransmitter *noradrenaline* in the brain.
3. Physical changes are incurred within the body that help an individual to fight or run away from the threatening stressor, for example, an attacker:
   - *Increased heart rate* – speeds up blood flow to vital organs and flow of adrenaline around the body
   - *Faster breathing rate* – increases oxygen intake
   - *Muscle tension* – improves reaction time and speed
   - *Pupil dilation* – improves vision
   - *Sweat production* – helps temperature control
   - *Reduced digestion and immune system functioning* – targets energy towards prioritised functioning, such as fighting and running.

Practical application
Oxytocin sprays have been used to treat autism, as oxytocin seems to stimulate areas of the brain associated with social interaction, something that autistic people often have difficulties with. The sprays are used to facilitate the effectiveness of therapies.

pp. 231–4

6 Biopsychology
Localisation of function in the brain

Description

The brain has two hemispheres (halves) that are linked by the *corpus callosum,* a bundle of nerve fibres that allows the two hemispheres to communicate.

Hemispheric lateralisation

Most people's brains are *contralateral,* where the right hemisphere deals with the left side of the body and vice versa. For example, information in an individual's right visual field is processed by their left hemisphere. When a function is dealt with by one hemisphere it is said to be *lateralised,* with the division of functions between the two hemispheres known as *hemispheric lateralisation:*

- **Left hemisphere** – for most people, language processing occurs in the left hemisphere. A stroke on the left side of the brain can therefore affect speech. The left hemisphere is also seen to focus on detail in visual information.
- **Right hemisphere** – *recognising emotions* in others occurs in the right hemisphere, as does dealing with *spatial information* (knowing where things are in relationship to each other in the visual field). The right hemisphere is also thought to process overall patterns in visual information.

Motor centres

- **Motor cortex** – movement is centred on the *primary motor cortex,* which sends information to the muscles via the brain stem and spinal cord. This brain area is important for complex movements and non-basic actions, such as coughing and crying. The spinal cord and brain co-ordinate movements, while the *premotor cortex* helps plan movements and the *prefrontal cortex* stores sensory information prior to a movement and assesses the probability of outcomes of movements.
- **Somatosensory centres** – touch is perceived in the *somatosensory cortex,* with processing of some body areas, like the face, involving larger parts of this brain area than others.
- **Visual centres** – the *primary visual cortex* is the main visual centre, with visual information conveyed along two pathways. One contains components of the visual field and the other the location of the components within the visual field.
- **Auditory centres** – the *primary auditory cortex* receives information from both ears via two pathways that transmit information about what a sound is and where it is.
- **Language centres** – *Broca's area,* located in the left temporal lobe, is responsible for production of speech, while *Wernicke's area,* close to the auditory cortex, is important for understanding language and accessing words.

> ### Focal study
> Domanski (2013) reported on neurologist Paul Broca, who conducted a post mortem on Louis Leborgne, who through epilepsy had lost the ability to speak (apart from the word 'Tan') and died aged 51. Broca found damage to the left temporal lobe, which suggests this brain area (now known as Broca's area – see Figure 6.5) has a localised responsibility for production of speech.

- Wernicke (1874) found that damage to an area next to the auditory cortex (now known as Wernicke's area) produced an impairment to the ability to comprehend language and *anomia*, a difficulty in finding a desired word. This suggests this brain area has a localised function in understanding and accessing language.

- Clarke *et al.* (1993) reported a case study of a woman who had damage to her right hemisphere, which resulted in her getting lost even in familiar surroundings. This suggests the right hemisphere processes spatial information.

- MacMillan (2002) reported on the case study of Phineas Gage, who had a much altered personality due to damage to a brain area that catered for the planning, reasoning and control of an individual. This supports the idea of localisation of function of brain areas.

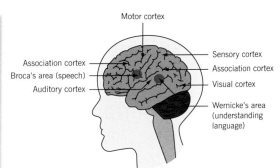

Fig 6.5 Broca's area and other localisation of cortical function

❌ Negative evaluation

✗ Some people seem able to recover functions after specific brain damage, which suggests that localisation of function may not exist universally.

✗ Much research in this area relies on case studies, which present problems of generalisation, as the results from single individuals cannot be said to be representative of all.

✗ The holistic theory of brain function argues against localisation of function. Lashley (1950) reported that work on rats' brains indicated no one specific brain area was responsible for memory, which suggests the idea of there being certain brain areas for specific tasks is wrong.

✔ Positive evaluation

✔ There is a wealth of research evidence to support the idea of localisation of function within specific brain areas.

✔ Modern brain scanning methods, such as PET and MRI scans, have backed up the idea of localisation of function by finding evidence of activation within specific brain areas when certain tasks are being performed.

Practical application
One practical application of research into brain functioning is a *corpus callosotomy*, an operation performed on epileptics where the nerve fibres at the corpus callosum are severed to separate the two hemispheres of the brain. This reduces the intensity of seizures, increasing the quality of life.

pp. 235–40

6 Biopsychology

Split brain surgery and plasticity and functional recovery of the brain after trauma

Split brain patients

Some sufferers of epilepsy who do not respond to drug treatment are given an operation that involves cutting the *corpus callosum* so that the effect of the disorder is reduced by containing it within one hemisphere of the brain. An effect of this is that the two hemispheres can no longer 'communicate' with each other and studies of such 'split brain' patients have allowed psychologists to investigate the role of each hemisphere. After surgery the hemispheres act separately, making an individual feel like two people in one body. Some patients develop techniques to allow the hemispheres to communicate with each other and strategies to compensate for the lack of connectivity, for example turning their heads so both hemispheres can perceive an environment.

Plasticity and functional recovery after trauma

Most people who incur brain damage can make some recovery and in some instances the brain can adapt and find another way to complete a function. Level of recovery is dependent on the type and severity of trauma.

Plasticity

Plasticity is the brain's ability to replace a function lost by anatomical damage. Cell bodies cannot be replaced, but in some instances axons (part of a nerve cell) can. There are three main anatomical ways that the brain can replace axon function:
1 *Increased brain stimulation* – if the undamaged hemisphere is stimulated, recovery from a stroke can improve.
2 *Axon sprouting* – damage to an axon results in lost connections to adjoining neurons, but their neighbouring neurons can grow extra connections to compensate. This can replace function if the damaged axon and the replacements perform similarly.
3 *Denervation supersensitivity* – axons that perform similarly to damaged ones can become aroused to a higher level to compensate.

Functional recovery of the brain after trauma

Rehabilitation can help the brain compensate for loss of function by an individual learning how to use their working faculties and functions to compensate for those lost to injury. Several factors affect recovery:
1 *Perseverance* – sometimes a function may appear lost, but it is because an individual isn't 'trying' hard enough. Perseverance can eventually restore some function.
2 *Physical exhaustion, stress and alcohol* – recovering function can be exhausting and stress and alcohol consumption can affect the ability to use recovered functions.
3 *Age* – recovering function can become more difficult with age.
4 *Gender* – women appear more able to recover from trauma as their function is not as lateralised (concentrated in one hemisphere).

Focal study

Schneider et al. (2014) investigated whether the amount of time spent in education affected recovery from brain injury. The amount of education of 769 patients receiving rehabilitation for head injuries was recorded. It was found that those receiving a lengthier education had greater recovery. This suggests that people remaining in education for longer have a greater 'cognitive reserve' that allows them to maintain function in spite of damage and to regain function after injury.

OTHER STUDIES

- Fleet & Heilman (1986) found that heightened stress levels and alcohol consumption lessened the ability to use regained function after brain injury, illustrating how environmental factors can affect the ability to recover from trauma.
- Sperry (1968) examined split brain patients to find that different functions are carried out by the two hemispheres of the brain. This supports the idea of lateralisation of function, that different brain areas are involved with differing tasks.
- Danelli (2013) reported on the case study of a boy who having lost his left hemisphere due to a tumour (which controlled his language abilities) recovered most of these abilities. This suggests the right hemisphere compensated for the loss, supporting the idea of the brain having plasticity.

❌ Negative evaluation

✗ Split brain research is carried out on people with severe epilepsy, so the extent to which findings can be generalised to people without such a disorder is questionable.

✗ The extent to which people can recover from brain injuries is subject to great individual differences, which suggests generalisable conclusions are difficult to draw.

✗ The level of function within specific brain areas before injury has taken place is generally unknown, making comparison with post-injury function levels difficult to achieve.

✓ Positive evaluation

✓ Split brain research has proved a useful means of investigating and understanding the functions of each hemisphere of the brain.

✓ Research indicates that recovery from brain injury is nearly always possible, giving hope for the future for those unfortunate enough to suffer brain traumas.

Practical application

Research into split brain and brain injury patients has contributed greatly to the establishment of effective rehabilitation programmes to help people recover lost function. This is especially beneficial to the large number of people suffering strokes.

pp. 240–45

89

6 Biopsychology
Ways of studying the brain
Post-mortem examinations

The earliest method of studying the brain was *post mortems,* where dead people's brains were inspected and dissected. However, it was difficult to reach valid conclusions about what roles different parts of the brain played in behaviour. Post mortems on people with brain damage did provide some information about the functioning of the brain. If a person had a specific deficit in functioning when alive, then dissection of the brain might suggest which brain area was related to that type of functioning.

Electroencephalogram (EEG) and event-related potentials (ERPs)

EEGs measure brain activity through electrodes on the scalp. ERPs measure brain activity in response to a stimulus, using the same equipment as that used for EEGs.

Scanning

The introduction of scanning techniques in the 1980s revolutionised the ways in which the brain was investigated, as for the first time it offered an opportunity to view a live brain actually functioning on everyday activities without the need for invasive techniques.

Magnetic resonance imaging (MRI)

This technique uses a powerful magnetic field and radio waves to record vibrations from various atomic nuclei within neurons. This allows measurements called *blood oxygen-level responses* to be taken of the blood flow to specific brain areas. This method of scanning produces static (non-moving) pictures of brain activity.

Functional magnetic resonance imaging (fMRI)

fMRIs work in the same way as standard MRIs but additionally show brain activity as it occurs. MRIs work by recording the energy produced by molecules of water, after the magnetic field is removed. With an fMRI the energy released by haemoglobin (the protein content of blood) is measured. When haemoglobin contains oxygen it behaves differently than when it does not contain oxygen. So when a brain area is active and therefore using more oxygen, the difference in the amount of energy released by the haemoglobin is detected by the scanner and the change is measured. This produces a dynamic (moving) picture of activity about 1 second after it occurs and is accurate to within 1–2 millimetres in the brain. fMRI scanning is the current dominant method of brain scanning and is used to map out brain areas involved in many types of behaviour and psychological processes.

Positron emission tomography (PET)

PET scanning is an invasive technique, as it involves injecting a radioactive substance, usually glucose, into the bloodstream. This travels to the brain where it is used as an energy source by neurons. The glucose emits radioactive particles that are picked up by sensors placed around the head, with active brain areas consuming more glucose. A computerised picture is then created of brain activity.

Computerised axial tomography (CAT)

CAT scanning was an early scanning technique. It produces a static three-dimensional picture of the brain using x-rays. It has mainly been replaced by PET, MRI and fMRI scanning as a means of investigating the workings of the brain.

✔ Positive evaluation

- **Post mortems:** these gave psychologists a method of mapping out the brain in terms of its component parts and gave some insight into its functioning.
- **EEG and ERPs:** both methods are cheaper, and therefore more available to researchers, than scanning.
- **MRI:** MRI scanning is more ethical as, unlike PET scans, for example, which require intravenous injection of radioactive materials, it is a non-invasive method.
- **fMRI:** fMRI scanning is non-invasive and is regarded as producing the most informative and detailed information concerning brain activity.
- **PET:** PET scans have specialised uses, such as using other tracking agents that bind to synaptic receptors to produce a map of serotonin receptors within the brain.
- **CAT:** CAT scanning is a useful technique for identifying structural changes in the brain, such as the detection of brain tumours.

✘ Negative evaluation

- **Post mortems:** as the brain is non-active after death, a post mortem is a much less informative method of study than scanning.
- **EEG and ERPs:** output needs to be analysed by a skilled technician, limiting which researchers can use these techniques.
- **MRI:** MRI scans are inferior to fMRI scans, as MRI scanning produces only static pictures of brain activity, while fMRI scans display moving pictures.
- **fMRI:** like PET and MRI scans, fMRI scans do not directly measure the electrical activity of neurons in the brain. The technique requires significant changes in glucose uptake for activity to be detected, so important small changes may be missed.
- **PET:** PET scanning is time consuming and its level of detail and speed of response are not as good as fMRI scans.
- **CAT:** compared with other forms of scanning, the technique is relatively uninformative about the workings of the brain, hence it is falling out of favour as a preferred method of investigation.

Practical application

Aside from providing a method of investigating the brain, scanning techniques are also useful in detecting brain tumours and assessing the degree of brain damage after a stroke, which helps form rehabilitation programmes.

pp. 247–49

6 Biopsychology
Biological rhythms

Focal study

Czeisler *et al.* (1999) criticised early sleep–wake cycle studies, where participants were generally kept in isolation with no time cues, as being negatively affected by exposure to high levels of artificial light, which may have continually re-set participants' internal body clocks. In their study 24 participants were kept in conditions of constant low-level light for 1 month with no clues as to the passage of time and were put on an artificial 28-hour sleep–wake cycle. Measurements were recorded in the form of regular body temperature readings and biochemistry levels through the analysis of blood chemicals. The findings showed that participants had adopted a sleep–wake cycle of 24 hours and 11 minutes, which differed from the earlier criticised studies that found a sleep–wake cycle closer to 25 hours. This suggests that the human sleep–wake cycle is close to the 24 hours that would logically be expected.

Description

Biological rhythms are *cyclical* behaviours, ones repeated periodically. These are controlled by *endogenous pacemakers*, functioning as internal biological clocks to regulate biological functioning, and *exogenous zeitgebers* in the form of external environmental cues. *Circadian* rhythms last around 24 hours, like the *sleep–wake cycle*, a free-running cycle controlled by an endogenous pacemaker operating as a body clock and facilitated by exogenous zeitgebers, such as time checks and regular mealtimes. *Infradian* rhythms last longer than 24 hours, for instance the *menstrual cycle*, regulated by hormonal secretions and controlled by the hypothalamus operating as an endogenous pacemaker and also facilitated by exogenous zeitgebers, like pheromones.

OTHER STUDIES

- Aschoff & Weber (1962) found that participants isolated in a bunker with no natural light formed sleep–wake cycles between 25–27 hours, suggesting endogenous pacemakers control the cycle in the absence of light cues.
- Russell *et al.* (1980) found that female participants' menstrual cycles synchronised after a donor's underarm sweat was applied to their upper lips, suggesting that pheromones act as an exogenous zeitgeber.
- Dement & Kleitman (1957) from EEG readings found that sleep consists of stages characterised by different levels of brain activity, with dreaming occurring in REM sleep, implying sleep is an ultradian rhythm.
- Stephan & Zucker (1971), by removing the SCN from rats, found that the usual rhythmic cycles of sleep and activity disappeared, suggesting that the SCN is the crucial endogenous pacemaker in the sleep–wake cycle.
- Luce & Segal (1966) found people in the Arctic Circle still slept 7 hours nightly, even though it was continually light in the summer, suggesting that social cues act as zeitgebers to regulate sleep.

✔ Research suggests that endogenous pacemakers do exist and are regulated by exogenous zeitgebers.

✔ Turke (1984) argues that there is an evolutionary advantage to women synchronising periods, in that it allows women living together to synchronise pregnancies and therefore share childcare duties. Also women working close to men have shorter menstrual cycles, giving them an evolutionary advantage in having more opportunities to get pregnant.

✔ The development of EEG readings gave psychologists an objective means of investigating sleep.

✔ There is an adaptive advantage to animals having endogenous pacemakers reset by exogenous zeitgebers, as it keeps them in tune with seasonal changes etc.

Ultradian rhythms last less than 24 hours, for instance the cycle of brain activity reflected in the stages of sleep occurring through the night. The main endogenous pacemaker involved in the circadian sleep–wake cycle is the *superchiasmatic nucleus* (SCN), a small group of cells in the hypothalamus generating a circadian rhythm reset by light entering the eyes. A rhythm is generated from several proteins interacting to form a biological clock. Exogenous zeitgebers help reset and synchronise the sleep–wake cycle, sunlight being the main one, with endogenous pacemakers responding to such zeitgebers to help regulate sleep behaviour in response to the external environment.

✘ Isolation studies of circadian rhythms have few participants, making generalisation difficult.

✘ Yamakazi *et al.* (2000) found that circadian rhythms persist in isolated livers, lungs, etc. grown in culture dishes without the influence of the SCN, suggesting that cells other than the SCN act as exogenous pacemakers.

✘ Findings from sleep studies are conducted in sleep laboratories with participants linked up to EEG machines, which implies findings lack external validity due to the artificial environment.

Practical application

One practical application of research into biological rhythms is that of the phase-delay system of rotating work shifts forward in time to reduce negative effects upon health and therefore improve output. There are also melatonin supplements to reduce the negative effects of jet lag.

pp. 249–54

7 Research methods
Experimental method and design

Description

With the experimental method researchers manipulate an *independent variable* (IV) between experimental conditions to see its effect on a *dependent variable* (DV), always a measurement of some kind. *Controls* prevent *extraneous variables* (variables other than the IV that could affect the value of the DV) from becoming *confounding variables* that 'confuse' the results. *Standardisation* involves each participant performing an experiment under the same conditions to reduce the chances of confounding variables. *Causality* (cause and effect relationships) is therefore established. For instance, caffeine consumption (IV) could be manipulated to assess the effect on reaction times (DV), with all other variables, such as amount of sleep, food consumed, etc., kept constant between participants.

Types of experiments

Laboratory experiments are performed in a controlled environment, permitting the control of most variables, with participants randomly allocated to testing groups.

Field experiments are performed in the 'real world' rather than in a laboratory, with the IV manipulated by researchers and other variables controlled. *Natural experiments* occur where the independent variable varies naturally, with the researcher recording the effect on the DV. Participants are not allocated randomly. *Quasi experiments* occur where the IV occurs naturally, for instance whether participants are male or female. Participants therefore are not allocated randomly. This method is often used when it is unethical to manipulate an IV.

Fig 7.1 Like a golfer selects the best club to play a shot, psychologists select the most appropriate research method to conduct a study

 Strengths of experiments

Laboratory

✔ With extraneous variables being controlled, causality can be established, i.e. that changes in the value of the DV are due to manipulation of the IV.

✔ Other researchers can exactly replicate the study to check results.

Field, natural and quasi

✔ As they occur in real-world settings, findings have high ecological validity and therefore are generalisable to other settings.

✔ As participants are often unaware that they are being studied, there are fewer demand characteristics, so participants behave naturally.

 Weaknesses of experiments

Laboratory

✗ High degrees of control are artificial, meaning results lack *ecological validity* and are not generalisable to other settings.

✗ *Demand characteristics* may occur, where participants attempt to guess the purpose of the study and respond accordingly.

Field, natural and quasi

✗ As it is more difficult to control extraneous variables, causality is harder to establish.

✗ It is difficult to replicate such experiments, as the lack of control means testing conditions are rarely the same again.

Experimental design

Experimental conditions have different forms of the IV, with the *control condition* acting as a comparison against the *experimental condition.* Three types of design exist, each with strengths and weaknesses:

- Repeated measures design (RMD) – the same participants perform each condition, therefore participants are tested against themselves under different forms of the IV.
- Matched participants design (MPD) – a special kind of RMD with participants pre-tested and matched on important variables into similar pairs. One of each pair is randomly allocated into the experimental condition and one into the control condition.
- Independent groups design (IGD) – different participants perform each testing condition, making them independent of each other, with participants randomly allocated to different conditions. Each participant therefore performs only one condition of an experiment.

✅ Strengths of experimental designs

RMD

✔ As each participant performs in all conditions, they are compared against themselves, so there are no *participant variables* (individual differences between participants) and differences in findings are due to manipulations of the IV.

✔ As participants perform in all conditions, fewer participants are needed.

MPD

✔ As participants do different conditions, there are no order effects.

✔ As participants do different conditions, there is less chance of demand characteristics by 'guessing' the purpose of the study.

IGD

✔ As different participants perform different conditions, there are no order effects.

✔ Demand characteristics are reduced, as participants perform only one condition each.

❌ Weaknesses of experimental designs

RMD

✗ *Order effects* occur where the order in which participants perform conditions affects findings, e.g. through learning or fatigue. Order effects are *counterbalanced*, where half the participants do one condition first and half the other condition first.

MPD

✗ As participants perform in only one condition, twice as many participants are required than with an RMD.

✗ MPD requires pre-testing and matching on important variables and therefore is time consuming.

IGD

✗ As participants perform only one condition, more participants are required to produce the same amount of data as with an RMD.

✗ There is a risk of *participant variables*, as findings may be due to participants' individual differences rather than manipulations of the IV.

pp. 258–62

7 Research methods
Non-experimental methods and design

Description

Non-experimental (*alternative*) research methods differ from experiments in that they do not have an IV or a DV, are not conducted under controlled conditions and are therefore difficult to replicate, and do not show causality (cause and effect relationships). Each has strengths and weaknesses and is more appropriate to different types of research aims.

Correlational analysis

Correlational analysis involves assessing the degree of relationship between two or more co-variables, for example between the number of hours' sleep and the score on a memory test. A *positive* correlation occurs when one co-variable increases as another co-variable increases, for example sales of umbrellas increase as the number of days it rains increases. A *negative* correlation occurs when one co-variable decreases while another increases, for example sales of bikinis decrease as the number of days it rains increases. *Zero correlations* occur when there is no association between co-variables. A *correlational co-efficient* is a numerical value expressing the degree to which co-variables are related. Measurements range between +1.0, a perfect positive correlation, and −1.0, a perfect negative correlation.

✓ Strengths

- ✔ Correlations do not require manipulation and are used when experiments would be unethical.
- ✔ Once correlations are established, predictions can be made, for example how many umbrellas will be sold on rainy days.

✗ Weaknesses

- ✘ Correlations are not conducted under controlled conditions and therefore do not show causality.
- ✘ Apparently low correlations can actually be statistically significant if the number of scores used is sufficiently high.

Observations

Naturalistic observations involve measuring naturally occurring behaviour in real-world situations, such as Festinger's (1957) study where he infiltrated a cult that was predicting the end of the world, while *controlled observations* are conducted under controlled laboratory conditions, for example Zimbardo's prison simulation (see **page 8**). *Participant observations* involve researchers being actively involved in the behaviour being assessed. *Non-participant observations* involve researchers not being actively involved in the behaviour being assessed. *Overt observations* involve the participants knowing they are being observed, while *covert observations* do not.

✓ Strengths

- ✔ Observations have high *external validity*, as they involve natural behaviour in a real-life setting and so can be generalised to other settings.
- ✔ As participants are usually unaware of being observed, there are few *demand characteristics*.

✗ Weaknesses

- ✘ It can be difficult to remain unobserved and make accurate, full observations.
- ✘ As observations are not conducted under controlled conditions, they are difficult to replicate to check the reliability and validity of findings.

Self-reports

Self-reports involve participants detailing information about themselves without researcher intervention.

Questionnaires are a self-report method where participants give answers to pre-set written questions, usually involving opinions, attitudes, beliefs and behaviour. *Closed* questions involve limited responses set by researchers, such as 'yes/no' tick boxes. Answers are easy to quantify, but restrictive. *Open* questions allow participants to answer fully in their own words and therefore give a greater depth and freedom of expression, but are less easy to quantify and analyse.

✔ **Strengths**

- ✔ Large samples can be generated by posting out questionnaires, which also means researchers do not have to be present when they are completed.
- ✔ Questionnaires obtain lots of data in a relatively quick time.

✖ **Weaknesses**

- ✖ There is a possibility of *idealised* and *socially desirable* answers, with participants answering how they think they should, rather than giving honest answers.
- ✖ Questionnaires, especially those with closed questions, are not suitable for sensitive issues requiring careful and detailed understanding.

Interviews involve asking participants face-to-face questions. *Structured* interviews ask identical, simple, quantitative questions to all participants, while *unstructured* interviews involve an informal discussion on set topics, producing mainly qualitative data. *Semi-structured* interviews use a mixture of structured and unstructured questions.

✔ **Strengths**

- ✔ Both quantitative and qualitative data are generated, producing a greater variety and depth of findings.
- ✔ With unstructured and semi-structured interviews, follow-up questions can be asked to explore interesting answers.

✖ **Weaknesses**

- ✖ Interviewers can bias responses through their appearance, age, gender, etc.
- ✖ Some participants may not have the verbal skills to fully express themselves.

Case studies

Case studies are detailed, in-depth investigations of one person or a small group, usually involving biographical details, behaviour and experiences of interest, for example Koluchova's (1972) study of twins suffering privation.

✔ **Strengths**

- ✔ Case studies allow 'difficult' areas to be investigated where other methods would be unethical, such as sexual abuse.
- ✔ Data relate specifically to one person, not an average produced from many people.

✖ **Weaknesses**

- ✖ Findings relate to only one person and cannot be generalised to others.
- ✖ Case studies are usually reliant on full and accurate memories, which can often be selective and affected by researcher bias.

pp. 262–69

7 Research methods

Aims, hypotheses, operationalisation of variables, demand characteristics and pilot studies

Aims

Aims are research objectives, exact statements of why studies are conducted, for instance to investigate whether differing amounts of sleep affect concentration levels. Aims should incorporate what is being studied and what studies are trying to achieve.

Hypotheses

Hypotheses are more objectively precise than aims and are testable predictions of what is expected to happen. There are two types of hypotheses:

1   The *experimental* hypothesis, which predicts that differences in the DV will be outside the boundaries of chance (known as *significant differences*) as a result of manipulation of the IV. The term 'experimental hypothesis' is used with experiments; other research methods refer to 'alternative hypotheses'. Example: 'that participants receiving 8 hours' sleep last night will perform significantly better on a test of concentration than those receiving 4 hours' sleep last night.'

2   The *null* hypothesis, which predicts that the IV will not affect the DV and that any differences found will not be outside the boundaries of chance, i.e. will not be significantly different. Example: 'that participants receiving 8 hours' sleep last night will not perform significantly better on a test of concentration than those receiving 4 hours' sleep last night. Any differences found will be due to chance factors.'

One of these two hypotheses will be supported by the findings and accepted while the other will be rejected.

There are two types of experimental/alternative hypotheses:

1   *Directional* (*one-tailed*) hypotheses, which predict the direction that the results will lie in. Example: 'that participants running 400 metres on an athletics track while being watched by an audience of their peers will run significantly quicker times than those running without an audience.'

2   *Non-directional* (*two-tailed*) hypotheses, which predict a difference in the results but not the direction in which the results will lie. Example: 'that there will be a significant difference in times achieved between participants running 400 metres on an athletics track while being watched by an audience of their peers and those running without an audience.'

Directional hypotheses are used when previous research gives an indication of which way findings will lay.

OPERATIONALISATION OF VARIABLES

Operationalisation concerns objectively defining variables in an easily understandable manner, so that an IV can be manipulated (altered between testing conditions) and its effect on a DV measured. For example, if researching the effect of sleep on concentration, the IV could be operationalised as the amount of sleep the previous night and the DV the score on a test of concentration. Without accurate operationalisation, results may be unreliable and invalid; therefore it is crucial to operationalise IVs and DVs accurately, but this can be difficult, for example how can 'anger' be accurately operationalised?

Demand characteristics

Research involves social interactions between investigators and participants, which can influence and bias findings so that they are not valid. One such research effect is demand characteristics, where participants form impressions of the research purpose and unknowingly alter behaviour accordingly. Demand characteristics affect research findings in several ways:

1 Where participants guess the purpose of research and try to please researchers by giving them their expected results.

2 Where participants guess the purpose of research and try to sabotage it by giving non-expected results.

3 Where participants, out of nervousness or fear of evaluation, act unnaturally.

4 Where participants respond to a *social desirability bias* and give answers/exhibit behaviour that shows them in a socially acceptable manner.

Demand characteristics are reduced by the *single-blind procedure*, where participants are not aware of which testing condition they are in, for example in a drug trial not knowing whether they have swallowed a real pill or a placebo.

INVESTIGATOR EFFECTS

Investigator effects concern the ways in which researchers can unconsciously influence research in several ways:

1 *Major physical characteristics* such as the age and gender of researchers.

2 *Minor physical characteristics* like their accent and tone of voice.

3 *Unconscious bias* in the interpretation of data.

The *double-blind technique* reduces investigator effects by neither participants nor researchers knowing which conditions participants are in.

Fig 7.2 The physical appearance of an investigator can unconsciously affect the behaviour of participants in studies

Pilot studies

Pilot studies are small-scale 'practice' investigations allowing procedural improvements and removal of methodological errors. Participants can point out flaws, such as the presence of demand characteristics. Pilot studies show what kinds of results are expected and whether there is any possibility of significant results. Pilot studies permit the quality of research to be improved and help avoid unnecessary time and effort being wasted, for example by performing lengthy studies only to find that due to unexpected errors and problems, the results are invalid and the study will have to be altered and repeated.

pp. 259–61, 271, 276

Research methods
Sampling and ethical issues
Sampling techniques

A sample is a part of a population and should be as representative as possible, i.e. possess the same characteristics as the population from which it is drawn. Several sampling techniques exist.

Random sampling occurs where all members of a target population have an equal chance of being selected. Computer-generated random number lists can be used.

✔ Strengths	❌ Weaknesses
✔ Selection for random sampling is unbiased and the sample should be fairly representative.	✗ Sometimes random sampling is impractical, e.g. not all members of a population are available. ✗ Samples can still be unrepresentative, for example all females are selected.

Opportunity sampling uses whoever is available.

✔ Strengths	❌ Weaknesses
✔ Opportunity samples are easy to obtain. ✔ It is the only sampling type available with natural experiments.	✗ Opportunity sampling is often unrepresentative, for example all students are selected. ✔ As participants can decline to take part, it can turn into self-selected sampling.

Self-selected sampling involves using volunteers, usually responding to advertisements.

✔ Strengths	❌ Weaknesses
✔ Self-selected sampling involves minimal effort to obtain participants. ✔ There is less chance of the 'screw you phenomenon' (where participants deliberately sabotage the study).	✔ Self-selected sampling often provides biased samples, as volunteers can be a certain 'type' of person and so eager to please that demand characteristics occur.

Systematic sampling involves taking every *n*th person from a list of the target population. This includes calculating the size of the population and assessing how big the sample needs to be to work out what the sampling interval should be (how big *n* is).

✔ Strengths
✔ Systematic sampling involves no bias in selection, so the sample should be fairly representative.

❌ Weaknesses
✗ Samples can still be unrepresentative if *n* coincides with a frequency trait, e.g. *n* = every fifth house in a street and every fifth house is flats occupied by young people.

Fig 7.3 Self-selected sampling involves participants volunteering to take part in a study

Stratified sampling is a small-scale reproduction of a population and involves dividing a population into its *strata* (sub-parts) and then random sampling from each strata. If one strata has 15 per cent of the population, then 15 per cent of the sample is drawn from that strata, and so on.

✔ Strengths

✔ Sampling is unbiased, and as selection occurs from representative sub-groups, the sample should be fairly representative.

✘ Weaknesses

✘ It is time consuming.

✘ A detailed knowledge of strata is required.

Ethical issues

To protect the dignity and safety of participants, as well as the integrity of psychology, research should be conducted in an ethical manner. Full details of research should be submitted to the appropriate ethical committee for approval before commencing. The British Psychology Society publishes a code of ethics that researchers should follow:

1 *Informed consent* – participants should be fully informed of the objectives and details of research to make a considered decision as to whether to participate. Parental consent is obtained for under 16s.
2 *Deception* – misleading of participants and withholding of information should be avoided.
3 *Protection of participants* – participants should not be put at risk of harm and should leave a study in the same state they entered it.
4 *Right to withdraw* – participants should be aware that they can leave at any time, including withdrawing their data in the future.
5 *Confidentiality* – participants' data should not be disclosed to anyone, unless agreed in advance.
6 *Anonymity* – participants are referred to by numbers, not names, so that data cannot be traced back to them.
7 *Inducements to take part* – participants should not be encouraged to participate through offers of financial gain or other gratification.
8 *Observational research* – observations should occur only in environments where people would expect to be observed.
9 *Cost–benefit analysis* – only if the benefits of research, in terms of knowledge gained etc., outweigh the costs, in terms of possible harm to participants etc., should the research be undertaken.

If deception is unavoidable there are measures that can be taken:

1 *Presumptive consent* – people of a similar nature are given full details of a study and asked whether they would have been willing to participate. If so it is presumed the real participants would not object.
2 *Prior general consent* – participants agree to be deceived but without knowing how it will occur.
3 *Debriefing* – immediately after a study finishes participants should be given full details and the right to withdraw their data. This applies to all studies, not just those involving deception, and also helps to alleviate possible psychological harm, so that participants leave in the same state they entered.

AQA
Psychology
For A-level Year 1 and AS
1

pp. 272–74, 278–79

7 Research methods

Observational design and questionnaire and interview construction

Observational design

There are several ways to gather data from observations, including visual and audio recordings, and 'on-the-spot' notetaking using rating scales and coding categories. Observational studies work best when time is taken to create effective behavioural categories.

- *Behavioural categories*: observers need to agree upon a grid or coding sheet that truly represents the behaviour being observed. For instance, if observers wish to observe the effect of age and gender on the speed of car driving, they might wish to create behavioural categories like *distracted, talking, using mobile phone* and *concentrating* (see Table 7.1) and then code individual drivers' behaviour using agreed scales. Coding can involve numbers, such as the apparent age of the driver, or letters to denote characteristics such as gender, e.g. 'M' for male, as well as observed behaviours, like using 'T' for a driver that was talking. Observed behaviours can also be rated on structured scales, for instance from 1 to 5 to indicate the degree of safe driving.

Table 7.1 Behavioural categories of driving behaviour

Driver	Sex (M/F)	Age (estimate)	Number of passengers	Observed behaviour	Type of car	Speed (estimate in km per hour)	Safe driving rating 1 = very unsafe 5 = very safe
A	M	55	0	M-P	Ford	40	2
B	F	21	2	T	VW	30	5
C	F	39	3	D	BMW	50	3
D etc.	M	70	0	C	Jensen	60	5

Observed behaviour code

D = Distracted **M-P** = Using mobile phone **T** = Talking **C** = Concentrating

- *Sampling procedures*: it is often difficult to observe all behaviour, especially continuous behaviour (non-stop). Placing behaviour into categories helps, but there are also different types of sampling procedures (methods of recording data) that can be used, which involve selecting some of the behaviour to observe and record, with the aim being to select representative behaviour. One sampling procedure is *event sampling,* where the number of times a behaviour occurs in a target individual (or individuals) is recorded. Another procedure is *time sampling,* where behaviour is recorded at a set interval, for instance what behaviour is seen every 30 seconds.
- *Inter-observer reliability*: this occurs when independent observers code behaviour in the same way. This lessens the chance of *observer bias* where an observer sees what they want/expect to see. To establish inter-observer reliability, clearly described behavioural categories need to be created that do not overlap. Video-taping observed behaviour means inter-observer reliability can be checked at a later date.

Questionnaires

A problem with questionnaires is their low response rate. Therefore it is important to construct questionnaires in a way that maximises the chances of participants completing and returning them.

- *Aim*: having a precise aim not only allows participants to understand the purpose of the questionnaire but also allows researchers to construct questions that fit the aim.
- *Length*: having unnecessary and over-long questions increases the chances that participants will not give the questions full consideration, or will not even complete the questionnaire.
- *Previous questionnaires*: questionnaires that have proved successful in gaining high return rates and generating useful answers should be used as a basis for the construction of a new questionnaire.
- *Question formation*: to generate meaningful answers and to increase completion rates, questions should be concise, unambiguous and easy to understand. It is also best if questions stick to single points to avoid becoming over-complex and confusing.
- *Pilot study*: a questionnaire should be tested out on a small group of individuals who provide detailed and honest feedback on all aspects of the questionnaire's design. This means corrections/adjustments can be made before the questionnaire is used on the actual sample of participants.
- *Measurement scales*: questionnaires often use measurement scales involving a series of statements, with participants choosing a score that reflects the statement they opt for. However, if participants do not fully understand a question, they will tend to choose the middle score, which can give a false impression of their actual attitude to that question. Therefore when constructing such questions it is important that the question and the statements to choose from are easy to understand.

Rate your level of agreement with the following statement:				
'Vigorous regular exercise is good for your health.'				
1	2	3	4	5
Strongly agree	Agree	Undecided	Disagree	Strongly disagree

Effective questionnaires also use a mix of *closed* questions, which allow a limited range of responses (such as yes/no answers) and therefore generate *quantitative data* (occurring as numbers), and *open* questions, which allow participants to answer fully in their own words and therefore generate *qualitative data* (non-numerical).

Design of interviews

The effectiveness of interviews is dependent on the appropriateness of the interviewer and the choice of such is affected by several factors, including:

- gender and age – can especially affect answers on questions of a sensitive sexual nature
- ethnicity – fuller, more honest answers are gained with an interviewer of the same ethnic background as the interviewee
- personal characteristics – an interviewer's appearance, accent, degree of formality, etc. can all affect the answers gained. Effective interviewers adapt their style to suit different interviewees.

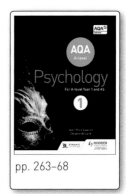

pp. 263–68

7 Research methods
The peer review process and implications of research for the economy

Peer review is essential to scholarly communication and the verification process. It involves the expert scrutiny of research papers to determine scientific validity. Only when perceived as valid may papers be published in respected journals, and therefore peer review is regarded as a 'gatekeeper', lessening the possibility that unscientific research is published and accepted as scientific fact. The process involves several experts being sent a copy of a research paper by a journal editor, with several possible outcomes: accept the work unconditionally; accept if modifications are made; reject, but suggest revisions; reject outright.

❌ Criticisms of peer review

✗ There are many organisations with interests in ensuring that only certain research is published, for example drug companies desiring studies published that suggest their products are effective, and this puts pressure on those involved in peer review to remain independent and unbiased.

✗ Research operates in a narrow social world that makes it difficult to peer review in an objective, unbiased way, due to jealousies, past differences, etc. that may occur between researchers.

✗ Reviewers have been accused of not validating research for publication so that their own work may be published first. Indeed, claims are even made of reviewers plagiarising research they were supposed to be scrutinising and passing it off as their own.

✗ Peer review can be slow, sometimes taking years to achieve.

Reporting psychological investigations

Psychologists communicate effectively by publishing research in peer-reviewed journals written in a prescribed manner to permit replication, so that findings can be validated. The *title* should be clear, relevant and fully informative. The *table of contents* lists all sections with page numbers. The *abstract* consists of a concise statement of aims, hypotheses, methodology, results, conclusions and suggestions for future research. The *introduction* presents the theoretical background and previous research, from an initial broader perspective down to a narrower one. The *aims* and *hypotheses* are then quoted in an unambiguous fashion, with justification for the direction of the experimental/ alternative hypothesis given. The *method* details all methodological requirements relating to the design and the participants, usually inclusive of ethical considerations, as well as materials, controls and the standardised procedure used. The *results* incur first as *descriptive statistics*, where measure of dispersion and central tendency are given and results summarised in appropriate graphs and tables, and second as *inferential statistics*, where statistical tests are justified and outcome of analysis quoted in terms of the hypotheses. The *discussion* explains findings in terms of aims and hypotheses and evaluates them in terms of previous findings and theoretical aspects. Sources of error are identified and strategies suggested to resolve them before implications of research and ideas for future research are presented. The *references* list all sources used, while the *appendices* detail standardised instructions, raw data, calculations and other relevant information.

The implications of psychological research for the economy

Psychological research continually leads to practical applications that benefit people's lives, which in turn benefits the economy. This is especially true for mental health. Ten per cent of people will spend time in a mental institution during their lifetime and 1 in 3 people will receive treatment for mental problems. Therefore, effective treatments, developed from psychological research, make huge savings in financial terms by enabling people to return to work and contribute more fully to the economy through the wages they earn and spend and through the increased taxes that they contribute. Effective strategies to deal with mental health also reduce the long-term financial costs on the health service from having to deal with people who would have remained ill without such treatments.

RESEARCH

- Koran et al. (2000) gave an additional treatment of the antipsychotic drug olanzapine to a group of OCD sufferers who had not responded to a course of treatment with the antidepressant drug fluoxetine, while treatment with the antidepressant continued. It was found that the combined treatment produced improvements in reducing OCD symptoms. This suggests that a combined drug therapy is useful in addressing treatment-resistant forms of OCD, thus benefiting the economy by getting people back to work and reducing the burden on the health services.
- Brosnan & Thorpe (2006) gave a group of participants who had a fear of using computers a 10-week course of systematic desensitisation (SD) and found that their fear levels became comparable to a control group of non-fearful participants. A second group of similarly treated participants were compared to a non-treated group of participants with a fear of using computers and were followed up for a year. Fear levels were significantly lowered in the fearful group, which suggests that SD is an effective treatment for reducing technophobia and therefore allows such people to work and contribute to the economy.

✔ Evaluation

- ✔ As well as producing a better functioning workforce and reducing costs to the health service, psychological research also cuts costs in policing, the judiciary, the prison services, etc., as psychologically healthy people are less likely to incur costs on these institutions.
- ✔ When conducting research, psychologists need to remember that ethical considerations come before profit and that psychology should not be used to exploit people, for instance by producing practical applications that have negative consequences, like manipulating social influences to get people to conform and carry out immoral practices in the workplace.
- ✔ In conducting research and producing practical applications, psychologists must ensure that they do not become divorced from the consequences of their actions. An example might be conducting research into psychoactive drugs, the results of which are then misused by drug companies to produce treatments that increase the companies' profits but have negative consequences for the people who use the drugs.

pp. 279–80

7 Research methods
Reliability and validity
Reliability

Reliability concerns the extent to which a test or measurement produces consistent results. To be reliable, if a study was repeated exactly, the same results should be obtained. Reliability can be improved by developing more consistent forms of measurement.

Types of reliability

There are two main types of reliability:

1 *Internal validity* concerns whether findings are consistent within themselves, for example, a measurement of height should measure the same distance between 2 metres and 4 metres as between 5 metres and 7 metres.

2 *External reliability* concerns whether findings are consistent over time, for example, an IQ test should produce the same level of intelligence for an individual on different occasions, as long as their level of intelligence remains the same.

WAYS OF ASSESSING RELIABILITY

- The *split-half method* measures internal reliability by dividing a test in two and having the same participant do both halves. If the two halves of the test provide similar results, then the test is seen as having internal reliability.
- The *test–re-test method* measures external reliability by giving the same test to the same participants on at least two occasions. If similar results are obtained, then external reliability is established.
- *Inter-observer reliability* measures whether different observers are viewing and rating behaviour similarly. This can be assessed by correlating the observers' scores, with a high correlation indicating they are observing and categorising similarly. Inter-observer reliability can be improved by developing clearly defined and separate categories of behavioural criteria.

The connection between reliability and validity

To be valid, results must first be reliable. However, results can be reliable without being valid. For example, if 1 + 1 was added up on several occasions and each time the answer was 3, then the findings would be reliable (consistent) but not valid (accurate). If 1 + 1 is added up on several occasions and the answer is always 2, then the results are both reliable and valid.

Validity

Validity concerns accuracy, the degree to which something measures what it claims to. Therefore validity refers to how accurately a study measures what it claims to and the extent to which findings can be generalised beyond research settings as a consequence of a study's *internal* and *external* validity (see below). Validity can be improved by increasing reliability and by improving internal and external validity.

Types of validity

There are two main types of validity:

1 *Internal validity* concerns whether findings are due to the manipulation of the IV or confounding variables. Internal validity can be improved by reducing investigator effects, minimising demand characteristics and by use of standardised instructions and a random sample. The more a study is controlled, the more sure we are that findings are due to the effect of the IV and not to poor methodology.

2 *External validity* concerns the extent to which findings from a study have *ecological validity* (can be generalised to other settings), *population validity* (can be generalised to other people) and *temporal validity* (can be generalised over time). External validity is improved by carrying out studies in more naturalistic settings.

WAYS OF ASSESSING VALIDITY

- *Face validity* involves 'eyeballing' items to assess the extent to which they look like what a test claims to measure.
- *Concurrent validity* assesses validity by correlating scores on a test with another test that is accepted as being valid.
- *Predictive validity* assesses validity by seeing how well a test predicts future behaviour – for instance, do school entrance tests accurately predict later exam results?
- *Temporal validity* evaluates to what extent research findings remain true over time.

pp. 280–81

7 Research methods
Features of science

Replicability

Replication involves repeating studies under identical conditions to check reliability and validity of findings. This occurs if research studies are written up in a designated manner. Fleischmann & Pons (1989) published research appearing to verify the existence of cold fusion, whereby limitless energy could be created very cheaply. Because the research was written up in the required manner, other scientists could replicate their work where unfortunately they discovered that the phenomenon does not exist, presumably due to methodological error. Replication performs the important function of ensuring that psychologists do not use practical applications in the real world until they have been shown to be based on empirically tested facts.

Description

The *scientific process* is a means of acquiring knowledge based on observable, measurable evidence, involving the generation and testing of hypotheses through *empirical methods*. These involve observations based on sensory experience rather than on thoughts and beliefs alone. A scientific fact is therefore one that has been subjected to empirical testing by rigorous observation of phenomena and must be explicable through theories testable by empirical means. Science

OBJECTIVITY

Objectivity concerns observations made without bias, as science requires that research be performed without the application of distorted personal feelings and interpretations. Objectivity is an element of empiricism, where observations are made through sensory experience rather than biased viewpoints formed from expectation and desire. To lessen the chances of bias, *standardised instructions*, *operational definitions of observed variables*, *physically defined measurements of performance* and *double-blind techniques* are used. Bias in research, making findings subjective rather than objective, is generally unconscious rather than deliberate fraud. For example, when Ganzfeld studies, which test for extra-sensory perception (ESP), are performed by believers in ESP, results tend to confirm that ESP exists, while when they are performed by sceptics, the exact same procedure tends to show that ESP does not exist.

requires predictions that are testable empirically, without bias or expectation of results, and under controlled conditions. Theories can therefore either be validated (seen to be true) or be falsified (seen to be untrue). The challenge for psychology is to achieve this in real-life settings.

PARADIGM SHIFTS

A *paradigm* is a shared set of assumptions about a subject matter and how it should be investigated. Psychologists then collect data that fit these assumptions and therefore find what they expect to find. *Paradigm shifts* occur when such old assumptions are rejected and new, revolutionary ones are adopted. Such changes occur only infrequently and often due to minority influence (see **page 20**).

pp. 282–85

7 Research methods
Reporting psychological investigations

Description

Progress in science depends on communication between researchers. It is therefore essential to describe the results of research as clearly and accurately as possible. To be published in peer-reviewed journals, research reports must be written in sections in a conventional manner, so that replication, to check the results, is possible. The basic requirements of a report are to say what was done, why it was done, what was found and what it means.

Sections of a report

- *Title* – should be clear, relevant and informative.
- *Table of contents* – lists sections in numerical page order.
- *Abstract* – summarises the study in one paragraph in terms of previous research, aims and hypotheses, methodology, results, conclusions and suggestions for future research.
- *Introduction* – details why the study was conducted. General theoretical background is supplied. Funnel technique is used, where a broad theoretical background is given that then narrows down to the precise study area, which leads on to the aims and hypotheses.
- *Aims* – the overall goals of the study are stated clearly and concisely.

HYPOTHESES

An experimental/alternative hypothesis and null hypothesis are stated precisely and unambiguously. A justification of the direction of hypotheses (one- or two-tailed) is also stated, as is the level of significance – normally 5 per cent.

Procedure/method

The procedure/method gives an outline of what was done, with methodological details reported so that replication could occur. This may involve details of the design, method, techniques used, identification of variables, sampling details or ethical considerations. It also includes materials used and controls. Details of standardised instructions etc. are included in the appendices.

Results

Findings are presented in the form of a table (with appropriate measures of central tendency and dispersion), graph and verbal summary (in words). Raw data are referenced but presented in the appendices. With inferential statistics, reasons for using a test are given, as well as what it tests for. Calculations are referenced but presented in the appendices. The outcome should be given, along with critical value, significance level and whether the test was one- or two-tailed. The outcome is then finally presented in terms of the hypotheses (rejected or accepted).

DISCUSSION

Findings are explained in several sub-sections:

1 *Explanation of findings* – key findings are related in terms of how they relate to the aims and hypotheses.

2 *Relationship to background research* – findings are discussed in relation to previous research findings presented in the introduction.

3 *Limitations and modifications* – possible sources of error, for example flawed sampling, are outlined and discussed, as well as possible means of rectifying them.

4 *Implications and suggestions for future research* – further research ideas that emerge from the findings are suggested, as well as any real-world implications and applications.

- *Conclusions* – a concise paragraph is provided, summarising key conclusions.
- *References* – full details of all sources used are provided in an accepted, conventional manner.
- *Appendices* – numbered appendices are given, containing full details of instructions given to participants, raw data, calculations, materials used, ethics form, etc.

pp. 285–88

7 Research methods

Quantitative and qualitative data

(See also presentation and display of quantitative data, **page 114**.)

Primary and secondary data

- *Primary data* refers to original data collected specifically for a research aim that has not been published before.
- *Secondary data* refers to data originally collected for another research aim that has been published before.

Primary data are more reliable and valid than secondary data, as the data have not been manipulated in any way. Secondary data drawn from several sources can help give a clearer insight into a research area than primary data can.

META-ANALYSIS

Meta-analysis is a process by which a large number of studies, involving the same research aim and research methods, are reviewed together, with the combined data statistically tested to assess the overall effect. For instance, Smith & Bond (1993) did a meta-analysis of 133 conformity studies using the Asch paradigm to assess conformity levels in different cultures. As meta-analyses use data combined from many studies, they allow identification of trends and relationships not possible with individual studies. Meta-analyses are helpful when individual studies find contradictory or weak results, as they give a clearer overall picture.

Description

Quantitative data are numerical (occur as numbers), such as counting the number of times something happens, while *qualitative data* are non-numerical (occur in forms other than numbers), such as someone describing their feelings. Quantitative data tend to be objective, reliable and simple, while qualitative data tend to be subjective, less reliable and more detailed. The two forms of data can be combined to give deeper understanding.

Qualitative data give insight into feelings and thoughts, but analysis can be affected by researcher bias (the researcher's interpretation of the data). However, qualitative data can be

Content analysis

Content analysis (CA) is a method of turning qualitative data, such as written, verbal and visual information, into quantitative data. Coding units are used to categorise the material being analysed, such as the number of times positive words occur in a written description. Coding units can involve *words*, *themes*, *characters* and *time and space*.

✔ Ease of application: CA is easy to do, inexpensive and does not require interaction with participants.

✔ Complements other methods: CA can be used to verify results using other research methods and is especially useful as a longitudinal tool to detect trends (changes over time).

✔ Reliable: it is easy to replicate, meaning checking reliability is simple.

converted into quantitative data through *content* and *thematic* analysis.

Quantitative data are generally produced from experiments, observations, correlational studies, structured interviews and closed questions in questionnaires. Qualitative data are generally produced from case studies and from unstructured interviews and open questions in questionnaires.

✘ Descriptive: being purely descriptive, CA does not reveal underlying reasons for behaviour, attitudes, etc.

✘ Flawed results – as CA is limited to available material, observed trends may not reflect reality.

✘ Lack of causality – as CA is not performed under controlled conditions, it does not show causality.

THEMATIC ANALYSIS

Thematic analysis (TA) is a means of identifying, analysing and reporting themes (patterns) within qualitative data, with themes being identified through data coding. TA goes beyond merely counting words and phrases and instead seeks to identify ideas within data. TA can involve comparing themes, identifying co-occurrences of themes and using graphs to show differences between themes.

Identified themes become categories for analysis, with TA performed by a process of coding involving six stages:

1 Familiarisation with data – involves intensely inspecting the data to become immersed in their content.

2 Coding – codes (labels) are generated that identify features of the data important to answering the research question.

3 Searching for themes – codes and data are inspected to identify patterns of meaning (potential themes).

4 Reviewing themes – potential themes are checked against the data to see whether they explain the data and fit the research aim. Themes are refined, which can involve splitting, combining or discarding them.

5 Defining and naming themes – each theme is intensively analysed so that it can be given an informative name.

6 Writing up – information gained from the TA is combined.

pp. 292–94, 299–300

7 Research methods

Presentation and display of quantitative data; distributions

Description

Quantitative data occur as numbers. They are often presented through graphs and tables, giving viewers an easily understandable visual interpretation of the findings from a study.

Graphs

Graphs should be fully and clearly labelled, on both the x-axis and the y-axis, and be appropriately titled. They are best presented if the y-axis (vertical) is three-quarters the length of the x-axis (horizontal). Only 1 graph should be used to display a set of data. Inappropriate scales should not be used, as these convey misleading, biased impressions. Different types of graphs exist for different forms of data.

Bar charts display data as separate, comparable categories, for example findings from young and old participants. The columns of the bars should be the same width and separated by spaces to show that the variable on the x-axis is not continuous. Data are 'discrete', occurring, for example, as the mean scores of several groups. Percentages, totals and ratios can also be displayed.

Histograms display continuous data, such as test scores, and these are displayed as they increase in value along the x-axis, without spaces between them to show their continuity. The frequency of the data is presented on the y-axis. The column width for each value on the x-axis is the same width per equal category interval so that the area of each column is proportional to the number of cases it represents on the histogram.

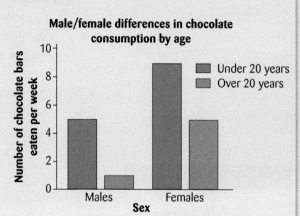

Fig 7.4 An example of a bar chart

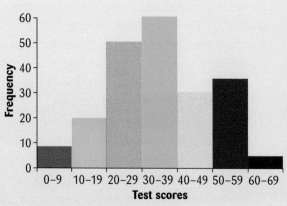

Fig 7.5 An example of a histogram

Frequency polygons (line graphs) are similar to histograms in that the data presented on the x-axis are continuous. A frequency polygon is constructed by drawing a line from the mid-point top of each column in a histogram to allow 2 or more frequency distributions to be displayed on the same graph, thus allowing them to be directly compared with each other.

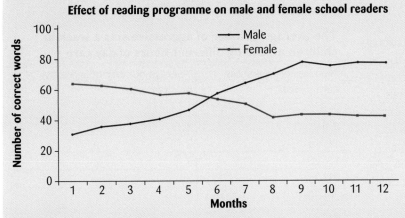

Fig 7.6 An example of a frequency polygon

Pie charts are used to show the frequency of categories of data as percentages. The pie is split into sections, each one representing the frequency of a category. Each section is colour coded, with an indication given as to what each section represents and its percentage score.

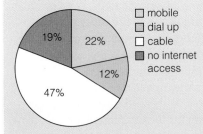

Fig 7.7 An example of a pie chart

Correlational data are plotted on *scattergrams*, which show the degree to which 2 co-variables are related.

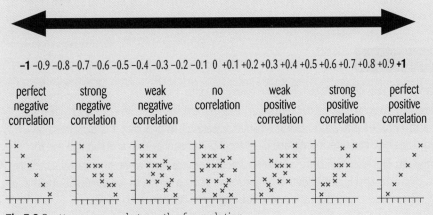

Fig 7.8 Scattergrams and strength of correlation

7 Research methods
Continued

Tables do not present raw, unprocessed data such as individual scores. Rather they are used to present an appropriate summary of processed data, such as totals, means and ranges. The unprocessed data are given in the appendices of a study as a data table (i.e. a presentation of the raw scores). As with graphs, tables should be clearly labelled and titled.

Table 7.2 An example of a table

The average number of aggressive acts a week in children attending different hours of day care	
Number of hours' day care a week	Average number of aggressive acts per week
0–5	1
6–10	3
11–15	2
16–20	4
21–25	2
26–30	3
31–35	9

Measures of central tendency

Measures of central tendency display the 'mid-point' values of sets of data.
- The *mean* is calculated by totalling scores and dividing by the number of scores. For example: 1 + 1 + 2 + 3 + 4 + 5 + 6 + 7 + 8 = 37; 37/9 = 4.2. Its strengths are that it is the most accurate measure of central tendency and includes all scores. Its weaknesses are that it is skewed by extreme scores and the mean score may not actually be one of the scores.
- The *median* is the central value of scores in rank order. For example: for the set of data 1, 1, 2, 3, 4, 5, 6, 7, 8 – the median is 4. With an odd number of scores this is the middle number, while with an even number of scores it is the average of the 2 middle scores. Its strengths are that it is not affected by extreme scores and is easier to calculate than the mean. Its weaknesses are that it lacks the sensitivity of the mean and can be unrepresentative in a small set of data.
- The *mode* is the most common value. For example: for the set of data 2, 3, 6, 7, 7, 7, 9, 15, 16, 16, 20 – the mode is 7. Its strengths are that it is less affected by extreme scores and, unlike the mean, is always a whole number. Its weaknesses are that there can be more than one mode and it does not use all scores.

Measures of dispersion are measures of variability in a set of data.
- The *range* is calculated by subtracting the lowest from the highest value. Its strengths are that it is easy to calculate and includes extreme values, while its weaknesses are that it is distorted by extreme scores and does not indicate if data are clustered or spread evenly around the mean.
- The *interquartile range* displays the variability of the middle 50 per cent of a set of data. Its strengths are that it is easy to calculate and is not affected by extreme scores, while its weaknesses are that it does not include all scores and is inaccurate if there are big intervals between scores.
- *Standard deviation* measures the variability (spread) of a set of scores from the mean. Its strengths are that it is more sensitive than the range, as all values are included and it allows the interpretation of individual values, while its weaknesses are that it is more complex to calculate and is less meaningful if data are not normally distributed.

Normal distribution

Normal distribution occurs when data have an even amount of scores either side of the mean. Normally distributed data are symmetrical – when such data are plotted on a graph they form a bell-shaped curve with as many scores below the mean as above. (See also **page 58**.)

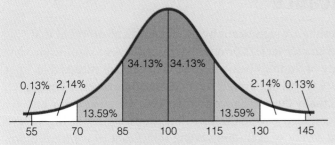

Fig 7.9 Normal distribution of IQ scores

Checking data for normal distribution

- *Examine visually* – inspect the data to see if scores are mainly around the mean.
- *Calculate measure of central tendency* – work out the mean, median and mode to see if they are similar.
- *Plot the frequency distribution* – put the data into a histogram to see if they form a bell-shaped curve.

SKEWED DISTRIBUTION

If data do not have a symmetrical distribution, the resulting graph is *skewed* and does not have an even amount of scores either side of the norm. *Outliers* ('freak' scores) can cause skewed distributions.

- A *positive* skewed distribution occurs when there is a high extreme score or group of scores.
- A *negative* skewed distribution occurs when there is a low extreme score or group of scores.

So a positively skewed distribution has more high than low scores in it, while a negatively skewed distribution has more low than high scores in it.

Checking data for skewed distribution

The same ways that data are checked for normal distribution are used. Plotting data on a histogram will show if a skew is negative or positive.

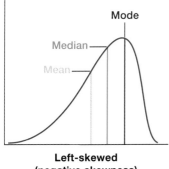

Left-skewed (negative skewness)

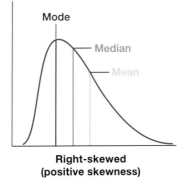

Right-skewed (positive skewness)

Fig 7.10 Skewed distributions

pp. 295–9

7 Research methods

Inferential testing

Probability and significance

Probability involves deciding whether results are significant by producing a cut-off point that determines whether findings are beyond chance factors or not. Psychology uses a significance level of $p \leq 0.05$, giving a 95 per cent assurance of findings being beyond chance. This means that 5 per cent of the time that significant results are found (seemingly beyond the boundaries of chance) they are in fact not significant and are actually due to chance factors. This is seen as being an acceptable level of error. In some instances, such as when testing new drugs, a more stringent level of $p \leq 0.01$ is used, entailing a 99 per cent certainty of findings being significant (this means there is only a 1 per cent chance of insignificant results that are actually explainable by chance factors being seen as significant and beyond the boundaries of chance). *Type I errors* occur when findings are accepted as significant but are not, as the significance level was too low, while *Type II errors* occur when findings are accepted as insignificant but are not, as the significance level was too high.

Inferential testing

Research produces data which are analysed by inferential statistical tests to see whether differences and relationships found between sets of data are significant or not. Three criteria need to be considered when choosing an appropriate statistical test:

1   What design has been used – whether an *independent groups design* or a *repeated measures design* (including a matched pairs design) has been used.

2   What types of outcome are being tested for – is a difference or a relationship between two sets of data being sought?

3   What level of measurement has been used – were the data produced of *nominal, ordinal* or *interval/ratio level?*

Table 7.3 Choosing an appropriate statistical test

Nature of hypothesis	Level of measurement	Type of research design	Independent (unrelated) Repeated (related)
Difference	Nominal data	Chi-squared	Sign test
	Ordinal data	Mann-Whitney U test	Wilcoxon (signed-matched ranks)
	Interval data	Independent t-test	
			Related t-test
Correlation	Ordinal data		Spearman's rho
	Interval data		Pearson product moment

- *Nominal data* – consist of *frequencies,* for example how many days of a week were rainy or not. Nominal data are relatively uninformative, for instance they would not tell us how rainy any particular day was.
- *Ordinal data* – involve putting data into *rank order,* for example finishing places of runners in a race. This is not fully informative, as although we know who are the *better runners, we do not know by how much they are better.*
- *Interval/ratio data* – involve data with standardised measuring distances, such as time. This is the most informative type of data. *Interval data* have an arbitrary zero point, for instance zero degrees temperature does not mean there is no temperature. *Ratio data* have an absolute zero point, for instance someone with zero pounds in their bank account has no money.

Statistical tests

- *Sign test* – used when a difference is predicted between two sets of data, data are of at least nominal level and an RMD/MPD has been used. The sign test works by calculating the value of *s* (the less frequent sign) and comparing this value to those in a critical values table to see whether the result is significant or not.
- *Chi-squared* – used when a difference is predicted between two sets of data, data are of at least nominal level and an IGD has been used. Chi-squared can also be used as a test of *association* (relationship).
- *Mann-Whitney* – used when a difference is predicted between two sets of data, data are at least of ordinal level and an IGD has been used.
- *Wilcoxon signed-matched ranks* – used when a difference between two sets of data has been predicted, data are of at least ordinal level and an RMD/MPD has been used.
- *Independent (unrelated) t-test* – used when a difference is predicted between two sets of data, data are normally distributed and of interval/ratio level, and an IGD has been used.
- *Repeated (related) t-test* – used when a difference is predicted between two sets of data, data are normally distributed and of interval/ratio level, and an RMD/MPD has been used.
- *Spearman's rho* – used when a relationship (correlation) is predicted between two sets of data, data are of at least ordinal level and consist of pairs of scores from the same person or event.
- *Pearson product moment* – used when a relationship is predicted between two sets of data, data are normally distributed, of interval/ratio level and consist of pairs of scores from the same person or event.

Interpretation of significance

Statistical analysis produces an *observed* value and this is compared to a *critical* value to see whether it is significant or not. To do this, critical value tables need to be referenced, taking into account whether a hypothesis was one- or two-tailed, how many participants or participant pairs were involved and what level of significance was used. The Mann-Whitney, Wilcoxon and sign tests require an observed value to be equal to or less than a critical value to be significant. The Chi-squared, independent t-test, dependent t-test, Spearman's rho and Pearson product moment require an observed value to be equal to or greater than a critical value to be significant.

pp. 301–11

8 Issues and debates
Gender and culture in psychology

Focal study

Sheridan & King (1972) assessed the degree to which males and females differ in levels of obedience. Milgram (1963) had found that 62.5 per cent of participants obeyed instructions to deliver electric shocks that increased up to 450 volts (the shocks weren't real) to a man in an adjacent room. However, critics argued that this was biased, as only male participants were used. Sheridan & King used Milgram's research procedure, but with a puppy visible in a glass tank, which received real electric shocks (the shocks were mild and did not increase in intensity, though the participants thought they did). Invisible anaesthetic gas was used to make the puppy collapse, as if injured or dead. 54 per cent of males gave the maximum shock, while 100 per cent of females did. This shows that Milgram's findings were androcentric and that females are more obedient than males, possibly as they are socialised to be so.

OTHER STUDIES

- Meeus & Raaijmakers (1986) used the Milgram paradigm to find the highest recorded obedience level of 90 per cent in Spanish participants, while Kilham & Mann (1974) used it to find the lowest obedience level of 28 per cent in Australian participants. This illustrates cultural relativism, as different cultural groups obey to different levels.

- Seyle (1936) reported on the fight-or-flight response, where individuals have a reflex response to perceived threats, permitting optimal functioning in fighting back or fleeing. He saw this as occurring in both genders, but Taylor (2000) found stress produces a 'tend-and-befriend' response in females, due to them producing more oxytocin, which promotes nurturing behaviour. Seyle's research is therefore an example of beta bias.

- Higgs (2011) reported on pibloktoq, a culture-bound syndrome found only among Arctic Eskimo communities, where individuals become excited, strip off, swear, break things and eat faeces. After enduring seizures and a coma, they awaken with no memory of the incident. This illustrates how behaviour can vary cross-culturally.

Description

Gender concerns the social and psychological characteristics of males and females. *Universality* means that all psychological research is assumed to apply equally to both genders. For this to be true, rigorous testing of males and females must occur when research is performed, if not *bias* will happen. There are three ways in which this can occur:

1 *Male (or female) samples* – research is conducted on one gender only but findings are generalised to the other gender.

2 *Male (or female) behaviour seen as standard* – if the opposite gender's behaviour is different it is seen as a deviation from the norm.

3 *Biological differences emphasis* – behavioural explanations tend to

Fig 8.1 It is important to consider the cultural context of behaviour before making a judgement

over-emphasise biology and under-emphasise social and external factors. *Androcentrism* is a form of male bias, where male behaviour is seen as the norm against which to compare female behaviour. *Alpha bias* occurs when differences between genders are exaggerated, while *beta bias* occurs when differences between genders are downplayed. *Cultural bias* occurs when findings from studies on one cultural group are generalised to all cultures. This can involve *ethnocentrism*, the assumption that the behaviour of one cultural group is the norm and superior to other cultures. *Cultural relativism* sees behaviour varying cross-culturally, with no one group being superior.

✖ Negative evaluation

✖ There is an issue of reactivity in human research as the gender of the researcher can alter the outcomes of the research; findings may be different if the researcher was female instead of male. This is also the case depending on whether the researcher is from the ethnic majority or ethnic minority of the culture in which research is conducted. This makes biases hard to avoid, although, again, an acknowledgement of this reactivity is important to ensure interpretation of findings is as fair as possible.

✖ Freud's psychodynamic theory can be seen as an example of alpha bias, as he saw females as morally weaker than males due to them identifying more weakly with their mothers to overcome their Electra complex than boys do when identifying with their fathers to overcome their Oedipus complex.

Practical application

A consideration of cultural relativism is important when diagnosing and advocating treatments for mental disorders. For this to be effective, full consideration of a patient's cultural background and norms should be undertaken.

pp. 28–33

8 Issues and debates
Free will and determinism

Focal study

Domanski (2013) reported on the case study of Louis Leborgne conducted by Paul Broca to assess the role of the left temporal lobe in producing speech. Leborgne suffered with epilepsy and lost the ability to speak (other than the word 'Tan'). He was hospitalised at age 30 and died there in 1861, aged 51 years. Broca performed a post mortem on Leborgne's brain and found a lesion (area of damage) on the left temporal lobe. This was the only area of damage visible, so Broca concluded that this brain area is responsible for the production of speech. The area is known to this day as Broca's area. The study indicates that there is a specific brain area for a specific form of behaviour, which is an example of biological determinism, as damage to Broca's area leads to impaired speech production that is beyond the control of an individual.

OTHER STUDIES

- Pavlov (1902) showed that dogs could be taught to salivate at the sound of a bell by presenting their food while simultaneously ringing a bell (on average for 7 presentations). He called this classical conditioning and it is an example of environmental determinism, as behaviour was controlled by environmental factors.

- Bandura (1961) showed that children observed and imitated a model who beat up a 'Bobo doll' if the model was reinforced. This involved thought processes, as children work out when they should imitate the behaviour, so is an example of soft determinism, as there is some personal control over the behaviour.

- Freud (1895) detailed his dream about a patient Irma who was not improving. In the dream another doctor injected Irma with a dirty needle and Freud interpreted this as wish fulfilment that he was not responsible for Irma's condition. This is an example of psychic determinism, where the unconscious mind (revealed by the dream) controls conscious behaviour.

Description

Is human behaviour a result of *free will*, where individuals have personal control over their behaviour, or is it a result of *determinism*, where factors outside of personal control motivate and maintain behaviour? There are different types and degrees of determinism that affect behaviour in varying ways and to varying extents. *Hard determinism* concerns the view that human behaviour is set by external forces and is beyond personal control. *Soft determinism* concerns the view that although behaviour is to some extent set by forces outside of personal control, individuals do retain some influence over what they choose to do. *Biological determinism* concerns the idea that behaviour is motivated and maintained by *physiological influences*,

Fig 8.2 Can we behave how we want, or are our actions determined?

✔ The idea of free will feels intuitively correct and it is this experience that means the debate continues. The subjective experience of most people is that they are in control of their actions and behaviours. The humanistic approach also acknowledges this feeling and argues that we do have free will.

such as genetics, biochemistry, evolution and brain mechanisms. *Environmental determinism* concerns the idea that behaviour is motivated and maintained by situational influences, with *behaviourism* being most associated with this idea, where behaviour is seen as responses stimulated by environmental stimuli. *Psychic determinism* is Freudian, a *psychodynamic* idea, whereby conscious behaviour is seen to be motivated and maintained by the *unconscious mind,* which develops in childhood by progression through a series of *psychosexual stages.* *Scientism* in psychology involves using controlled laboratory experiments to find *causal* (cause and effect) *explanations.*

✗ Negative evaluation

✗ Free will is practically impossible to test. It is a non-physical concept and as such is difficult to quantify and measure. As psychology is a science, the idea that something without a physical presence can affect behaviour is at odds with the discipline. This means that a resolution of the debate is not currently likely. If, at some point in the future, measurement becomes possible, the scientific discipline of psychology may be able to resolve the debate. Of course, the argument is that free will is not measurable because it does not exist.

✗ Although laboratory experiments allow the establishment of causality for phenomena, because they are conducted under such artificially controlled conditions they can be said to lack ecological validity, where results cannot be generalised to real-life situations in which such conditions do not exist. However, other research methods are not as strictly controlled and do not allow the establishment of causality.

Practical application

Environmental determinism has practical applications in teaching desired skills to animals and people. For example, target behaviours can be reinforced through operant conditioning. Conditioning techniques are also used in therapies, such as systematic desensitisation in reducing phobias.

pp. 33–38

8 Issues and debates
The nature–nurture debate

Focal study

Grootheest *et al.* (2005) conducted a twin study to assess the degree to which OCD is an inherited condition under genetic control. The researchers conducted a meta-analysis of two types of twin studies: first, ones conducted between 1929 and 1965 using outdated diagnostic criteria (9 studies comprising 37 twin pairs) and, second, ones conducted since 1965 using modern diagnostic criteria (19 studies comprising 9,997 twin pairs). It was found that in children, OCD had a heritability influence (the degree to which the condition was genetic in nature) of 45–65 per cent, while in adults OCD was found to have a heritability influence of 27–47 per cent. It was concluded that, especially in children, there is a genetic component to OCD. However, as OCD was not found to be totally genetic in origin, it supports the interactionist approach that OCD occurs through a mixture of genetic and environmental influences.

OTHER STUDIES

- Plomin *et al.* (2013) used gene-mapping techniques with a sample of 3,154 pairs of 12-year-old twins to find that genetics accounted for about 66 per cent of the heritability of the cognitive features of depression, such as negative schemas, which suggests that depression is largely a result of nature.

- Turnbull (1961) reported on Kenge, a pygmy who had lived all his life in dense rainforest. When taken to wide open savannah grasslands he perceived buffalo miles away as ants, but a short distance away. It seemed that learning experiences (from living in dense rainforest) had shaped his perceptual abilities, supporting the nurture viewpoint.

- Skodak & Skeels (1949) found the correlation between IQ (intelligence) scores of adopted children and their biological mothers rose from 28 per cent at age 4 to 44 per cent at age 13, supporting the nature viewpoint. However, Scarr & Weinberg (1983) found adopted children's IQ levels moved away from those of their biological parents towards those of their adoptive parents, supporting the nurture viewpoint.

Description

The *nature–nurture debate* focuses on the degree to which behaviour is inherited or learned. The nature part of the debate sees behaviour as being determined by the genes an individual inherits, with no input at all from environmental factors. The *nurture* part of the debate, however, sees all behaviour as determined solely through learning via environmental influences, with no hereditary genetic influences. Research does not indicate that behaviour is genetically determined, so nature, by itself, cannot explain the causation of behaviour. However, research does show that many behaviours have a genetic component, so the debate mainly

Fig 8.3 Does our behaviour stem from our genetics or our upbringing?

✔ The nature–nurture debate in recent times has moved from the argument between the extreme viewpoints of nature and nurture to the general acknowledgement that an interactionist stance is seen to be appropriate. The argument now is based on the relative influence of nature and nurture.

✔ Research on the relative heritability of a characteristic varies greatly. This could be due to many things such as sample size, methodology and age. It may indeed possibly be due to the fact that some people are more susceptible to environmental influence than others. For example, with intelligence, the higher an individual's genetic potential for intelligence (nature), the more environmental learning experiences (nurture) play a part in determining that individual's actual level of intelligence.

focuses on the relative importance of heredity and environment in determining behaviour. Research has focused on twin studies, where the nature point of view is favoured if MZ twins (genetically identical) are more similar in behaviour than DZ twins (50 per cent genetically similar), and adoption studies, where nature is favoured if adopted children's behaviour is more similar to their biological parents, as well as gene mapping studies, which try to identify specific genes associated with specific behaviours. The *interactionist approach* sees individuals as having genetic potentials for different behaviours, with environmental factors determining how much of the genetic potential is realised for each behaviour.

✗ **Negative evaluation**

✗ Assessing the relative influence of nature and nurture is fraught with difficulties. Even using twin studies is problematic due to the assumption that the only difference between MZ and DZ twins is their genetic similarity. Parenting styles differ in that MZ twins are treated more similarly than DZ twins. This means the difference in concordance rates could be due to nurture rather than nature.

Practical application
Because intelligence has been shown to be considerably affected by environmental factors (nurture), it has allowed researchers to identify the types of interactions that can be made to help boost children's IQ, such as diet, exercise and social stimulation, as well as teaching.

pp. 40–44

8 Issues and debates
Holism and reductionism

Focal study

Davis et al. (2013) assessed the role that genetics played in the causation of OCD and Tourette's syndrome. The researchers used a study method called genome-wide complex trait analysis, which allows simultaneous comparison of genetic variation across the entire genome, rather than the usual method of testing genes one at a time. The genetic data sets of 1,500 participants with OCD were compared against 5,500 non-OCD controls. (The study also compared the data sets of 1,500 Tourette's syndrome sufferers with 5,200 non-Tourette's controls.) The results showed that both OCD and Tourette's syndrome had a genetic basis, though more so in Tourette's syndrome, and that although there were some shared genetic characteristics, the two disorders had distinct genetic architectures. This suggests the two are separate disorders with some overlap. The findings also fit a reductionist explanation, as they reduce the understanding of the disorders to a single biological explanation.

OTHER STUDIES

- Pichichero (2009) reported that case studies from the US National Institute of Health showed that children with streptococcal (throat) infections often displayed OCD symptoms shortly after becoming infected. This supports the idea that such infections may be having an effect on neural mechanisms underpinning OCD. Again this is a biological reductionist explanation, as it reduces OCD to a single biological explanation.

- Di Gallo (1966) reported that 20 per cent of people experiencing traumatic car accidents developed a phobia of travelling in cars, which is explicable by classical conditioning, as the neutral stimulus of the car became associated with a fear response. Not travelling by car is negatively reinforcing, as it reduces anxiety, which is explicable by operant conditioning. These are therefore examples of environmental reductionism.

- Boury (2001) found that depressives misinterpret facts and experiences in a negative fashion and feel hopeless about the future, supporting a cognitive explanation for depression, which is more of a holistic explanation than a biological one would be.

Description

Holism concerns the viewpoint that, to be understood, behaviour should be considered in its entirety, as a whole, while reductionism concerns the viewpoint that behaviours should be reduced (broken down) into their basic components in order to be comprehended. Levels of explanation relate to what type of explanation is required. At a more reductionist level this would involve understanding behaviour from more of a biological standpoint, such as from a biochemical, neural, evolutionary or genetic viewpoint. At a more holistic level this would involve comprehension of behaviour from more of a psychological standpoint, such as learned associations, mental processes, emotions and socio-cultural

Practical application

Biological reductionism has led to biological therapies, such as drugs, that help sufferers of mental disorders. The improvement such treatments incur often then allows more psychological therapies, for example CBT, which are more rooted in holism, to be delivered, creating an interactionist approach to treatment.

✔ Reductionist explanations mean that an explanation can be rigorously scientifically tested under controlled conditions as there are fewer factors to consider. This means that empirical work can be conducted on an explanation and this gives it academic weight.

✔ Humanistic psychology uses holism, as humanism believes that people can be understood only by being viewed in their entirety, rather than through single aspects.

influences. The holism–reductionism debate has implications for what kind of academic discipline psychology should be. If a reductionist stance is adopted, it places greater emphasis on scientifically determined, biological explanations, while if holism is adopted, greater emphasis is placed on other factors and levels of explanation, such as behaviourist, cognitive and social psychological ones. *Biological reductionism* involves explaining behaviour using biological systems, such as genetics or biochemistry, while *environmental (stimulus–response) reductionism* involves learned associations, such as those seen in classical conditioning, operant conditioning and social learning theory, which form the behaviourist perspective.

✘ Many psychologists acknowledge that the likelihood that a behaviour has a purely biological explanation is low. The complexity involved in every behaviour means that a purely reductionist explanation is rarely accepted as sufficient.

✘ A reductionist explanation may mean that other explanations are ignored and underplayed. In the case of mental illness this could lead to a recurrence of the disorder, as all the factors have not been considered. For example, the behaviourist explanation of anorexia nervosa sees it as being learned through conditioning experiences. Therefore the treatment involves patients being positively reinforced for weight gain. However, once a target weight is reached and the patient is released from hospital, they will often relapse because the explanation (and the treatment) did not address the underlying non-behaviourist reasons for the patient being anorexic.

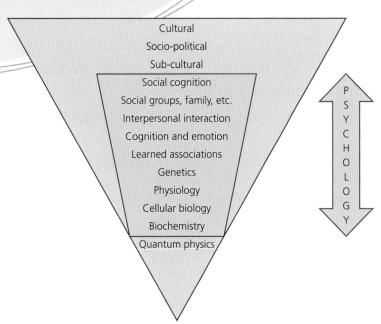

Cultural
Socio-political
Sub-cultural
Social cognition
Social groups, family, etc.
Interpersonal interaction
Cognition and emotion
Learned associations
Genetics
Physiology
Cellular biology
Biochemistry
Quantum physics

P S Y C H O L O G Y

AQA

AQA A-level

Psychology ②

Jean-Marc Lawton
Eleanor Willard

DYNAMIC | HODDER

pp. 44–49

Fig 8.4 Various levels available to consider a behaviour

8 Issues and debates

Idiographic and nomothetic approaches to psychological investigation

Focal study

Thigpen & Cleckley (1954) reported on the psychotherapeutic treatment of 25-year-old Eve White, who was referred to the clinicians due to her 'blinding headaches'. A case study was conducted that consisted of interviews with Eve and her family members, hypnosis sessions, observations, EEG readings and psychological tests, such as memory, IQ and personality tests. Emotional difficulties were revealed, mainly concerning Eve's marital difficulties and personal frustrations. During hypnosis (and sometimes spontaneously) an alternative personality called 'Eve Black' appeared, a totally different person characterised by irresponsibility, violence and a selfish desire for pleasure. Eve White had an IQ of 110 to Eve Black's 104. Eve White also had superior memory ability to Eve Black. A third personality, called Jane, then appeared, with all three personalities showing different EEG readings. It was concluded that Eve had multiple personality disorder. This was an example of an idiographic approach, as it related to Eve as a unique example.

Description

The idiographic versus nomothetic approaches debate concerns whether it is best to study and understand a person as being unique or as sharing the similarities of others. *Idiographic* refers to when an explanation centres on a person as an individual, seeking to find what uniqueness that person has that makes them who they are. *Nomothetic*, meanwhile, concerns the idea that people have similarities that allow them to be grouped together. Nomothetic explanations can therefore be generalised to all members of a group, while idiographic explanations are non-generalisable. Research based on

OTHER STUDIES

- Scoville (1957) reported on HM, an epileptic, who after surgery developed anterograde amnesia where he could not encode new long-term memories, though his short-term memory was intact. His brain was dissected on his death aged 82 to reveal damage to his hippocampus. As this related to a fairly unique case, it can be considered an idiographic approach.

- Herlitz et al. (1997) assessed LTM abilities in 1,000 Swedish participants, finding that females outscored males on tasks requiring episodic LTM. This suggested a gender difference in episodic LTM ability and, as it was an experiment performed on many participants, used a nomothetic approach, with the findings generalisable to the general population.

- Wagenaar (1986) found he had excellent LTM recall when testing himself on his diary entries of 2,400 events over 6 years. This self-report method of diary usage involves the idiographic approach, as it relates only to Wagenaar as an individual, with the findings not necessarily generalisable.

- ✔ An idiographic stance, such as a case study, is often the seed prompting ideas for further research. It looks at behaviour and phenomena in detail from an idiographic, in-depth perspective that leads to research ideas. Inevitably, though, a nomothetic stance will be adopted at some point.
- ✔ Those in the field who perceive psychology as, or wish it to be, a science use the nomothetic approach, as it fits the empirical research methods used in the established natural sciences, such as physics and chemistry, where the search is for general rules applicable to all. Those who prefer a less scientific approach, such as those who favour the psychodynamic and humanistic approaches, adopt a more idiographic approach.

the idiographic approach is unlikely to be performed on large numbers of people, as in experiments, as it would not be trying to establish universal laws generalisable to all members of a population. Case studies are an example of an idiographic study method, as they seek to assess only one person. The idiographic approach tends not to favour quantitative methods, where numerical data are generated, but instead qualitative methods, where non-numerical data are generated concerning attitudes, beliefs and self-reflections, often from self-report measures, such as interviews, questionnaires and diaries. The nomothetic approach seeks to classify people into groups, establish universal laws and create continuums upon which people can be placed.

✘ Negative evaluation

- ✘ Idiographic viewpoints seek to find behavioural patterns applicable to all. Conversely, a nomothetic stance means that theories often do not fit everyone and therefore we cannot adopt a one-size-fits-all approach. This inevitably makes them inappropriate for some people. This argument can also be applied to interventions and means that people are forced to use interventions not really applicable to them, which may have only a moderate effect on them, or no effect at all.

Practical application

Most psychological research is nomothetic, which has a practical application in the therapies, treatments and interventions that are created, which can be successfully administered to great amounts of people. Interventions and treatments incurred from idiographic research are generally only applicable to that one individual.

AQA
AQA
A-level
Psychology
2

Jean-Marc Lawton
Eleanor Willard

pp. 51–55

8 Issues and debates
Ethical implications of research studies and theory

Focal study

Hamer *et al.* (1993) assessed the role of genetics in male homosexuality. Incidence rates of male homosexuality were assessed in families of 114 homosexual male participants. DNA linkage analysis was also conducted on 40 families that had two gay brothers and no evidence of maternal transmission. It was found that increased rates of same-sex orientation were found in the maternal uncles and male cousins of participants, but not in their fathers or paternal relatives. DNA analysis revealed a positive correlation between homosexual orientation and the inheritance of genetic markers on the X chromosome in 64 per cent of participants. Hamer concluded that male homosexuality was genetic in origin and used the term 'gay gene' to describe this. His speculation that his research would lead to greater tolerance of homosexuals did not occur; instead there were calls for screening of foetuses and aborting of 'gay' ones. Hamer had not considered the social sensitivity of his research.

OTHER STUDIES

- Yerkes (1915) found on tests of his design that white Americans had a higher IQ than black people and immigrants. But the tests were flawed as they were based on white American culture. The findings were used to justify using black people as 'cannon fodder' in the First World War, which was highly socially insensitive.

- Perry (2012) claims that in Milgram's famous 1963 study of obedience, debriefing of participants (he eventually used nearly 3,000 participants) did not always occur, as he thought debriefings might confound his results. If true, this would have resulted in highly unethical levels of harm.

- Harlow (1959, 1965) performed a series of experiments that resulted in terrible levels of damage to the infant monkey participants. Harlow suffered from depression and alcoholism, which may have stimulated his interest in the origins of mental disorders, with the accusation being that his co-workers knew this was fuelling his unethical research and so should have stopped him.

Description

Before and during the carrying out of research studies psychologists should consider the ethical implications that their research might incur. It would not be acceptable to claim 'Well, I didn't know that was going to happen' if an ethically unacceptable, but foreseeable, consequence was to occur. Therefore all reasonable steps should be taken to ensure that negative ethical implications do not occur. As well as ensuring that informed consent has been gained, that the right to withdraw has clearly been made, that no deceit has been used, that no harm to participants will occur, that full briefings and debriefings have occurred and that anonymity and confidentiality

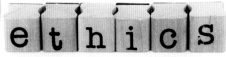

Fig 8.5 It is important for psychologists to consider the ethical implications of their research, as it can have far-reaching social consequences

✔ The code of ethics governed by the British Psychological Society together with university ethics boards means that ethical implications of research have to be considered if research is to be conducted. Stringent guidelines are in place to protect all people who may be involved in the process. The guidelines have become more careful as time has passed so the chances of research causing problems has been reduced.

have been ensured, researchers should ensure other researchers adhere to ethical guidelines, that no inducements to participate are given and, possibly most importantly, that issues of *social sensitivity* have been considered. Social sensitivity refers to psychological research that has wider ethical implications that impact outside of the narrow research context. Such considerations include the impact of findings upon participants, their family and friends, upon researchers and the institutions they represent, as well as groups of people, such as cultural and sub-cultural ones, who may also be impacted upon. Ethical committees can be useful in considering potential ethical implications.

✗ Negative evaluation

✗ Sometimes it is not possible to see what the effects of research might be on the researcher, the participants and society. This makes it hard to judge. It is also not an objective decision, so there is potential for bias from within the decision makers. This means that socially sensitive research still causes problems from time to time.

✗ The ethical guidelines set for research permission are seen by some to be too strict. There are areas of research which could elicit helpful findings that could benefit a lot of people. However, the research cannot be conducted due to the research process potentially causing issues for the participants or researcher. Reaching a balance is therefore problematic.

Practical application

The main practical application of the consideration of ethical implications is that it has led to research that is conducted in a much more sensitive manner, which has resulted in the protection of the health and dignity of participants, as well as the reputation of psychology.

pp. 55–59

9 Relationships
The evolutionary explanation for partner preferences

Focal study

Schutzwohl & Koch (2004) tested the idea that males fear sexual infidelity while females fear emotional infidelity. 100 males and 100 females were presented with four imaginary scenarios involving social situations, each with two alternative responses. The important scenario was: 'Imagine you discover your partner formed a deep emotional and sexual relationship with another person. Which aspect of your partner's involvement would make you more jealous: (1) the deep emotional relationship, (2) the passionate sexual relationship?'

Both sexes reported more jealousy over emotional involvement, but more males (37 per cent) than females (20 per cent) selected their partner's sexual involvement as making them more jealous. Women who selected emotional infidelity reached their decision faster than women selecting sexual infidelity. Men selecting sexual infidelity reached their decision faster than men selecting emotional infidelity. Therefore, men and women who choose their adaptively primary infidelity type – sexual for men, emotional for women – rely on their initial response tendency suggested by their respective jealousy mechanism.

Description

Evolutionary theory sees differences in male and female sexual behaviour as having arisen due to different selective pressures. Males are not certain of paternity, so their best strategy to pass on their genes is to impregnate as many females as possible, which has little reproductive cost, as males produce lots of sperm. Males therefore seek signs of fertility in women, such as youth, healthiness and child-bearing hips, and indulge in intra-sexual competition with other males to obtain high-quality females. Females are certain of maternity but produce few eggs, so reproductive activity has a greater cost for them. Therefore their best strategy is to indulge in intersexual competition and select

OTHER STUDIES

- Cartwright (2000) found females with symmetrical breasts were more fertile than those with non-symmetrical breasts, supporting the idea of body symmetry as indicating reproductive fitness. This was supported by Penton-Voak et al. (2001) finding females prefer males with greater facial symmetry.

- Pawlowski & Dunbar (1999) found women aged 35–50 years were more likely to not disclose their true age in personal advertisements, which suggests they do so in order to not be judged by males as being less fertile and therefore increase their reproductive opportunities.

- Toma et al. (2008) found that in personal advertisements men were more likely to lie about their education and income, while Kurzban & Weeden (2005) found women were more likely to lie about their weight being less than it really was, supporting the idea of resource richness being attractive in males and physical indicators of fertility being attractive in females.

Fig 9.1 Evolutionary theory predicts differences in types of jealousy between males and females

- ✔ Evolutionary predictions about sexual behaviour are generally supported by research into animals, with behavioural variations understandable by reference to differences in environmental pressures. This suggests that differences in sexual behaviour have evolved.

- ✔ The practice of checking partners' emails and mobile phones can be seen as a modern form of mate-guarding, where checks are made on partners to see whether they are being sexually and emotionally faithful, which would reduce our reproductive fitness.

- ✔ Females finding males who take drugs, drink alcohol and engage in risky activities as attractive may occur due to such males advertising their reproductive fitness by being able to safely consume toxins and survive potentially dangerous situations.

fit males to produce healthy children. A female therefore seeks wealth and resources in males, indicators that they will be able to provide for her and her children. Females also get males to spend time, effort and resources in courtship, to reduce the chances of males deserting and leaving childcare to females. Males indulge in courtship rituals to compete and display genetic potential and have evolved to be bigger to compete with other males. Both males and females benefit from copulation with non-partners, males by increasing chances of reproductive success and females by widening the genetic diversity of their children, increasing survival chances.

- ✖ The evolutionary explanation cannot account for romantic relationships where couples choose not to have children or homosexual relationships that cannot result in pregnancy.

- ✖ Younger males desiring substantially older females goes against evolutionary predictions – though this could be explicable as males wanting to mate with females proven to be fertile.

- ✖ The fact that many women today have resources of their own and therefore do not need resource-rich males goes against the evolutionary explanation.

- ✖ Female choosiness and male competitiveness can be explained by gender role socialisation, as well as through evolution.

Practical application

Learning that jealousy is a natural, evolutionary response to perceived sexual and emotional threats could help partners in relationships threatened by intense feelings of jealousy to come to terms with it and therefore save their relationship.

AQA
A-level

Psychology 2

Jean-Marc Lawton
Eleanor Willard

DYNAMIC   HODDER

pp. 64–72

9 Relationships

Factors affecting attraction in romantic relationships

Focal study

Shaw-Taylor et al. (2011) used profiles and photographs from an online dating site to assess the matching hypothesis in a series of studies. In one of the studies, the attractiveness of 60 males and 60 females was measured and their interactions were monitored. The people with whom they interacted were then monitored to see who they interacted with and returned messages to. What the researchers found was different from the original construct of matching. People contacted others who were significantly more attractive than they were. However, it was found that the person was more likely to reply and to agree to 'communicate' if they were closer to the same level of attractiveness. This suggests the matching hypothesis applies more to later stages of the dating process rather than explaining initial attraction, as first proposed.

OTHER STUDIES

- Kleinke (1979) found that individuals who were perceived as being selective about who they disclosed personal information to were seen as more attractive, as recipients of the information felt specially chosen, illustrating the importance of self-disclosure as a factor affecting attractiveness. This was further supported by Wortman et al. (1976) reporting that when individuals believed they had been specially selected for intimate disclosure, they felt trusted and admired.

- Taylor et al. (2010) reported that 85 per cent of Americans who got married in 2008 married someone of their own ethnic group, supporting the social demographic notion that partner choice is limited to those of a similar background.

- Sadalla et al. (1987) found that women are attracted to males who are reliable, socially dominant, self-confident and extrovert, as such qualities indicate an ability to achieve relatively high positions in society, therefore meeting their need for provision of resources. This supports the idea that complementarity is an important limiting factor in which individuals are perceived as potential partners.

Description

Several factors influence who we are attracted to. *Self-disclosure* involves revealing personal information about oneself to another, which helps relationships become more intimate. *Physical attractiveness* is important because it is an immediate and accessible way to rate someone, with those having greater physical attractiveness seen as possessing more desirable personality characteristics. An important consideration with physical attractiveness is the idea of the *matching hypothesis*, which sees individuals as seeking partners with similar levels of physical attractiveness to themselves, as this reduces the chances of rejection or abandonment for someone more attractive. *Filter theory* sees partner choice as affected by factors limiting the availability of those

Fig 9.2 Self-disclosure of personal information helps to build closer, more intimate relationships

✔ Personality is important in self-disclosure, as individuals who self-disclose above their normal level of disclosure are seen as most attractive because recipients perceive themselves as special to have received such intimacy.

✔ People without physical attractiveness can compensate for it through pairing up with a more physically attractive partner by having other attractive qualities, such as wealth or domestic skills.

✔ Age is another limiting factor in whom is available to us as potential partners. The average age difference between individuals in romantic relationships is 2–3 years, with generally the female partner being younger.

possible to select from. *Social demography* focuses upon how potential partners tend to be limited to those who live nearby, work and socialise, etc. with us and have a similar ethnic, religious, educational and economic background to ourselves. Such people seem more attractive because similarity aids communication and therefore development of a relationship. *Similarity of attitudes* concerns the degree of likeness between individuals' viewpoints, with those possessing similar attitudes being seen as more compatible. *Complementarity* concerns the degree to which individuals meet each other's needs, especially emotional ones, as this helps 'deepen' a relationship.

✘ Much research into self-disclosure does not distinguish between friendship/companionship relationships and romantic relationships, making it difficult to assess the role of self-disclosure solely in romantic relationships.

✘ Evolutionary theory opposes the matching hypothesis because it sees physical attractiveness as more important in females, as advertising their health and fertility, with resource richness being seen as more desirable than physical attractiveness in males.

✘ Filter theory does not really consider that males and females filter out different things due to different needs. Filter theory is also culturally biased, as most research into it applies mainly to individualistic cultures, with relationships in collectivist cultures affected by different limiting factors.

Practical application
In order for relationships to have more chance of success, dating agencies should take into consideration individuals' relative levels of physical attractiveness, as well as demographic variables, similarity of attitudes and complementarity. Individuals should also be encouraged to self-disclose in order to develop deeper levels of intimacy.

AQA
A-level
Psychology
2

pp. 72–78

9 Relationships
Theories of romantic relationships

Focal study

Yum *et al.* (2009) investigated whether equity theory predicts heterosexual relationship maintenance behaviours in six different cultures: the USA, Spain, Japan, South Korea, the Czech Republic and China. As predicted by equity theory, maintenance strategies differed, with individuals in perceived equitable relationships engaging in most maintenance strategies, followed by those in perceived over-benefited and under-benefited relationships. Over the entire sample most people who perceived being equitably treated within their relationship reported greater use of maintenance strategies than those who perceived not being equitably treated. Therefore cultural factors had little effect, suggesting that equity theory can be applied to relationships across cultures.

OTHER STUDIES

- Rusbult (1983) got participants to complete questionnaires over a 7-month period concerning rewards and costs associated with relationships. She found that social exchange theory did not explain the early 'honeymoon' phase of a relationship when balance of exchanges was ignored. However, later on, relationship costs were compared with the degree of personal satisfaction, suggesting that the theory is best applied to the maintenance of rather than the formation of relationships.

- Rusbult *et al.* (1998) gave the Investment Model Scale (IMS) questionnaire to student participants in relationships, to find that commitment in relationships was positively correlated with satisfaction level, negatively correlated with the quality of alternatives and positively correlated with investment size, supporting all 3 factors of Rusbult's investment model of commitment.

- Hatfield *et al.* (1984) reported that when an individual experiences initial dissatisfaction with a relationship they are burdened by resentment and feelings of being 'under benefited', which leads to social withdrawal so that the individual can consider their position, therefore supporting the notion of an intrapsychic phase within Duck's phase model of relationship breakdown.

Description

Social exchange theory sees relationship maintenance based on maximisation of profits and minimisation of costs. Individuals perceive feelings for others in terms of profit (the rewards obtained from relationships minus the costs). Rewards are assessed through the *comparison level*, by assessing rewards against costs for an existing relationship, and the *comparison level for alternative relationships*, by assessing rewards and costs for possible alternative relationships. Relationships continue if rewards exceed costs and the profit level is not exceeded by possible alternative relationships. *Equity theory* sees individuals motivated to achieve fairness in relationships, with maintenance occurring through balance and stability. Inequity, where individuals put in more or less than they receive, leads to motivation

Fig 9.3 Equity theory sees relationship maintenance occurring through balance and stability

Positive evaluation

✔ Social exchange theory applies to those who 'keep score'. Murstein (1977) devised the *exchange orientation tool*, which identified such individuals as suspicious and insecure, suggesting the theory applies to those lacking confidence and mutual trust.

✔ Equity theory especially applies to females, as women often do most of the work to make relationships equitable.

✔ Research indicates that Rusbult's model, with its focus on commitment and what individuals have invested, is a better predictor of long-term maintenance in relationships than social exchange or equity theory.

✔ Duck's phase theory has face validity as it is an account of relationship breakdown that most people can relate to from their own and/or others' experiences.

to make adjustments to return to equity. *Rusbult's investment model* is composed of 3 factors of relationship: *commitment*, *satisfaction level*, concerning the degree to which partners meet each other's needs, and *investment size*, concerning the amount and importance of resources associated with a relationship. *Duck's phase model* sees relationship breakup occurring in four stages: *intrapsychic*, where a partner becomes dissatisfied, *dyadic*, where the dissatisfaction is discussed between partners, *social*, where the dissatisfaction becomes publicly acknowledged, and *grave dressing*, where a post-relationship view of the breakup is established that protects self-esteem and rebuilds towards new relationships.

Negative evaluation

✘ Fromm (1962) argues against social exchange theory, defining true love as characterised by unselfish giving, rather than 'marketing' where individuals expect favours returned.

✘ Mills & Clark (1982) believe equity cannot be assessed in relationships, as most input is unquantifiably emotional and to attempt to do so diminishes the quality of love.

✘ Support for Rusbult's investment model is over-reliant on self-report measures that are prone to socially desirable and idealised answers, as well as researcher bias.

✘ Duck's four phases are not universal – they do not apply to all breakups, nor do they always occur in a set order.

Practical application

Relationship counselling is based on research into theories of romantic relationships. Sex therapy, workshops and mediation between dissatisfied partners are all based on proven psychology. This even stretches to advice on separation and divorce, including counselling for children of such relationships.

pp. 80–90

137

9 Relationships
Virtual relationships in social media

Focal study

McKenna *et al.* (2002) assessed virtual relationships by getting participants to interact either for 20 minutes with a partner in person on 2 'real' occasions or via an internet chat room first before meeting face to face. In the final condition participants interacted with 1 partner in person and another via an internet chat room, but unbeknown to both partners they were actually the same participants (the order in which people met in this final condition was counterbalanced). Each participant was paired with an opposite-sex partner on 10 occasions. It was found that partners liked each other more when they met via the internet than face to face in all situations because communications were seen as more intimate. This supports the idea that in face-to-face interactions superficial gating features, such as degree of physical attractiveness, dominate and overwhelm other factors that lead to more intimate disclosure and greater attraction.

Description

Virtual relationships involve non-physical interactions between people communicating via social media, with the advent of the internet providing increased opportunities for such relationships to develop. Virtual relationships can produce high levels of intimacy, especially between less socially skilled individuals, as they are not confined by the barriers that face-to-face relationships involve. *Self-disclosure* involves the revelation of personal information about oneself to another, with the anonymity of virtual relationships allowing such self-disclosures to occur without fear of embarrassment. Therefore intimacy develops more quickly and deeply than with face-to-face relationships, as the relationship is based more on meaningful factors, such as attitudes and interests,

OTHER STUDIES

- Mishna *et al.* (2009) found that most 16–24 year olds considered virtual relationships to be as real as their physical relationships and that the internet played a crucial role in adolescents' sexual and romantic experiences, illustrating the importance and acceptance of virtual relationships by the younger generation.

- Schouten *et al.* (2007) found that people high in social anxiety revealed greater self-disclosure in virtual relationships due to the lack of non-verbal cues in online communications, supporting the idea that people who have problems socialising in the physical world are able to self-disclose more in virtual relationships.

- Bargh *et al.* (2002) found that intimacy developed more quickly with virtual than with face-to-face relationships because of a lack of gating features that typically prevent intimate disclosures in face-to-face relationships. This supports the idea that a lack of gating helps virtual relationships to grow more quickly and intimately than face-to-face ones.

Fig 9.4 The growth of the internet and other social media has seen a huge increase in virtual relationships

✔ Positive evaluation

- ✔ Self-disclosure in virtual relationships can be more honest and intimate as there is little danger of such disclosures being revealed to one's real-life social circle.
- ✔ Online interactions take four times longer than face-to-face interactions but give individuals time to evaluate what has been communicated to them and to consider a 'perfect' response, making the quality of interactions superior to that of face-to-face communications.
- ✔ The absence of gating features in virtual relationships means there are potentially lots more people to form relationships with online as virtual relationships focus on common interests, attitudes, etc. rather than on more superficial gating features, such as level of physical attractiveness.

than on superficial factors, like levels of physical attractiveness. The fact that virtual relationships are not restricted by the usual gating (limiting) factors found with face-to-face relationships is a great benefit to those who lack physical attractiveness, social skills, etc. as it gives them a chance to build intimacy through self-disclosure, with such relationships often progressing to becoming real-life relationships. There is a danger, though, of individuals misrepresenting themselves in order to exploit others, as well as the issue of partaking in risky behaviour, such as sexting, where sexually explicit images are shared. There is also a danger of individuals substituting face-to-face relationships for virtual ones.

✗ Negative evaluation

- ✗ Research has not considered that limiting gating features differ between different groups of people, for instance age and level of physical attractiveness are more important gating factors for females than for males.
- ✗ A danger of self-disclosure in virtual relationships is that individuals may present their ideal-self to their virtual partner, rather than their real-self, faults and all. This leads to idealisation of a virtual partner, which the person cannot live up to in reality.
- ✗ Social media may create pressure for individuals to conform to acts of intimacy they are reluctant to do, for example being pressured to send sexually explicit pictures via the internet.

Practical application

Virtual relationships could be used as a therapy for the socially inept to learn social skills essential for developing real face-to-face relationships. They could also be used to help those suffering from a fear of social situations to overcome such phobias.

AQA A-level Psychology 2

Jean-Marc Lawton
Eleanor Willard

pp. 91–97

9 Relationships
Parasocial relationships

Focal study

McCutcheon & Houran (2003) assessed whether interest in celebrities divides into pathological and non-pathological cases. 600 participants completed a personality test and were interviewed about their level of interest in celebrities. Participants had to rate statements, such as 'If she/he asked me to do something illegal as a favour, I would probably do it'. One-third of participants showed pathological *celebrity worship syndrome*; 20 per cent were extroverts who followed celebrities for entertainment–social reasons, 10 per cent were neurotic, moody types who had intense attitudes towards celebrities bordering on addiction, while 1 per cent were impulsive, anti-social types, classed as borderline-pathological, who were prepared to hurt themselves or others for their idol. The findings indicate that rather than division into pathological and non-pathological types, there is a sliding scale in which celebrity fans become progressively more fascinated by their idols. Worshipping celebrities does not make people dysfunctional, but it increases the chances of them becoming so.

Description

Parasocial relationships are one-sided relationships that occur with celebrities outside of an individual's real social network, usually without the personalit knowledge. McCutcheon *et al.* (2002) developed the *Celebrity Attitude Scale*, which measures items within 3 levels o parasocial relationships: (1) *entertainme social sub-scale*, which measures social aspects of parasocial relationships, (2) *intense-personal sub-scale*, which measu strength of feeling about celebrities, an (3) *borderline-pathological sub-scale*, wh measures levels of uncontrollable feelir and behaviour towards celebrities.

The *absorption–addiction model* sees a individual's fascination with a celebrity potentially progressing from admiratic for a celebrity's skills in most people to a delusion of a real-life relationship in

OTHER STUDIES

- McCutcheon *et al.* (2002) found a negative correlation of −0.4 between the level of education achieved by participants and the degree to which they idolised celebrities, which suggests that celebrity interest is linked to the amount of schooling received.

- Maltby *et al.* (2004) found those in the entertainment–social category of the celebrity attitude scale were mentally healthy, but those in higher categories often had poor mental health, suggesting that different parasocial levels correlate with different levels of mental stability.

- Kienlen *et al.* (1997) found 63 per cent of stalkers experienced loss of primary caregivers during childhood, usually due to parental separation, while more than 50 per cent reported childhood emotional, physical or sexual abuse by primary caregivers. This supports the idea that disturbed attachment patterns relate to extreme forms of parasocial relationships.

- MacDougal (2005) believes the adoration given to dead celebrities is like that in charismatic religions, suggesting that religious worship and extreme levels of parasocial relationships fulfil similar needs in some individuals.

Fig 9.5 Parasocial relationships are inter by purchasing memorabilia relating to a personality

✔ Research into stalking may help to understand the behaviour, leading to the formation of effective therapies, such as psychotherapy to address underlying causes, with a role also for drug treatments, to reduce obsessive tendencies.

✔ The idea of attachment being related to parasocial relationships is supported by a key component of attachment theory – that of seeking proximity to the attachment figure. Those in parasocial relationships will often seek 'closeness' to their admired media personality.

✔ Younger people may be more attracted to celebrities as they have less involvement in face-to-face relationships and spend more time interacting with media sources than older people do.

individuals dissatisfied with themselves and their own lives. In rare cases involvement in parasocial relationships can become addictive and may involve criminal behaviour such as stalking and physical violence against the celebrity. Alternatively, *attachment theory* sees a tendency for parasocial relationships to be formed by individuals with insecure childhood attachments. Such individuals have a need for close emotional relationships, but without fear of rejection – as celebrities are not aware of such relationships, they will not 'reject' the individual. There is also the possibility that parasocial relationships help young people with identity formation, through observation and imitation of positive role models, which celebrities can help provide.

✘ **Negative evaluation**

✘ Research into parasocial relationships often use questionnaires, which can be negatively affected by idealised and socially desirable answers, with findings therefore lacking validity.

✘ Legal interventions, such as trespassing orders, are effective in dealing with celebrity stalkers, but can make stalkers even more obsessive and persecutory towards their target.

✘ Ross & Spinner (2001) indicated that there is variation in attachment styles across significant relationships. If this also applies to parasocial relationships it would mean that linking a specific attachment pattern to such relationships is not valid.

Practical application

West & Sweeting (2002) recommend media training in schools to highlight the dangers of idolising celebrities, such as developing eating disorders to emulate super-slim body images of some celebrities.

AQA
A-level

Psychology
②

Jean-Marc Lawton
Eleanor Willard

pp. 97–103

10 Gender
Sex and gender

Focal study

Burchardt & Serbin (1982) assessed whether androgyny was associated with positive health in normal and psychiatric populations. 106 female and 84 male undergraduates and 48 female and 48 psychiatric patients were given the BSRI and a personality questionnaire in order to be classified as masculine, feminine or undifferentiated personalities. It was found that androgynous females scored lower for depression and social introversion than feminine females, and in the college sample also scored lower on schizophrenia and mania scales than masculine females. In the male psychiatric patients, this pattern was generally sustained, with androgynous and masculine participants less deviant than feminine males and lower on depression. Within undergraduate males, androgynous males scored lower on social introversion than feminine males. It was concluded that being androgynous is positively correlated with good mental health, especially concerning depression levels, although masculine types scored equally well, which suggests masculinity also aids mental health.

OTHER STUDIES

- Langlois & Downs (1980) compared peers' and mothers' reactions to pre-schoolers playing with opposite-gender toys. When boys played with girls' toys, mothers accepted it, but male peers ridiculed and even hit such boys, demonstrating the intolerance of male peers towards cross-gender behaviour and therefore the strength of their influence on establishing gender roles.

- Eccles et al. (1990) reported that children were encouraged by their parents to play with gender-typical toys, supporting the idea that parents reinforce sex-role stereotypes. This was supported by Lytton & Romney (1991) finding that parents praised sex-role stereotypical behaviour in boys and girls, such as what activities they participated in.

- Flaherty & Dusek (1980) found androgynous individuals have higher degrees of self-esteem, greater emotional wellbeing and more adaptable behaviour, supporting the idea of psychological androgyny indicating psychological wellbeing. Lubinski et al. (1981) also found that androgynous individuals report greater emotional wellbeing.

Description

Sex concerns whether an individual is biologically male or female, while *gender* concerns the social and psychological characteristics of males and females. *Sex-role beliefs* concern the types of qualities and characteristics that are expected of males and females, with these beliefs becoming *sex-role stereotypes* when they are seen as 'rules' to be obeyed by all individuals. Therefore individuals are born biologically male or female, but sex-role stereotypes teach what qualities are masculine and feminine and create norms for individuals to conform to. Sex-role expectations are taught from an early age, with different-sex children being handled differently and taught different games, and this continues at

Fig 10.1 Androgyny involves having both male and female characteristics

school with gender-specific subjects. The ways in which males and females are portrayed in the media are also powerful sources of sex-role stereotyping.

Androgyny involves the idea that male and female characteristics can co-exist in the same person, with Olds (1981) arguing that androgyny is a higher developmental state reached by only a few individuals. Androgyny can be achieved by individuals only when they perceive the world without gender stereotypes. Bem (1975) developed the *androgynous hypothesis*, which saw androgyny as a positive state, and devised the Bem Sex Role Inventory (BSRI), a 60-item self-report to measure androgyny.

✅ Positive evaluation

✔ The fact that sex-role stereotypes can differ substantially cross-culturally suggests that the characteristics associated with sex roles are culturally transmitted, which implies that environmental learning experiences are stronger than biological forces in determining sex-role stereotypes.

✔ The BSRI test has good test–re-test reliability, as it produces consistent results when used on different occasions with the same participants.

✔ It may be that because of masculine bias in Western cultures, where masculine qualities, such as independence and competitiveness, are more valued than feminine ones, like co-operation and nurturing, masculine qualities are seen as superior even within androgynous individuals.

❌ Negative evaluation

✘ Categorising behaviours, occupations, etc. as masculine or feminine may place restrictive barriers on positive roles that males and females can play in society, such as males nurturing children (only 3 per cent of nursery teachers are male) or females being scientists (only one British woman has ever won a Nobel prize for science).

✘ Although the BSRI has good test–re-test reliability, there are doubts about its validity, due to it being created from data from 1970s' American students about what they perceived as desirable characteristics in men and women. The test may therefore lack external validity in terms of being relevant to people today and to people from other cultures.

Practical application

Because evidence suggests sex-role stereotypes are mainly learned from experience, it suggests that negative sex-role stereotyping could be countered by giving positive learning experiences that reinforce positive sex roles as equally applicable to males and females.

pp. 108–115

10 Gender
The role of chromosomes and hormones

Focal study

Stochholm *et al.* (2012) assessed whether males with KS had a greater incidence of criminality by investigating criminal patterns in 1,005 Danish men with standard KS and an XYY version. It was found that men with KS had higher conviction rates for sexual abuse, burglary and arson and lower conviction rates for traffic and drug offences than non-KS controls and these findings were even greater for those with the XYY version of KS. However, when adjustments were made for socioeconomic variables (such as level of education, fatherhood, cohabiting with a partner, etc.), conviction levels were similar to the controls (apart from sexual abuse and arson). This suggests that KS is associated with increased criminality, but through poor socioeconomic conditions endured by sufferers rather than the condition itself.

OTHER STUDIES

- Money & Ehrhardt (1972) reported on girls whose mothers took drugs containing testosterone during pregnancy. The girls showed male-type behaviours, like playing energetic sports, and an absence of female-type behaviours, such as playing with dolls, which suggests that testosterone influences gender behaviour.

- Alonso & Rosenfield (2002) found oestrogen necessary for the normal development of body tissues, such as the neuroendocrine–gonadal axis, associated with puberty in males and females. This supports the idea that oestrogen is associated with the transformation into being sexually active in females and males too.

- White-Traut *et al.* (2009) measured oxytocin levels in saliva produced by females before, during and after breastfeeding. Oxytocin levels were highest just before feeding, decreased at initiation of feeding and rose again 30 minutes after feeding, illustrating oxytocin's role in promoting breastfeeding.

- Price *et al.* (1986) performed a longitudinal study for 17 years of 156 females with TS, finding 9 per cent died compared with 3 per cent in matched non-TS females. Most died of cardiovascular and circulatory conditions, which suggests TS sufferers have a short lifespan due to organ abnormalities.

Description

Biological sex is determined by the sex chromosomes X and Y – XX for females and XY for males – with sex chromosomes containing genetic material that controls development as a male or female, a process assisted by sex hormones, such as testosterone, oestrogen and oxytocin. Testosterone stimulates development of male sexual characteristics and is associated with masculinisation of the brain, for example the development of spatial skills, and male-type behaviours, such as competitiveness. Oestrogen promotes the development of female sexual characteristics and assists in the feminisation of the brain, as well as female-type behaviours, for instance co-operation. Oxytocin is involved

Fig 10.2 The sex chromosomes X and Y determine human biological sex

✔ Testosterone is not exclusively a male hormone or oestrogen and oxytocin exclusively female hormones – research shows all three exert influences on both males and females.

✔ Isotocin is a type of oxytocin found in non-mammals, which causes females to respond to male mating songs. It acts primarily on auditory stimuli in females, so may explain why women are attracted to male 'crooning' singing voices.

✔ As both KS and TS are biological conditions caused by atypical chromosome patterns, research into them is justifiable on the basis that it could bring about effective gene therapies to correct the conditions.

in reproductive behaviours – it controls contractions during childbirth, stimulates milk production during breastfeeding and is involved in pair bonding.

Klinefelter's syndrome (KS) is a male genetic condition involving an extra X chromosome. KS occurs during meiosis, where egg or sperm cells produce an extra copy of the X chromosome. Males produce insufficient levels of testosterone to allow physical male sexual characteristics to fully develop. Psychological effects include poor language skills and a passive temperament. Turner's syndrome (TS) is a female genetic condition, occurring at conception, which involves having an extra Y chromosome. Non-functioning ovaries result in underdevelopment of female sexual characteristics, for example fertility. There are physical effects, such as down-slanting eyes, as well as potential abnormalities of the heart and kidneys.

✘ **Negative evaluation**

✘ It is simplistic to regard single hormones as having exclusive effects on sex and gender. Hormones are part of biological mechanisms exerting multi-faceted and complex actions upon the body and behaviour, for example the interaction of sex chromosomes, the SRY gene and gonadal hormones.

✘ Much research into the role of hormones is conducted on animals, presenting problems in generalising findings to humans.

✘ Both KS and TS are diagnosed prenatally on cytogenetic analysis of a foetus. However, ethically this may be socially sensitive, as such a diagnosis could lead prospective parents to demand an abortion.

Practical application

Oxytocin is given during childbirth to reduce bleeding, decreasing death rates in both mothers and newborn babies. Testosterone is given to men with problems in achieving and sustaining erections, while oestrogen protects post-menopausal women against osteoporosis.

pp. 115–123

145

10 Gender
Cognitive explanations for gender development

Focal study

Slaby & Frey (1975) assessed Kohlberg's theory of gender constancy by giving questions to 55 children aged between 2 and 5.5 years to assess their level of gender constancy and then several weeks later showed them a film of a man and woman performing gender-stereotypical activities. It was found that 97 per cent had achieved gender identity, 75 per cent gender stability and 50 per cent gender consistency. Children with high levels of gender constancy paid more attention to same-sex models than children with low levels of gender constancy, which suggests that high-gender-constancy children watch their own gender to acquire information about gender-appropriate behaviour, supporting Kohlberg's theory that gender development is an active process. The results show that the stages of development are sequential, as Kohlberg stated, and also support Kohlberg's claim that gender constancy is a cause of the imitation of same-sex models, rather than an effect.

Description

Cognitive explanations of gender focus on how children's thinking about gender occurs in qualitatively different stages. Kohlberg's (1966) theory of gender constancy sees children developing an understanding of gender in stages, with gender-role behaviour apparent only after an understanding emerges that gender is fixed and constant. In the gender labelling stage (18 months–3 years), children's recognition of being male or female allows them to categorise and understand their world, though mistakes are made, such as not realising that boys become men. In the gender stability stage (3–5 years), children realise their gender is for life but rely on superficial, physical signs to determine

OTHER STUDIES

- McConaghy (1979) found that if a doll was dressed in transparent clothing so that its genitals were visible, children of 3–5 years judged its gender by its clothes, not its genitals, supporting Kohlberg's belief that children of this age use superficial physical indicators to determine gender.

- Martin & Halverson (1983) asked children to recall pictures of people, finding that children under the age of 6 years recalled more gender-consistent ones – for example, a male footballer – than gender non-consistent ones – for example, a male nurse – in line with gender schema theory predictions.

- Campbell (2000) found that even the youngest infants between 3 and 18 months had a preference for watching same-sex babies and by 9 months boys demonstrated an increasing tendency to pay attention to 'boy toys'. This shows that young children pay more attention to their same-sex group, supporting the idea of gender schemas forming early on.

Fig 10.3 A child with gender constancy understands that a woman with a shaved head is still female

- ✓ Research evidence suggests that the concepts of gender identity, stability and constancy occur in that order across many cultures, lending support to Kohlberg's theory and suggesting a biological mechanism.
- ✓ Kohlberg's theory is an holistic explanation, as it combines social learning and biological developmental factors.
- ✓ Gender schema theory explains why children's attitudes and behaviour concerning gender are rigid and lasting. Children focus only on things that confirm and strengthen their schemas, ignoring behavioural examples that contradict the theory.
- ✓ Gender schema theory explains why children are more likely to model gender-appropriate behaviour rather than imitating a same-sex model demonstrating non-gender appropriate behaviour.

gender. Therefore a girl who cuts her long hair short could be mistaken for having changed her gender. In the gender constancy stage (6–7 years), children recognise gender is permanent over time and across situations.

Gender schema theory sees gender identity alone as providing children with motivation to assume sex-typed behaviour patterns. Gender schema begins to develop at 2–3 years when children organise accumulated knowledge about the sexes into schemas that provide a basis for selecting gender-appropriate behaviours and therefore children's self-perceptions become sex-typed. Children now have expectations about male and female behaviour.

✗ Negative evaluation

- ✗ Kohlberg's theory concentrates on cognitive factors and overlooks cultural and social factors, such as the influence of parents and friends.
- ✗ Kohlberg's theory is descriptive – it outlines the process of gender development but does not explain how these developments occur and so lacks depth of explanation.
- ✗ When children perform activities not normally stereotypical of their gender, like a boy cooking, they adjust their thinking so the activity becomes acceptable. This implies that thinking is affected by behaviour, while gender schema theory predicts the opposite, weakening the theory.
- ✗ Gender schema theory is reductionist, as it neglects the influence of biological factors, assuming that all gender-orientated behaviour is created through cognitive means.

Practical application

A practical application of cognitive explanations is that they permit a universal indication of how gender identity develops, giving guidelines to practitioners, such as teachers and parents, as to what activities and materials will be suitable for boys and girls to interact with at different ages.

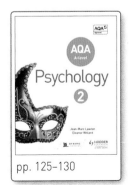

pp. 125–130

10 Gender
Psychodynamic explanation for gender development

Focal study

Freud (1909) developed his theory of gender development by performing a case study of 'Little Hans', a 5-year-old boy with a phobia of horses, especially ones with black bits around their mouths, which Freud interpreted as horses being representative of the boy's father (the black bits being his moustache). Therefore Hans was actually scared of his father, not horses, which was seen to fit the concept of the Oedipus complex, whereby Hans was fearful of his father castrating him because Hans desired his mother. Hans was also seen to have overcome his Oedipus complex by having two fantasies, one where a plumber came and exchanged his bottom and 'widdler' (penis) for larger ones and a second one where he fathered several children. This fitted Freud's theory of gender development, as Hans was seen as having identified with his father and therefore internalised his male gender to gain a sense of male gender identity.

OTHER STUDIES

- Hyman (1921) reported that 22 of 31 female manic-depressive patients were diagnosed as suffering with an unresolved Electra complex, with 12 of the 22 having regressed to an earlier stage of psychosexual development, providing support for Freud's theory.

- Snortum et al. (1969) reported that 46 males exempted from military service for being homosexual had more close-bonding and controlling mothers and rejecting, detached fathers than a comparable sample of heterosexual men. This supports the idea that males who fail to resolve their Oedipus complex by identifying with their fathers become homosexual.

- Wiszewska et al. (2007) got females to rate the attractiveness of pictures of different kinds of men and assessed the quality of their relationships with their fathers. The researchers also compared the similarity of the images females found attractive to those of their fathers, finding that women who were well treated by and had close relationships with their fathers were attracted to men resembling their fathers physically, supporting Freud's idea of the Electra complex.

Description

Freud's psychoanalytic theory is an explanation of gender development that sees gender identity and gender role as acquired during the phallic stage of psychosexual development (3–5 years), where the focus of the libido (sexual energy) is on the genitals. In the earlier oral and anal stages children are seen as bisexual, as different gender identities do not exist for boys and girls. In the phallic stage boys experience the Oedipus complex, where they develop an unconscious sexual desire for their mother and dislike and fear their father, who has access to the mother. Boys overcome the Oedipus complex by identification with the father, acquiring

Fig 10.4 Freud developed the psychoanalyt[ic] theory of gender development

his characteristics, so that the father is incorporated into his own personality, permitting a boy a sense of male gender identity. Girls simultaneously experience the Electra complex, where they develop an unconscio[us] desire for their father and loa[...] has access t[...] complex is c[...] with the m[...] her charac[...] is incorpo[...] allowing[...] identity.[...] and Ele[...] believe[...]

pp. 130–133

10 Gender
Social learning theory as applied to gender development

OTHER STUDIES

- Quiery (1998) found that fathers interact in a more achievement-orientated way and give more attention to sons, while mothers attend equally to sons and daughters. This suggests that fathers reinforce sex typing more than mothers do.

- Lamb & Roopnarine (1979) found peers reward sex-appropriate play in preschool children and ridicule sex-inappropriate play, demonstrating the influence that peers have in reinforcing gender behaviour.

- La Fromboise *et al.* (1990) found gender roles among North American Indian tribes different from those in Western cultures. Women were often 'warriors', illustrating that aggressive roles are not universally male, indicating gender to be more of a social construction.

- Williams & Best (1990) found universal agreement across cultures about which characteristics were masculine and which were feminine, with men perceived as dominant and independent and women as caring and sociable, and children from these cultures exhibiting the same attitudes. This suggests gender roles are universal and biological in nature.

Description

Social learning theory (SLT) sees gender development as occurring through the observation and imitation of influential models, such as parents and peers. Behaviour seen to be reinforced for being gender-appropriate is copied and that which is punished for being gender-inappropriate is not copied. From such observational learning children acquire their gender roles. SLT sees girls and boys learning different gender roles, as parents only reinforce gender-appropriate behaviour. Children, through a gradual process of immersion, take on their parents' gender schemas. Peers act as role models for gender-role stereotypes, with children more likely to imitate same-sex models. Children soon show a preference for same-sex groups, with peers policing

Fig 10.5 Does TV portray females as scientists?

✔ Studies of SLT tend not to be gender biased, as they consider the different effects of peers, parents and the media upon gender development of both boys and girls.

✔ Although parents exert a strong influence when children are young, peers probably have a stronger role in shaping gender development, as children interact more with peers in social situations and police gender behaviours more, for example ridiculing children displaying non-gender-stereotypical behaviour.

✔ As gender stereotypes and gender roles are fairly consistent across human populations, it seems that gender is more biological. However, there is also evidence of gender roles varying considerably across cultures, indicating some influence of social learning.

gender behaviour by reinforcing gender-appropriate behaviour and punishing, through ridicule, gender-inappropriate behaviour. The media is also a powerful socialising agent, with TV, magazines, social media, etc. portraying both sexes in gender-stereotypical ways. There is an argument, though, that the media could also be used as an efficient tool to break down stereotypical gender behaviour by providing examples of, and reinforcing, non-gender stereotyped behaviour. Studying cultural influences on gender roles allows psychologists to assess whether gender is biological or a social construct. If gender is biological, then different cultural influences would have no impact on gender development: it will be the same in all cultures.

✘ Negative evaluation

✘ SLT cannot explain gender changes with age; indeed, SLT assumes there are no developmental stages, while evidence suggests there are.

✘ It is simplistic to regard children as passive recipients of media. Children actively select characters and events to respond to, suggesting more of a cognitive input than a purely social learning effect.

✘ Cross-cultural research is often prone to the problem of an imposed etic, where researchers, in assessing other cultures, use research methods and tools which are applicable only to their own cultures, resulting in flawed conclusions.

Practical application

If media influences have a negative effect on gender stereotyping, they should also be able to create and promote positive non-gender stereotypes, such as successful female scientists, business women and sports stars.

pp. 135–142

10 Gender
Atypical gender development

Focal study

Garcia-Falgueras & Swaab (2008) investigated the possibility of GID being a biological condition caused by abnormal hormonal activity during the masculinisation/feminisation of the brain process. The researchers collected and compared post-mortem data from 17 deceased individuals who when alive had undergone gender reassignment surgery with 25 controls who had not undergone such surgery. It was found that the hypothalamic uncinate nucleus brain area was similar in male-to-female gender-reassigned participants to female controls and was similar in the one female-to-male gender-reassigned participant to male controls. The results support the idea of GID having a biological origin, with structural differences in brain areas, such as the hypothalamic uncinate nucleus brain area, possibly occurring due to abnormal hormonal activity during masculinisation and feminisation of the brain.

Description

Gender identity disorder (GID) is a condition in which the external sexual characteristics of the body are perceived as opposite to the psychological experience of oneself as either male or female. The personal experience of this discomfort is referred to as gender dysphoria. About 1 in every 5,000 people have the condition, with more males affected than females. Prejudice and negative feelings of anxiety and distress are often experienced, leading to depression, self-harm and even suicide. Most gender dysphoria occurs in childhood, but for the majority it does not persist after puberty. However, those for whom it does persist tend to have stronger gender dysphoric symptoms in childhood. Social explanations see

OTHER STUDIES

- Gladue (1985) reported that there were few, if any, hormonal differences between gender-dysphoric, heterosexual and homosexual men. As similar findings are reported for women, it suggests that a social rather than a biological explanation may better explain gender dysphoria.

- Rekers (1995) reported that in 70 gender dysphoric boys there was more evidence of social than biological factors, as there was a common factor of a lack of stereotypical male role models, suggesting that social learning factors play a role in the condition.

- Hare et al. (2009) examined gene samples from male gender dysphorics and non-dysphorics. A correlation was found between gender dysphoria and variants of the androgen receptor gene, implying the gene to be involved in a failure to masculinise the brain during development in the womb, supporting a biological explanation.

Fig 10.6 Gender identity disorder affects individuals unhappy with their biological sex

GID as learned through operant conditioning, where individuals are reinforced (rewarded) for exhibiting cross-gender behaviour, with parents encouraging and complimenting their children for such behaviour. Social learning may also play a part, with the disorder being learned by observation and imitation of individuals modelling cross-gender behaviour. Biological explanations are more supported by evidence, with research suggesting a genetic vulnerability to the condition. The biochemical explanation sees a role for hormonal imbalances during foetal growth in the womb and in later childhood development. The two explanations combine, with hormonal imbalances being genetically influenced.

Practical application

As research suggests that GID is mainly a biological condition, with a large role for abnormal hormonal levels, this has allowed the condition to be addressed with hormonal therapies that enable individuals to undergo successful gender reassignment so that their external biological sex matches their internal feelings about their sex.

pp. 143–146

11 Cognition and development
Piaget's theory of cognitive development

Focal study

Piaget & Inhelder (1956) assessed at what age children are egocentric. Infants aged 4–8 years explored a model of three mountains by walking around it, then sat on one side with a doll on the opposite side. The children were shown ten pictures of different views of the model, including the doll's and their own. They were asked to select the picture representing the doll's view. 4 year olds chose the picture matching their own view. 6 year olds showed some understanding of other viewpoints, but often selected the wrong picture. 7 and 8 year olds consistently chose the picture representing the doll's view. It was concluded that children below 7 years are egocentric, while older children can *decentre*, see things from another's viewpoint.

OTHER STUDIES

- Bower & Wishart (1972) found that 1-month-old babies show surprise when toys disappear, suggesting that Piaget witnessed immature motor skills, not a lack of object permanence.

- Piaget (1952) got 7-year-old children to agree that two identically shaped beakers A and B contained equal amounts of liquid. Having witnessed beaker A being poured into beaker C, a taller, thinner beaker that contained the same amount, the children stated that C contained more, which suggests they could not conserve.

- Inhelder & Piaget (1958) asked participants to consider which of three was the most important in assessing the speed of swing of a pendulum. The solution was to vary 1 variable at a time and children in the formal operations stage were able to do this, but younger children could not, as they tried several variables at once. This suggests that children in the formal operation stage can think logically in an abstract manner in order to see the relationships between things.

Description

Piaget saw knowledge as discovered using: (1) *functional invariants*, structures remaining the same throughout development. There are two of these: (a) the process of *adaption* – involving *assimilation* (fitting new environmental experiences into existing schemas) and *accommodation* (altering existing schemas to fit in new experiences), and (b) the process of *equilibration* – involving swinging between *equilibrium*, a pleasant state of balance, and *disequilibrium*, an unpleasant state of imbalance motivating a return to equilibrium. (2) *Variant structures* – structures that develop as knowledge is discovered. There are two of these: a) *schemas* – ways of understanding the world, and b) *operations* – logical strings of schemas. Therefore, cognitive development involves constantly swinging between equilibrium and disequilibrium, through

Fig 11.1 Jean Piaget was possibly the most influential psychologist of all time and his theory of cognitive development is still held in high regard

11 Cognition and development

Positive evaluation

✔ Cross-cultural evidence implies that the stages of development (except formal operations) occur as a universal, invariant sequence, suggesting cognitive development is a biological process.

✔ Piaget's theory became the starting point for many later theories and research. Schaffer (2004) argues it is the most comprehensive account of how children come to understand the world.

✔ Piaget was not rigid in his beliefs. His theory was constantly adapted in response to criticism. In later life he referred to his stages of development as 'spirals of development' to reflect evidence that there were transitional periods in which children's thinking was a combination of the stage they were leaving and the stage they were progressing on to.

continuous series of assimilation and accommodation.

There are four stages of cognitive development: the *sensorimotor stage* (0–2 years), where *object permanence*, an understanding that objects which are not being perceived or acted upon still exist, develops; the *pre-operational stage* (2–7 years), where children are *egocentric* (cannot see a situation from another's point of view); the *concrete operational stage* (7–11 years), where *conservation*, an understanding that changing the appearance of something does not affect its mass, number or volume, develops, and *class inclusion*, an understanding that some sets of objects or sub-sets can be sets of other larger classes of objects, also develops; and the *formal operational stage* (11+ years), where abstract reasoning develops.

Negative evaluation

✘ Piaget's often poor methodology, such as using research situations that were unfamiliar to children (for example, the Swiss Mountain study), led him to underestimate what children of different ages could achieve.

✘ Piaget neglected the important role of emotional and social factors in intellectual development and in doing so over-emphasised cognitive aspects of development.

✘ Piaget saw language ability as reflecting an individual's level of cognitive development, while theorists like Bruner argued it was the other way round, with language development preceding cognitive development.

Practical application

Piaget's theory has wide applications in primary education, especially in *discovery learning*, where children learn through independent exploration, and the idea of *curriculum*, where certain skills are taught at certain ages to reflect a child's level of cognitive development.

pp. 151–58

11 Cognition and development
Vygotsky's theory of cognitive development

Focal study

Woods & Middleton (1975) assessed the role of the zone of proximal development by observing mothers using various strategies to support 4 year olds in building a model that was too difficult for the children to do themselves. Mothers who were most effective in offering assistance were ones who varied their strategy according to how well a child was doing, so that when a child was progressing well they gave less specific help, but when a child struggled they gave more specific guidance until the child made progress again. This highlights the concept of the ZPD and shows that scaffolding is most effective when matched to the needs of a learner, so that they are assisted to achieve success in a task that previously they could not have completed alone.

OTHER STUDIES

- Wertsch et al. (1980) found that the amount of time children under 5 years of age spent looking at their mothers when assembling jigsaws decreased with age, illustrating the progression through scaffolding to self-regulation.

- McNaughton & Leyland (1990) observed mothers giving increasingly explicit help to children assembling progressively harder jigsaws, which illustrates how scaffolding and sensitivity to a child's ZPD aids learning.

- Freund (1990) asked children aged 3 and 5 years to help a puppet decide what furniture should be put in different rooms of a doll's house. Half the children worked alone, while half worked with their mothers providing guidance. The results showed that children given guidance performed best, which suggests that Vygotsky's idea of scaffolding, where children work with guidance, is superior to Piaget's idea of discovery learning, where children learn through independent exploration.

- Berk (1994) found that children talked to themselves more when doing difficult tasks, supporting the idea of egocentric speech. This decreased with age in line with Vygotsky's idea of progression to inner speech.

Description

Vygotsky saw cognitive development as affected by the learning of norms and attitudes of the culture a child is raised in. At the *cultural level* children benefit from the knowledge of previous generations, gained through interactions with caregivers, while at the *interpersonal level* cognitive development occurs first on a social level, through interaction between people, (*interpsychological*) and second on an individual level within a child (*intrapsychological*).

A key part of Vygotsky's theory is the *zone of proximal development* (ZPD), the distance between current and potential ability. Cultural influences and knowledgeable others acting as mentors push children through the

Fig 11.2 Scaffolding involves children being assisted by mentors who give clues as to how to solve a problem rather than giving actual solutions

ZPD and on to tasks beyond their current ability. Another key concept is *scaffolding*, where cognitive development is assisted by sensitive guidance, with children given clues as to how to solve a problem, rather than being given the actual solution. Vygotsky saw *semiotics* as assisting cognitive development through the use of language and other cultural symbols, acting as a medium for knowledge to be transmitted, which turn elementary mental functions into higher ones. Such development occurs in several phases: *social speech* (birth to 3 years) – involving pre-intellectual language, *egocentric speech* (3–7 years) – involving self-talk/thinking aloud, and *inner speech* (7+ years) – where self-talk becomes silent and internal and language is used for social communications.

✗ Negative evaluation

✗ Although there is relatively less research evidence to support Vygotsky's theory, the fact that it focuses more upon the processes involved in, rather than the outcomes of, cognitive development makes it harder to test.

✗ Vygotsky's theory was developed within a collectivist culture and is more suited to such cultures, with their stronger element of social learning, than individualistic Western cultures. The theory can also be accused of over-emphasising the role of social factors at the expense of biological and individual ones. Learning would be faster if development depended on social factors only.

Practical application

Similarly to Piaget's theory, Vygotsky's theory has applications in education, especially his concepts of scaffolding and peer tutoring, where a child is perceived as an apprentice learner who is assisted in their learning rather than being taught directly.

pp. 159–64

11 Cognition and development
Baillargeon's explanation of early infant abilities

Focal study

Baillargeon *et al.* (1985) familiarised 5-month-old infants with a drawbridge that was moved through 180 degrees. A coloured box was then placed in the path of the drawbridge. The infants then either witnessed a 'possible event' where the drawbridge stopped at the point where its movement would be stopped by the box, or an 'impossible event' where the drawbridge appeared to pass through the box and ended up lying flat, with the box apparently having disappeared. It was found that the infants spent longer looking at the impossible event, which suggests the infants were surprised that their expectations (about the properties of physical objects) were violated and that they knew a solid object cannot pass through another solid object. This supports the idea that children develop an understanding of the properties of objects at a much younger age than Piaget thought.

OTHER STUDIES

- Baillargeon (1987) found that 3-month-old infants looked for longer at an impossible event – where a block was placed where it would stop a truck's movement but didn't – than they did at a possible event – where the block was placed to the side of the truck where it would not stop its movement. This suggests children develop an understanding of the properties of objects much earlier than Piaget believed.

- Baillargeon & DeVos (1991) found 3.5-month-old infants spent longer looking at an impossible scenario of a tall carrot that did not appear in a window as it moved along a track than at a possible scenario of a shorter carrot. This suggests children develop object permanence earlier than Piaget stated.

- Cashon & Cohen (2000) used Baillargeon-type scenarios with 8-month-old children to find that the children looked for longer at more 'interesting' scenarios (ones that had more novelty) than 'impossible' scenarios, suggesting humans do not have an innate understanding of object representation.

Description

Renee Baillargeon devised the *violation of expectation technique*, which tests whether infants develop object permanence earlier than Piaget believed. The technique is based on the idea that infants look for longer at things not expected. A child is repeatedly shown a scenario new to them until they demonstrate, by looking away, that the technique is no longer novel to them. Then the child is shown an impossible example of the scenario, such as an object appearing to pass through a solid object without being damaged. The time spent looking at this is compared to the time spent looking at a possible example of the scenario. Using this technique, Baillargeon consistently

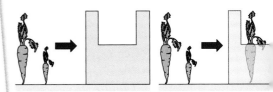

Fig 11.3 Children expect to see the top of the tall carrot in the window – when they don't it violates the expectation and they stare at that scenario longer

✔ Baillargeon's 'violation of expectation' technique has become a paradigm method, the accepted method of assessing children's understanding of the physical properties of objects, which is a testimony to the high regard in which the procedure is held.

✔ Investigating the cognitive developmental abilities of infants is problematic, as infants cannot communicate verbally what abilities they have. Therefore Baillargeon's paradigm technique is useful as it allows insight into what skills infants possess.

✔ Research based on Baillargeon's methodology has produced consistent results, which allowed the CKT to be widely accepted as a valid explanation.

found results that suggested children much younger than Piaget thought demonstrate object permanence and have intuitive knowledge concerning the properties of objects and their relationships to each other. Baillargeon's research has permitted investigation of the *Core Knowledge Theory* (CKT), the belief that humans have an innate understanding of inanimate objects and their relationships with each other. Baillargeon's findings have suggested this is true, but more recent research, such as that by Cara Cashon (2000), has cast doubt on this by suggesting that infants look longer at scenarios that are more 'interesting' rather than impossible.

✗ **Negative evaluation**

✗ Schoner & Thelen (2004) argue that all that violation of expectation studies demonstrate is that infants notice a *difference* between the 'possible' and 'impossible' scenarios they have been shown, which does not necessarily mean they are *surprised* by what they have witnessed. For instance, in the drawbridge study infants may be attracted to the fact that the 'impossible' scenario has more movement in it than the 'possible' scenario. Therefore what Baillargeon sees as evidence of infants having innate knowledge of object representation may actually be just the effects of confounding variables. This viewpoint is supported by research such as Cashon & Cohen (2000).

Practical application

The main practical application of Baillargeon's research has been in providing a useful method of investigating very young children's cognitive developmental abilities, something that was not possible before Baillargeon developed the technique.

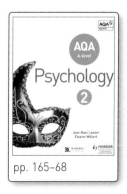

pp. 165–68

11 Cognition and development
The development of social cognition

Focal study

Baron-Cohen *et al.* (1985) assessed whether a lack of ToM could explain autism. 20 autistic children with an average age of 12 years, 14 Down's syndrome children with an average age of 11 years and 27 normally developed children with an average age of 4.5 years witnessed a doll, Sally, place a marble in her basket. While she was away, Anne, another doll, hid the marble in her box. When Sally returned the children were asked: where is the marble? (reality question), where was the marble originally? (memory question) and where will Sally look for it? (belief question). All children passed the reality and memory questions. 85 per cent of normally developed children and 86 per cent of Down's syndrome children passed the belief question, but only 20 per cent of autistic children. This suggests that a lack of a ToM is a plausible explanation for autism, as autistic children cannot attribute beliefs to others.

Description

Social cognition concerns the mental processes by which information about oneself and others is processed and understood. Selman (1980) devised *role-taking theory* as an explanation of *perspective taking*, the ability to comprehend from another's viewpoint. The theory was devised from children's answers to *moral dilemmas* and has five levels: *egocentric viewpoint* (3–6 years), *social informational role taking* (6–8 years), *self-reflective role taking* (8–10 years), *mutual role taking* (10–12 years) and *social and conventional system role taking* (12–15+ years). The theory sees children move from not realising others have different experiences and feelings to understanding the processes involved in

OTHER STUDIES

- Selman (1971) found children aged 4–6 years made a prediction concerning a child's behaviour in a situation they had information about but the child had not, based on the information they were given. This suggests they were in the egocentric viewpoint, in line with Selman's theory, as they could not see the situation from the child's perspective.

- Gurucharri & Selman (1982) performed a 5-year longitudinal study, using Selman's methodology of interpersonal dilemmas, to assess the development of perspective-taking abilities in 41 children. 40 of the children developed perspective taking, as predicted by Selman's stages, supporting his theory.

- Shatz *et al.* (1983) reported that children under 4 years old can differentiate between different mental states. At 2 years of age they can name emotional states, and by 3 years of age they can demonstrate knowledge of what thinking is, suggesting that acquisition of a ToM is a developmental process.

Fig 11.4 Selman conducted research based on interpersonal dilemmas, such as that of Holly, who breaks her promise not to climb trees in order to save a cat

others developing different viewpoints, by adopting the outlook of others to experience their feelings and thoughts.

Theory of Mind (ToM) concerns the ability to attribute mental states to oneself and others, with some seeing *autism*, a developmental disability characterised by problems in communicating and relationship building, as linked to a lack of a ToM. This was researched through the *Sally-Anne test*, a method of assessing an individual's social cognitive ability to attribute false beliefs to others. ToM is not present at birth but develops over time and is similar to Piaget's idea of how children move from seeing the world only from their own perspective to being able to perceive other viewpoints.

AQA

AQA
A-level
Psychology
②

Jean-Marc Lawton
Eleanor Willard

DYNAMIC   HODDER EDUCATION

pp. 169–78

11 Cognition and development
The role of the mirror neuron system in social cognition

Focal study

Dapretto *et al.* (2006) assessed mirror neuron ability in autistic and normally developed children. 80 facial expressions representing 5 emotions of anger, fear, happiness, neutrality and sadness were randomly presented for 2 seconds each to 10 high-functioning autistic children and 10 normally functioning children aged 10–14 years. fMRI scans were performed as participants either observed or imitated the faces presented. Symptom severity of autism was measured through the Autism Diagnostic Interview-Revised Scale A. Both groups were able to observe and imitate the facial expressions. However, the autistic children showed no mirror neuron activity in the frontal gyrus brain area and a correlation was found between degree of autism and mirror neuron activity in other brain areas associated with mirror neuron activity. This suggests differences exist in the neural pathways used by typically developing and autistic children and that there is a biological basis to social cognition and the development of autism.

Description

Mirror neurons are nerves in the brain that are active when specific actions are performed or observed in others, allowing observers to experience the action as if it was their own. Mirror neurons may therefore allow individuals to share in the feelings and thoughts of others by empathising with and imitating others, therefore permitting them to have a ToM. The action of mirror neurons is such that when individuals experience an emotion, for instance disgust, or observe an expression of disgust on another's face, the same mirror neurons are activated. This permits the observer and the person being observed to

OTHER STUDIES

- Stuss *et al.* (2001) reported that individuals with damage to their frontal lobes often had an inability to empathise with and read other people's intentions and were easy to deceive, which suggests damage to the mirror neuron system and emphasises its importance to normal human social cognition.

- Gallese (2001) used fMRI scanning to find that the anterior cingulate cortex and inferior frontal cortex are active when individuals experience emotion or observe another person experiencing the same emotion, supporting the idea of mirror neuron-type activity occurring in humans.

- Iacoboni *et al.* (2005) recorded the activity of single neurons in the inferior parietal lobule, to find that different neurons fired off when a monkey grasped an object to eat it as opposed to grasping an object to place it, even though both required similar hand movements. This suggests mirror neurons allow intentions of others' behaviour to also be understood.

Fig 11.5 Do mirror neurons allow humans to directly experience other people's feelings and thoughts?

✔ Studies using fMRI scans have found evidence of mirror neuron systems in humans in the same brain areas as macaques (though there seems to be a wider network of brain areas in humans, especially the *somatosensory cortex*), which suggests the findings of animal studies into mirror neurons are relevant to humans.

✔ Research into mirror neurons has indicated a possible biological explanation for autism and greater understanding may pave the way for developing methods of counteracting the social deficits associated with the disorder.

have direct experiential understanding of each other. The mirror neurons for disgust 'fire up' in both individuals, creating a sensation within the mind of the feeling associated with disgust, allowing immediate empathy with what the other person is experiencing. Research has suggested that mirror neurons also permit the understanding of others' intentions as well as their behaviour. Mirror neurons are found in brain areas involved with social cognition and therefore may be the biological mechanism by which the comprehension of our own and the mental states of others occurs. Defective mirror neuron systems may explain conditions such as autism.

✖ **Negative evaluation**

✖ Heyes (2012) argues that even if mirror neurons do exist, it is not established yet whether they actually have evolved purely to permit the understanding of actions through the process of natural selection, or whether they are merely a biological by-product of social interaction between individuals.

✖ Kosonogov (2012) argues that if individuals can understand the motivation behind other people's actions by mirror neurons firing off when observing a goal-directed action or a pantomime of a goal-directed action (such as someone acting in a film), how is it possible to know when an action is real and not a pantomime of an action (for example, telling the difference between someone really crying and someone pretending to cry)?

Practical application
Research into mirror neurons may not just allow us a greater understanding of autism and how it develops but may also lead to effective treatments and therapies to counteract the disorder, especially in terms of how sufferers struggle to empathise with and understand the mental state of others.

pp. 178–81

12 Schizophrenia
Classification of schizophrenia

Focal study

Rosenhan (1973) assessed the validity of schizophrenia diagnosis using DSM-II. 8 sane volunteers presented themselves at mental hospitals claiming to hear voices. All were admitted and thereafter acted normally. Reactions to them and time taken to be released were recorded. It took between 7 and 52 days for them to be released, diagnosed as 'schizophrenics in remission'. Normal behaviours were perceived as signs of schizophrenia by clinicians, though 35 out of 118 real patients suspected they were imposters. Rosenhan concluded that diagnosis lacked validity, but clinicians protested that people do not usually fake insanity to get admission into hospital. Therefore Rosenhan informed hospitals that an unspecified number of imposters would try to gain admission during a 3-month period. Of 193 patients admitted during this time, 83 aroused suspicions as being imposters. No imposters were sent. This backed up Rosenhan's claim that diagnosis of schizophrenia lacks validity.

OTHER STUDIES

- Beck (1962) reported only a 54 per cent concordance rate between practitioners' diagnoses, while 43 years later Soderberg (2005) reported a concordance rate of 81 per cent, which suggests reliability of diagnosis has improved over time as diagnostic criteria have been updated.

- Sim et al. (2006) reported that 32 per cent of hospitalised schizophrenics had an additional mental disorder, illustrating the problem that co-morbidity presents in achieving reliable and accurate diagnoses.

- McGovern & Cope (1977) reported that two-thirds of patients detained in Birmingham hospitals were first- and second-generation Afro-Caribbeans, suggesting a cultural bias to over-diagnose schizophrenia in the black population.

- Lewin et al. (1984) found that if clearer diagnostic criteria were applied, the number of female schizophrenia sufferers became much lower, suggesting a gender bias in the original diagnosis.

- Ophoff et al. (2011) found that of 7 gene locations on the genome associated with schizophrenia, 3 of them were additionally associated with bipolar disorder, suggesting a genetic overlap between the 2 disorders.

Description

Schizophrenia affects thought processes and the ability to determine reality. *Type I* is characterised by *positive symptoms*, with better prognosis for recovery. *Type II* is characterised by *negative symptoms*, with poorer prognosis for recovery. Positive symptoms involve displaying behaviours concerning loss of touch with reality, such as *hallucinations*, where sufferers hear voices in their head, and *delusions*, false beliefs resistant to confrontation with reality. Negative symptoms involve displaying behaviours concerning disruption of normal emotions and actions, such as *speech poverty*, characterised by brief replies to questions with minimal elaboration, and *avolition*, a general lack of energy resulting in loss of goal-directed behaviour. Schizophrenia is diagnosed by

Fig 12.1 David Rosenhan's classic study brings the validity of schizophrenia diagnosis into question

✔ Positive evaluation

✔ Evidence generally suggests that reliability of diagnoses has improved as classification systems have been updated.

✔ The high level of certain co-morbid disorders found in schizophrenics suggests that such co-morbidities might actually be sub-types of the disorder.

✔ Females tend to develop schizophrenia on average 4–10 years later than males, and females can develop a later form of post-menopausal schizophrenia, which suggests there are different types of schizophrenia to which males and females are vulnerable.

reference to classification systems, for example the DSM-V. Diagnosis should be reliable and valid. *Reliability* refers to the consistency of diagnosis, over time (test–re-test reliability) and by different clinicians (inter-rater reliability). *Validity* refers to the accuracy of diagnosis, like predictive validity, where diagnosis leads to successful treatment. *Co-morbidity* concerns the presence of additional disorders simultaneously occurring with schizophrenia, while *culture bias* refers to the tendency to over-diagnose members of other cultures as suffering from schizophrenia. *Gender bias* concerns the tendency for diagnostic criteria to be applied differently to males and females, while *symptom overlap* involves the perception that symptoms of schizophrenia are also symptoms of other mental disorders.

✘ Negative evaluation

✘ Being labelled schizophrenic has a long-lasting, negative effect on social relationships, work prospects, self-esteem, etc., which is unfair when diagnoses of schizophrenia have generally low levels of validity.

✘ Schizophrenics with co-morbid conditions are often excluded from research and yet form the majority of sufferers. This suggests that research findings cannot be generalised to the majority of schizophrenic patients.

✘ Research suggests there is a case for different diagnostic considerations when diagnosing males and females. However, this would cast doubts on the validity of schizophrenia as a separate disorder.

✘ Misdiagnosis due to symptom overlap can lead to delays in receiving proper treatment or to even receiving inappropriate treatment. This could lead to further suffering, degeneration of condition and even suicide.

Practical application

The fact that there is genetic overlap between mental disorders suggests that gene therapies might be developed to simultaneously treat different disorders.

pp. 186–97

12 Schizophrenia
Biological explanations for schizophrenia

Focal study

Avramopoulos *et al.* (2013) assessed the contribution of genetics to the development of schizophrenia. They sequenced genes associated with the neuregulin signalling pathway, which relays signals within the nervous system. The researchers found that some families with high levels of schizophrenia had multiple neuregulin signalling-related gene variants while others had none. Schizophrenics with neuregulin signalling gene variants experienced more hallucinations but had less impairment than the other schizophrenia patients. The findings therefore suggest that individually harmless genetic variations, which affect related biochemical processes, may unite to increase vulnerability to schizophrenia, but additionally provide support for the idea that schizophrenia is not a single disorder at all but is actually a group of related disorders. Patients without neuregulin signalling-related variants have variants in a different pathway and therefore different symptoms.

OTHER STUDIES

- Gottesman & Shields (1976) reviewed 5 twin studies and reported a concordance rate of between 75 per cent and 91 per cent for MZ (identical) twins with severe forms of schizophrenia, suggesting that genetics plays a larger role with chronic forms of the disorder. Torrey *et al.* (1994), reviewing evidence from twin studies, found that if 1 MZ twin develops schizophrenia, there is a 28 per cent chance that the other twin will too, again supporting the idea that schizophrenia is inherited.

- Kessler et al. (2003) used PET and MRI scans to compare people with schizophrenia with non-sufferers, finding that the schizophrenics had elevated dopamine receptor levels in the basal forebrain and substantia nigra/ventral tegemental brain areas. Differences in cortical dopamine levels were also found, suggesting that dopamine is important in the onset of schizophrenia.

- Tilo (2001) used fMRI scans to find that severity of thought disorder, a core symptom of schizophrenia, was negatively correlated with activity in the Wernicke brain area, associated with producing coherent speech. This suggests specific brain areas are linked to schizophrenia.

Description

Biological explanations see schizophrenia as physiologically determined. The *genetic explanation* sees the disorder as transmitted through hereditary means. It is not thought that there is a single 'schizophrenia gene' but instead that several genes are involved – the more of these genes an individual has, the more vulnerable they are to developing schizophrenia, though an environmental trigger would also be needed for the onset of the condition. The *dopamine hypothesis* sees the development of schizophrenia as being related to abnormal levels of the hormone and neurotransmitter dopamine. High levels of dopamine in the mesolimbic dopamine system are associated with positive symptoms,

Fig 12.2 Several genes are suspected of being involved in the development of schizophrenia

✔ Positive evaluation

✔ Adoption studies show that adopted children with a high genetic risk of developing schizophrenia (as there was a high incidence of the disorder among biological relatives) are more sensitive to non-healthy rearing practices by adopted families, illustrating how genetic and environmental factors interact in the development of schizophrenia.

✔ Several neurotransmitters, not just dopamine, may be involved in the development of schizophrenia. More newly developed anti-schizophrenia drugs suggest that glutamate and serotonin also have an influence.

✔ Some patients may not respond to treatment as structural brain damage does not permit anti-psychotic drugs to have an effect in reducing symptom levels.

while high levels in the mesocortical dopamine system are associated with negative symptoms. It is probable that genetic factors are linked to faulty dopaminergic systems in sufferers of the condition. The idea of *neural correlates* is that abnormalities within specific brain areas may be associated with the development of schizophrenia. Scanning has found enlarged ventricles in central brain areas and the prefrontal cortex, especially in those suffering negative symptoms. Abnormalities have also been found in the Wernicke brain area, which with its role in language abilities may explain the difficulties many schizophrenics have in producing coherent speech.

✗ Negative evaluation

✗ Although twin studies suggest a genetic component to the development of schizophrenia, they do not consider the influence of social class and socio-psychological factors between twins, nor do they consider shared environmental influences, which lowers the validity of the evidence for the genetic explanation.

✗ Differences in the biochemistry of schizophrenics, such as with dopamine levels, may be an effect of being schizophrenic rather than a cause.

✗ Some non-schizophrenics have enlarged ventricles in brain tissue, but not all schizophrenics do, which refutes the idea of schizophrenia being linked to loss of brain tissue. It may be that loss of brain tissue is a result of schizophrenia rather than a cause.

Practical application

The main practical application of biological explanations is in drug therapies. Anti-schizophrenic drugs, such as phenothiazines, work by decreasing dopamine activity, with the effectiveness of such drugs giving support to the dopamine hypothesis.

AQA
A-level
Psychology
②

Jean-Marc Lawton
Eleanor Willard

pp. 198–204

12 Schizophrenia
Psychological explanations for schizophrenia

Focal study

Patino *et al.* (2005) assessed the effectiveness of the family dysfunction explanation for the development of schizophrenia in migrant families. The researchers used self-reports to identify common factors in family interactions that were associated with the development of schizophrenia. They found that migrants who had experienced at least 3 out of the following 7 problems associated with family dysfunction – (1) poor relationship between adults in the household; (2) lack of warmth between parents and child; (3) visible disturbance of the mother–child (4) father–child, or (5) sibling–child relationship; (6) parental overprotection; and (7) child abuse – had four times the normal level of vulnerability to developing schizophrenia, compared to the double level of risk for migrants not experiencing family dysfunction. This suggests that family dysfunction increases the likelihood of life stressors triggering the onset of schizophrenia, especially in migrant families.

OTHER STUDIES

- Tienari *et al.* (2004) found that the level of schizophrenia in adopted individuals who were the biological children of schizophrenic mothers was 5.8 per cent in those adopted by healthy families compared with 36.8 per cent for children raised in dysfunctional families, which supports the family dysfunction theory and supports the idea that individuals with high genetic vulnerability to schizophrenia are more affected by environmental stressors.

- O'Carroll (2000) found that cognitive impairment is found in 75 per cent of schizophrenics, particularly in memory, attention, motor skills, executive function and intelligence, supporting the cognitive explanation. Cognitive impairments often pre-dated illness onset, did not occur as a result of substance abuse and were related to social and functional impairments.

- Brune *et al.* (2011) reviewed 20 years of evidence to report that many symptoms of schizophrenia and the resulting impairments in social functioning result from poor metacognition, especially the ability to self-reflect and empathise with others, which suggests that metacognition dysfunction is an important part of schizophrenia, therefore supporting the idea of dysfunctional thought processing.

Description

Psychological theories focus on non-physiological explanations for schizophrenia. The *family dysfunction* explanation sees maladaptive relationships and patterns of communication within families as sources of stress, which can cause or influence the development of schizophrenia. Parents of schizophrenics often display three types of dysfunctional characteristics: (1) high levels of interpersonal conflict, (2) communication difficulties and (3) being excessively critical and controlling of their children. Another feature of family dysfunction is *expressed emotion*, where families which persistently exhibit criticism and hostility exert a negative influence, especially upon recovering schizophrenics, who may then relapse. *Cognitive explanations* see schizophrenia as developing due to

Fig 12.3 Dysfunctional families are associated with high levels of schizophre[nia] (photo posed by models)

Positive evaluation

- The family dysfunction explanation is supported by the fact that therapies which successfully focus on reducing expressed emotions within families have low relapse rates compared with other therapies.
- Although there is a lack of general support for family dysfunction as a causal factor of schizophrenia, research evidence into expressed emotion does suggest that family dysfunction plays a major role in maintenance of the disorder.
- A strength of the cognitive explanation is that it can account for both positive and negative symptoms. It can also be combined with the biological explanation to give a fuller understanding of the causes of schizophrenia.

irrational thought processes. Abnormalities within brain functioning are seen as increasing vulnerability to stressful life experiences, which in turn may lead to dysfunctional beliefs and behaviour. Cognitive deficits then occur, with sufferers experiencing problems of attention, communication and information overload. *Dysfunctional thought processing* concerns the idea that the development of schizophrenia is related to abnormal ways of thinking. Metacognition (the monitoring of one's own thoughts) allows individuals to 'view' their mental states and the intentions of others. Schizophrenics though experience metacognitive dysfunction, which affects executive functioning, the higher level cognitive processes that control and manage cognitive and behavioural processes.

Negative evaluation

- Although dysfunctional thought processing seems linked to impairments in memory ability, research indicates that deficits occur only in specific areas of memory functioning, especially the central executive component of working memory and specifically tasks for which the visuospatial system is needed for central executive control.
- Having a schizophrenic within a family can be problematic and stressful on family relationships, therefore rather than dysfunctions within families causing schizophrenia, it could alternatively be that having a schizophrenic within a family leads to dysfunctions.
- A problem with the family dysfunction explanation is that it cannot explain why all children in such families do not develop schizophrenia.

Practical application

The family dysfunction explanation has led to the development of family therapy, the treatment of schizophrenia by alteration of communication systems within families. The treatment has proven to be effective.

pp. 204–9

12 Schizophrenia
Therapies for the treatment of schizophrenia

Focal study

Bagnall *et al.* (2003) compared the clinical effectiveness, safety and cost effectiveness of typical and atypical drugs in the treatment of schizophrenia, as well as assessing their effectiveness against treatment-resistant schizophrenia and first-onset schizophrenia. Data were compiled from 171 randomly controlled and 52 non-randomly controlled trials of the effectiveness of drug treatments. Additional data were compiled from 31 economic evaluations of antipsychotic drug treatments for schizophrenia. The data were analysed by two independent researchers to establish inter-rater reliability. It was found that atypical drugs were generally more effective than typical drugs in symptom reduction. Clozapine and zotepine were more effective treatments of treatment-resistant schizophrenia. No differences were found between typical and atypical antipsychotics in treating first-onset schizophrenia. Both treatments had differing forms of side-effects. Atypical drugs were more expensive. It was concluded that atypical drugs are generally more effective, no single drug is superior and different drugs suit different patients.

OTHER STUDIES

- Tarrier (2005) reviewed 20 controlled trials of CBT using 739 patients, finding persistent evidence of reduced symptoms, especially positive ones, lower relapse rates and a speedier recovery rate of acutely ill patients. However, these were short-term benefits, with follow-ups needed to assess CBT's long-term benefits.

- McFarlane *et al.* (2003) reviewed available evidence to find that family therapy results in reduced relapse rates, symptom reduction in patients and improved relationships among family members that leads to increased wellbeing for patients. This suggests that family therapy is an effective treatment, with an indication that better family relationships are the key element.

- Dickerson *et al.* (2005) reviewed 13 studies of token economy, finding it useful in increasing the adaptive behaviour of patients, which implies that it is an effective treatment. Token economy worked best in combination with psychosocial and drug therapies, though the specific benefits of the technique when used as a combination treatment were not identified, suggesting an area for future research.

Description

Drug therapies involve the chemical treatment of schizophrenia through tablets and intravenous means. Anti-psychotic drugs come in two types: (1) *typical*, such as chlorpromazine, which arrests dopamine production through blocking receptors in synapses that absorb dopamine, to reduce positive symptoms like hallucinations and delusions, and (2) *atypical*, such as clozapine, which acts on serotonin as well as dopamine production systems, affecting negative symptoms, like reduced emotional expression. *Cognitive behavioural therapy* (CBT) treats schizophrenia by modifying thought patterns to alter behavioural and emotional states. CBT aims to change the maladaptive thinking and distorted perceptions that are seen as underpinning the condition in order to modify hallucinations and

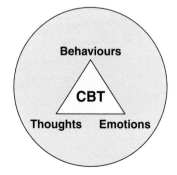

Fig 12.4 Cognitive behavioural therapy is a common psychological treatment of schizophrenia, but how effective is it?

- Antipsychotics are effective, as they are relatively cheap to produce, easy to administer and have positive effects on many sufferers, allowing them to live relatively normal lives outside of mental institutions. Less than 3 per cent of people with schizophrenia in the UK live permanently in hospital.
- Token economies generally lead to a safer and more therapeutic environment, with staff injuries reduced, therefore leading to lower staff absenteeism rates.
- The Schizophrenia Commission (2012) estimates family therapy is cheaper than standard treatments for schizophrenia by £1,004 a patient over 3 years, which suggests it is more cost effective.

delusional beliefs. Antipsychotic drugs are usually given first to reduce psychotic thought processes, so that CBT will be more effective. *Family therapy* treats schizophrenia by altering communication systems within families. It aims to (i) improve positive and decrease negative communication, (ii) increase tolerance levels and decrease criticism levels between family members, and (iii) decrease feelings of guilt among family members for causing the disorder. *Token economies* are a method of behaviour modification that reinforces target behaviours by awarding tokens that can be exchanged for material goods. It is targeted especially at low motivation, poor attention and social withdrawal among schizophrenic patients.

✖ Negative evaluation

- ✖ Evidence that atypical drugs are more effective than typical ones is generally of poor quality, based on short-term trials and difficult to generalise to all schizophrenic patients.
- ✖ CBT is not suitable for all patients, especially those too disorientated, agitated or paranoid to form trusting alliances with clinicians.
- ✖ Although family therapy is proven to be effective and is therefore desirable, due to cost restraints it is often not possible to offer it to all patients.
- ✖ Token economies are frowned on by some clinicians, as they see them as humiliating and that their benefits do not generalise to real-life settings when tokens are withdrawn.

Practical application

Research into treatments of schizophrenia allows psychologists to not only assess the effectiveness of individual therapies in relieving symptoms, but also assess their comparative cost effectiveness, potential side-effects, as well as determining which treatments best suit which types of patient.

AQA
AQA A-level
Psychology
2

Jean-Marc Lawton
Eleanor Willard

pp. 211–21

12 Schizophrenia

The importance of the interactionist approach in explaining and treating schizophrenia

Focal study

Murray (1996) assessed the interactionist approach by reviewing evidence concerning the degree to which pregnant mothers contracting flu impacted on individuals' vulnerability to developing the disorder in later life. Data were collected by assessing how many schizophrenics' mothers had contracted flu while pregnant and at which point in the pregnancy they had contracted flu. It was found that children who were born after flu epidemics where their mothers had contracted the disease while pregnant, especially in the second trimester (pregnancy months 4–6), had an 88 per cent increased chance of developing schizophrenia than children born in the same time period whose mothers had not contracted flu. Exposure to flu during the second trimester is suspected of causing defects in neural brain development, which leads to increased vulnerability to schizophrenia due to brain damage, which has a knock-on effect on dopamine functioning. This illustrates how schizophrenia could result from an interaction of factors.

OTHER STUDIES

- Walker (1997) reported that schizophrenics have higher levels of cortisol than non-sufferers and that cortisol levels are related to severity of symptoms, with stress-related increases in cortisol levels heightening genetic-influenced abnormalities in dopamine transmission that underpin vulnerability to schizophrenia, triggering the onset of the disorder. This illustrates the interaction of biological and environmental factors in the development of schizophrenia in line with the diathesis-stress model.

- Barlow & Durand (2009) reported that a family history of schizophrenia, indicating a genetic link, coupled with a dysfunctional stressor elevated the risk of developing schizophrenia, supporting the diathesis-stress model.

- Guo et al. (2010) reported that patients in the early stages of schizophrenia who receive a combination of antipsychotics and a psychological therapy have improved insight, quality of life and social functioning and are therefore less likely to discontinue treatment or relapse than those taking antipsychotics alone, illustrating the value of combined treatments.

Description

Rather than seeing the development of schizophrenia as being due to a specific biological or psychological explanation, it is better to regard the mental disorder as being a product of several interacting factors, both biological and psychological. This is the *interactionist approach*, which encompasses the *diathesis-stress model*, where a schizophrenic episode is perceived as being triggered or worsened when environmental stressors (stress) combine with an individual's level of biological vulnerability (diathesis) to developing the condition. The interactionist approach sees schizophrenia as having an underlying genetic component, not from possessing a single 'schizophrenia gene', but from the cumulative effect of several genes, with the more of these genes an individual possesses, the greater their biological

Fig 12.5 The flu theory of schizophrenia perceives the disorder as occurring due to an interaction of biological and environmental factors

✔ The *differential susceptibility hypothesis* extends the diathesis-stress model to include positive as well as negative environments. This sees exposure to positive factors, such as having a loving, supportive family background, as reducing the chances of someone developing schizophrenia.

✔ As schizophrenia often has both biological and psychological components, combined treatments are often desirable, where biological treatments like drugs address the biological elements and psychotherapeutic treatments the psychological elements.

✔ Although combining therapies increases the cost of treatment, the increase in effectiveness of treatment can make combination therapies more cost effective in the long term.

vulnerability to developing the mental disorder. However, even having a high genetic vulnerability does not mean an individual will develop schizophrenia. For that to happen environmental stressors, such as family dysfunction, substance abuse, critical life events, etc., have to occur, with the greater the genetic vulnerability to developing schizophrenia, the easier it is for environmental stressors to trigger an episode. Biological vulnerability can also be due to abnormal brain functioning or biochemistry. The interactionist approach also sees a combination of biological and psychological treatments as being more effective than any single biological or psychological treatment.

❌ Negative evaluation

✘ Stressors that may contribute to a risk of developing schizophrenia include biological, environmental, psychological, and social factors. However, it is not known precisely how these risks contribute to the diathesis-stress interaction for any one person because specific causes for schizophrenia may differ between individuals.

✘ Combination treatments can have a down side too: patients receiving CBT sometimes interpret the side effects of simultaneous drug treatment in a delusional manner, increasing their mistrust and resistance to further treatment.

✘ Combination treatments, although desirable, cost more than individual treatments and so may not be made available to all patients.

Practical application

The main application of research into the interactionist approach is in developing tailor-made combination therapies that suit an individual's specific needs, for example initial treatment with drugs followed by family therapy for a patient with dysfunctional family relationships.

pp. 221–24

13 Eating behaviour
Explanations for food preferences

Focal study

Go *et al.* (2005) assessed the role of bitter taste preferences by examining the presence of genes that allow detection of bitter tastes in both humans and other primates. The researchers looked at the prevalence of the bitter taste receptor genes T2R in humans and 12 other primate species to test for an evolutionary ability to detect bitter tastes. The results showed humans have accumulated more pseudogenes (dead genes) than other primates, indicating that humans' bitter tasting capabilities have deteriorated more rapidly. T2R molecules play a key role in the avoidance of bitter, toxic substances, so the modification of the T2R gene may reflect different responses to changes in the environment resulting from species-specific food preferences during evolution. It was concluded that although humans possess the ability to detect and avoid bitter tasting foodstuffs, perhaps due to environmental changes, natural selection is acting to reduce humans' ability to detect bitter tastes.

OTHER STUDIES

- Denton (1982) found an innate preference for salt in many animal species, suggesting the preference has a survival value and is evolutionarily determined.

- Birch *et al.* (1987) found that 2 year olds given the most exposure to unfamiliar fruits and cheeses reduced their neophobia of the foodstuffs more quickly, illustrating the role of learning in reducing food neophobia.

- Bernstein & Webster (1980) demonstrated taste aversion in humans by finding that adults given ice-cream before receiving chemotherapy developed a subsequent aversion to eating ice-cream as they had a biological preparedness to associate the nausea with food they had eaten rather than the chemotherapy that had actually caused the nausea.

- Menella *et al.* (2005) found that although genetic influences shape children's food preferences, by adulthood cultural influences over-rode genetic ones, especially in the degree of preference for sweet-tasting foods. This suggests that genetic influences shape early food preferences, but culture influences later ones.

Description

The *evolutionary explanation* sees food preferences as occurring due to their adaptive survival value and having been shaped by natural selection to become widespread in the population. Sweet tasting foods are preferred due to their high-energy and non-poisonous content, while salty taste preferences evolved, as salt is essential for maintaining neural and muscular activity and water balance. An ability to detect and reject bitter and sour tastes evolved, as such tastes indicate the possible presence of toxins. Meat eating is not an innate tendency, it has to be introduced into children's diets, with many reluctant to do so. *Neophobia* concerns the tendency

Fig 13.1 There is a preference for sweet foods as they are associated with high-energy, non-poisonous content

✔ Positive evaluation

✔ The idea of an evolutionary determined preference for sweet tastes has much research support, including cross-cultural evidence. Bell (1973) reported that Inuit people, who had never tasted sweet foodstuffs before, accepted them on their first presentation.

✔ Some children appear less neophobic than others, which has an adaptive value, as they would be more willing to eat unfamiliar foods. If they found them non-toxic their behaviour would be observed and imitated by more neophobic children.

✔ There is an adaptive survival value to observing and imitating others' eating practices; if others safely consume novel foods, this indicates they are safe to eat, which helps break down food neophobias.

for infants to dislike or be distrustful of unfamiliar foods. This has an evolutionary protective function, as unknown foods could be toxic. *Taste aversion* occurs when individuals eat foodstuffs that makes them ill and therefore avoid those foodstuffs in the future. This involves *biological preparedness,* where individuals are primed by evolution to develop taste aversions more easily to toxic foodstuffs. *Learning experiences* reduce food neophobia and learning also occurs via *social influences,* where others' food preferences impact upon our eating behaviour, and *cultural influences,* where specific eating practices are transmitted to members of cultural groupings.

✖ Negative evaluation

✖ Kendrick (1982) studied cultural groups noted for longevity, finding a common factor was their vegetarianism, which suggests there is a price to pay for meat eating, that of having a shorter lifespan.

✖ With the increase in world population mobility, developments in transport systems and modern food hygiene practices, like the wider availability of refrigeration, eating behaviours are more global and less based on individual cultural locations.

✖ There are individual differences in salt preference, which is puzzling as evolution would predict a standard universal preference. This lowers support for the idea of an evolved salty taste preference.

Practical application

As many medicines are bitter tasting, children, with their evolved preference to avoid such tastes as they indicate the possibility of toxins, find it difficult to swallow or keep them down. But as children have an innate preference for sweet tastes, sweetening bitter-tasting medicines helps them swallow them.

AQA
AQA A-level
Psychology 2

Jean-Marc Lawton
Eleanor Willard

pp. 228–39

13 Eating behaviour

Neural and hormonal mechanisms involved in the control of eating behaviour

Focal study

Nakazato et al. (2001) assessed the role of the hormone ghrelin in eating behaviour, especially its involvement with the stimulation of appetite and feeding. Injections of ghrelin were given to normal rats and to rats bred to be genetically deficient in growth hormone. It was found that the injections strongly stimulated feeding in the normal rats, leading to significant increases in body weight. Feeding also increased in the genetically deficient rats. Subsequently, injections of anti-ghrelin immunoglobulin G robustly suppressed feeding behaviour in both groups of rats. This illustrated the important role that ghrelin plays in promoting eating and releasing growth hormone. As ghrelin was also seen to influence NPY gene expression and to decrease the influence of the hormone leptin (which is known for its role in decreasing appetite) the findings additionally suggest that there is a competitive interaction between ghrelin and leptin.

Description

Neural mechanisms concern the influence of brain components in regulating eating behaviour. The *dual control theory* is based on the idea of a homeostatic perception of hunger and satiety (fullness), whereby when the level of glucose (blood sugar) is low, the liver sends signals to the lateral hypothalamus, creating a sensation of hunger that motivates an individual to eat. When food is eaten, glucose is released, activating the ventromedial hypothalamus (VMH), producing a sensation of satiety, which stops further eating. Alternatively *set-point theory* (SPT) suggests everyone has a 'set-point' weight their body is shaped towards,

OTHER STUDIES

- Teitelbaum (1957) got rats to push a bar an increasing number of times to get food. Lesioned VMH rats initially work hard in line with dual control theory (DCT), but work less hard as more presses are required. VMH lesioned rats were also fussy eaters and ate less than normal rats if food tasted stale or bitter. These findings do not support DCT.

- Powley & Keesey (1970) found rats that lose weight through starvation and then have lesions made to their LH do not lose further weight, supporting SPT as it indicates that the rats had slimmed down to a new set-point before the lesions were created.

- Baicy et al. (2007) found that leptin binds to NPY neurons in the arcuate nucleus brain area, decreasing the activity of these neurons, which signals to the hypothalamus to produce a sensation of satiety. This illustrates the key role leptin plays in controlling eating.

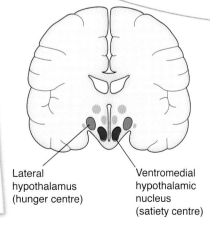

Lateral hypothalamus (hunger centre)

Ventromedial hypothalamic nucleus (satiety centre)

Fig 13.2 The hypothalmic nuclei involved in the regulation of appetite

- ✔ Dual control theory does not have universal research support, while set-point theory has a wealth of evidence to back it up, which suggests that set-point theory is a more valid explanation of eating behaviour.
- ✔ Much research into neural mechanisms has involved animal experimentation, which creates problems in generalising findings to humans. However, Quaade (1971) found that stimulating the ventromedial hypothalamus in obese people made them hungry, and findings from post-mortem studies also back up those from animal studies, which suggests that results of animal studies are therefore generalisable to humans.

determined by the rate at which calories are consumed. Set-points alter depending on several factors, including eating patterns and exercise. *Hormonal mechanisms* are chemical messengers within the body that influence eating behaviour. *Leptin* is a hormone produced by fat cells which signals to the hypothalamus that calorific storage is low and so is associated with decreasing appetite. *Ghrelin* is a hormone secreted from the lining of the stomach, whose concentration in the blood falls after eating and rises until the next. Ghrelin signals to the hypothalamus to increase the sensation of hunger and stimulates eating. As leptin also helps stimulate hunger, it may be that leptin helps regulate ghrelin levels.

❌ **Negative evaluation**

- ✘ Perceiving the lateral hypothalamus (LH) as a 'feeding centre' is oversimplified, as it is possible to recover from LH lesions and LH lesions also produce disruptions in aggression levels, sexual behaviour and reinforcement behaviour.
- ✘ The various signals sending information to the hypothalamus are only part of the complex systems regulating eating, as other factors apart from neural mechanisms play a role too, like biological rhythms.
- ✘ Although hypothalamic mechanisms are important in controlling hunger and satiety, they're not fully understood. For example, it is not clear how ghrelin and leptin reach targets in the brain, as both are large peptides that do not cross the blood–brain barrier readily.

Practical application

As leptin is seen to reduce appetite, leptin therapy was devised to treat obesity. However, although leptin injections reduce weight in some obese people, it is not universally effective. Current thinking is that leptin therapy may be more helpful in preventing weight regain than in achieving weight loss.

pp. 239–43

13 Eating behaviour
Explanations for anorexia nervosa

Focal study

Oberndorfer *et al.* (2013) assessed the role brain structures play in the development of anorexia. 14 female recovered anorexics (recovered anorexics were used to avoid the confounding variable of altered nutritional state) and 14 non-anorexic females fasted overnight and then each received a standardised breakfast of 604 calories, before having an fMRI scan to test neurocircuitry by measuring brain responses to sweet tastes, where participants were given 120 doses of either sucrose or sucratose (to distinguish between neural processing of calorific and non-calorific sweet tastes). It was found that anorexic participants had greatly reduced responses to sweet tastes, especially the taste of sucrose, in the right anterior insula brain area, which is associated with whether people feel hungry or not. The findings confirmed results from earlier studies that linked anorexia with neural processes in the insula brain area. This suggests that altered functioning of neural mechanisms contributes to the restricted eating feature of anorexia.

OTHER STUDIES

- Hakonarson (2010) compared DNA material from anorexics and non-anorexics to find variants of the OPRD1 and HTR1D genes were associated with anorexia, supporting the genetic explanation.

- Strauss & Ryan (1987) found that anorexics had less autonomy than non-anorexics, as well as poorer self-concept and disturbed family interactions, supporting the family systems theory.

- Bemis (1978) found that the weight of centrefolds in 'Playboy' magazine progressively decreased over a 20-year period, while Garner & Garfinkel (1980) found beauty queen winners had become slimmer over time, supporting the SLT idea that anorexia results from observing and imitating media models of ultra-slim women.

- Bemis-Vitousek & Orimoto (1993) found that anorexics had a consistently distorted body image and felt that they must continually lose weight to be in control of their bodies, supporting cognitive theory, especially the key role that distortions play in the maintenance of anorexia.

Description

The *neural explanation* sees anorexia resulting from abnormally functioning brain mechanisms, especially the insula brain area, which develops differently in anorexics. The neurotransmitter serotonin is associated with the onset and maintenance of anorexia, with leptin and noradrenaline also attracting interest. The *genetic explanation* sees anorexia as having an inherited component, with several genes involved. The more of these you have, the more vulnerable you are to developing anorexia. The *family systems theory* sees anorexia resulting from dysfunctional patterns of family interaction. This includes *enmeshment,* a family interactive style that inhibits each family member's sense of individuality, and *autonomy and control,* which

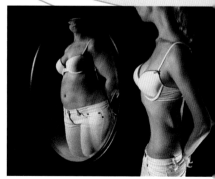

Fig 13.3 Anorexics often have a distorted body image in line with the cognitive theory

involve the lack of experience of choice and freedom in relation to oneself and others. *Social learning theory* (SLT) sees anorexia as being learned through the observation and imitation of anorexic behaviour. This involves *modelling,* where learning occurs vicariously by observation of others, *reinforcement,* where models incur positive consequences for their anorexic behaviour, and *media,* where anorexia is portrayed as desirable in public forms of communication. *Cognitive theory* sees anorexia resulting from maladaptive thought processes, involving *distortions,* errors in thinking that negatively affect perceptions of body image, and *irrational beliefs,* maladaptive ideas that lead to the development and maintenance of anorexia.

pp. 245–55

13 Eating behaviour
Explanations for obesity

Focal study

Stunkard *et al.* (1990) assessed the role of genetics in the development of obesity. The researchers compared body mass similarities between twins in a sample of 154 pairs of MZ (identical) twins who had been reared together, 93 pairs of MZ twins who had been reared apart, 208 pairs of DZ (non-identical) twins who had been reared together and 218 pairs of DZ twins who had been reared apart. If obesity had a genetic component, then MZ twins should have a higher concordance rate for obesity than DZ twins. Twins reared apart aroused special interest, as they would not have experienced identical environmental influences. It was found that the highest concordance rate for obesity was between MZ twins reared together, but MZ twins reared apart (0.68 concordance rate) was only slightly lower. This strongly suggests that body weight, and therefore obesity, is heavily influenced by genes.

Description

The *genetic explanation* sees obesity as having an inherited component, with several genes involved. The more of these you have, the more vulnerable you are to developing obesity. The *neural explanation* sees obesity as resulting from abnormally functioning brain mechanisms, with attention focused on the ventromedial hypothalamus, as well as the action of leptin upon the POMC and NPY neurones, due to their roles in regulating appetite. *Restraint theory* perceives obesity as resulting from the placing of unsustainable limits on food intake, which results in *disinhibition* where overeating and weight gain occurs due to the loss of restraint. The *boundary model* proposes that hunger motivates

OTHER STUDIES

- Yang *et al.* (2012) found that an increase in signalling in POMC neurons was positively correlated to age-dependent obesity in mice, suggesting neural factors may be able to explain why obesity increases with age.

- Bryant *et al.* (2008) report that disinhibited eaters have lower self-esteem, low physical activity and poorer psychological health and also experience lower success at dieting and incur greater weight regain, suggesting that disinhibition is strongly linked to vulnerability to obesity.

- Bartlett (2003) found dieting success occurs best with a target of reducing calorific intake of between 500 and 1,000 calories a day, resulting in weight loss of about 1–2 pounds a week, supporting the idea that achievable goal setting is a strong motivational force.

- Jeffery (2000) found obese people start regaining weight after 6 months due to failing to maintain behavioural changes, suggesting factors such as loss of motivation and social pressure have negative influences.

Fig 13.4 Can obesity be explained by biological or psychological explanations?

✔ Evolutionary theory offers support for the genetic explanation, as it sees obesity as occurring through a tendency to overeat when food is available and store excess energy as fat for times of food scarcity, something that rarely occurs in the modern world of ever-available food. Such a tendency would be genetically transmitted.

✔ Disinhibition is a major factor in weight gain leading to obesity, because of the high daily number of eating opportunities to be found in Western cultures.

✔ Research suggests that social support is an important factor in dieting success. Organisations like Weight Watchers see their effectiveness as heavily due to the social support members offer to each other.

individuals to intake food above a set minimum level and that satiety (fullness) motivates individuals to keep intake below a set level. Obesity arises, because once restrained eaters exceed their self-imposed eating target, they continue to eat to satiety, as their physiological set-point boundary overrides the self-imposed cognitive boundary. Diets fail due to being unsustainable, setting unrealistic targets, loss of motivation and hunger pangs. Diets succeed when weight is lost in an attainable manner and a stable energy balance is achieved around a new lower weight. Social support helps, as does positive reinforcements for achieving weight loss targets.

✗ **Negative evaluation**

✗ Genes cannot explain the upsurge in obesity. Genes have not changed, but environmental factors like the availability of food have, which lowers the validity of the genetic explanation.

✗ Research into dieting is gender biased, as most research has centred on females and so cannot be generalised to males, who may have different reasons for dieting and be affected by different factors.

✗ Ogden (2009) reviewed research into restraint theory and concluded that as restraint is detrimental to the physical and psychological health of normal weight individuals, it should not be used by overweight individuals vulnerable to becoming obese.

Practical application
Research into explanations for obesity have helped form effective weight-reduction programmes, with the central factor being to achieve weight loss gradually over time and then to stabilise weight around an ideal target weight.

AQA
AQA A-level
Psychology
2
Jean-Marc Lawton
Eleanor Willard

pp. 255–65

14 Stress
The physiology of stress

OTHER STUDIES

- Leshem & Kuiper (1996) found that applying different stressors to plants, like heat and drought, made them produce a similar stress response of retarded growth and lower yields, which suggests that GAS can be applied to plants as well as animals, illustrating the biological nature of stress responses.

- Taylor *et al.* (2000) found that acute stressors produce a 'flight or fight response' in males, but a 'tend and befriend' response in females, arguably because females produce more oxytocin, a chemical that promotes relaxation and nurturing, suggesting a gender difference in the workings of the SMP.

- McCarty (1981) found that older and younger rats had equal blood plasma levels of stress hormones before being subjected to stress, but that older rats had lower levels after being stressed, which implies that the SMP has diminished responsiveness with age.

- Heim *et al.* (2000) found elevated PAS responses to stress in females who had endured sexual abuse in childhood, suggesting that PAS hyper-sensitivity, due to corticotropin-releasing factor (CRF) hypersecretion, results from childhood abuse, but that CRF-receptor antagonist drugs could be used to treat conditions related to such early-life stress.

Description

The general adaptation syndrome (GAS) describes in three stages the body's physiological reaction to stress:
1 *Alarm reaction* – the body responds to emotional reactions.
2 *Resistance* – the body fights the stressor.
3 *Exhaustion* – bodily resources become depleted.
The *sympathomedullary pathway* (SMP) comprises the *sympathetic nervous system* (SNS) and the *sympathetic adrenal medullary system* (SAM). Acute stressors activate the two divisions of the *autonomic nervous system* (ANS): the SNS, which responds to stimuli and is responsible for emotional states and elevated arousal, and the *parasympathetic nervous system* (PSNS), which maintains equilibrium and reduces bodily processes.

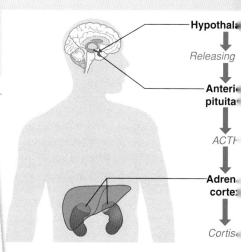

Fig 14.1 The hypothalamic–pituitary–adrenal axis

On exposure to acute stressors, the SNS becomes activated, while simultaneously the SAM system stimulates production of the hormone adrenaline into the bloodstream from the adrenal glands in the adrenal medulla, preparing the body for 'fight or flight' by increasing available oxygen and glucose to the brain and muscles, while suppressing non-emergency processes, like digestion.

The *hypothalamic pituitary-adrenal system* (PAS) is activated by chronic stress, prompting the *hypothalamus* to stimulate production of *corticotrophin-releasing hormone* (CRH) into the bloodstream. This activates the pituitary gland to produce *adrenocorticotropic hormone* (ACTH), which goes to the adrenal glands, stimulating the production of stress-related hormones, like *cortisol,* allowing a steady supply of energy to permit individuals to deal with stressors. Cortisol helps greater pain toleration, but also incurs diminished cognitive ability and immune system performance.

pp. 268–72

14 Stress
The role of stress in illness

Focal study

Kiecolt-Glaser (1984) assessed immune system functioning in response to stressful events. 49 male and 26 female volunteer first-year medical students gave blood samples 1 month before sitting their final exams and then again on the first day of their exams, after sitting 2 exam papers. Blood samples were analysed for leucocyte activity, specifically *killer cell* activity, which are known to fight off viruses and cancerous cells. Questionnaires were also completed to assess psychiatric conditions, loneliness and life events. Killer cell activity was found to be greatly reduced in the second blood samples compared to the first blood samples. Immune activity was also found to be lowest in participants who scored highly for loneliness, stressful life events and psychiatric conditions, such as depression and anxiety. Therefore it was concluded that stress is particularly associated with immunosuppression, especially in those individuals who are exposed to certain types of stressor.

OTHER STUDIES

- Cobb & Rose (1973), from comparison of medical records, found that air traffic controllers (in a very stressful job) had higher levels of hypertension and risk of heart disease than other air traffic personnel, illustrating how chronic stress is linked with CVDs.

- Melamed et al. (2006) found that burn-out, characterised by physical, emotional and cognitive fatigue, resulting from prolonged exposure to work-related stress, was associated with heightened levels of CVDs and other cardiovascular-related ailments, illustrating the link between chronic stress and CVDs.

- Kiecolt-Glaser et al. (1995) found that the healing process in women given small wounds took longer in those who cared for senile relatives, suggesting that prolonged, chronic stress weakens immune system functioning.

- Cohen et al. (1993) found that participants were more likely to develop a cold after being subjected to the virus if they had high stress scores, suggesting that stress leads to immunosuppression.

Description

The immune system is a collection of billions of cells, which help defend the body against *antigens* (foreign agents), like bacteria, viruses and cancerous cells, with the major type of cells being *leucocytes* (white blood cells). Some immune cells produce *antibodies*, which bind to antigens and destroy them. When stressed the body's ability to resist antigens is weakened, increasing vulnerability to infection. Stress does not cause infection, but increases the body's susceptibility to infectious agents through *immunosuppression*, the temporary reduction of immune functioning. Stress is associated with conditions like influenza, herpes and chronic-fatigue disorder. Occasional release of cortisol does not damage the immune system, but if produced continually, as with chronic

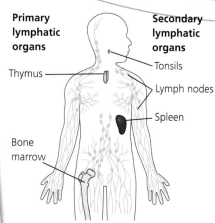

Fig 14.2 The immune system produces cells in the body that help fight infection

- Although prolonged, chronic stress can lead to immunosuppression and infection, short-term acute stress can be enjoyable, like watching horror films, and actually strengthen the immune system and therefore incur greater protection against immunosuppression and illness.
- Research has allowed psychologists and clinicians to gain a greater knowledge of how the immune and cardiovascular systems function and, more importantly, how they are affected by short-term and long-term stressors.
- There is a wealth of evidence to suggest that stressful lifestyles can have a negative impact upon the immune and cardiovascular systems, which has led to initiatives to encourage people to live more healthy and stress-free lifestyles.

stress, it impairs leucocyte activity and the production of antibodies. Therefore cortisol etc. helps protect against viruses and heal damaged tissues, but too much cortisol etc. suppresses the immune system's ability to protect the body. Stress also causes damage to the heart and blood vessels, which can result in *cardiovascular disorders* (CVDs), like hardened arteries, hypertension (high blood pressure) and coronary heart disease, which results from arteries becoming clogged up with fatty deposits. Stress can lead to CVDs directly by bodily stress systems, or indirectly through unhealthy lifestyle, like smoking and drinking.

✖ Negative evaluation

- ✗ Research investigating the immune system and stress is only correlational and cannot show cause and effect relationships. Other factors may be involved, such as smoking.
- ✗ Individual differences in personality, age and gender have been seen to affect vulnerability to developing CVDs in response to prolonged stress, which means there is no universal explanation for the role of stress in illness.
- ✗ Changes in immune system functioning as a response to stress can take time to occur and are not immediately identifiable by research. Longitudinal studies could help to show the functioning of the immune system, in response to stress, over extended periods.

Practical application

A practical application of research into stress and the immune system is that health practitioners can use knowledge gained to help anticipate problems that occur as a response to stressful situations, like post-operative stress, and use appropriate treatments.

AQA A-level Psychology 2

pp. 272–76

14 Stress
Sources and physiological measures of stress

Focal study

Holmes & Rahe (1967) investigated the effect of life change stressors, after Holmes noticed he developed a cold every time his mother-in-law came to stay. They examined 5,000 patients' medical records, making a list of 43 life events, of varying seriousness, which clustered in the months preceding illness. 100 judges were told 'marriage' had a score of 500 and they then gave values to the other life events. From this the SRRS was developed, which measures the amount of stress experienced in a given time, as *life change units* (LCUs). Only six events were seen as more stressful than marriage, like death of a spouse. Individuals with high LCU scores for the last year were vulnerable to developing stress-related illnesses in the next year, a score of over 300 LCUs being classed as a major crisis, incurring an 80 per cent risk of illnesses like heart attacks, leukaemia and sports injuries.

OTHER STUDIES

- Kanner et al. (1981) found by studying 100 participants aged 45–64 years over a 12-month period that, although the effects of uplifts were unclear, daily hassles correlated with undesirable psychological symptoms and were a better predictor of illness than life events. This suggests that daily hassles do contribute to stress-related illness.

- Kivimaki (2006) performed a meta-analysis of 14 studies involving 80,000+ participants, to find that workload was positively correlated with risk of developing coronary heart disease, demonstrating the influence of workload upon stress-related illness.

- Marmot et al. (1997) found employees with low job control three times more likely to have heart attacks than those with high job control, suggesting that low job control negatively impacts on health.

- Villarejo (2012) found that SCR readings were able to measure participants' stress levels when performing tasks involving varying levels of stress with 76.5 per cent accuracy, illustrating that SCR is a capable, though not perfect, method of measuring stress.

Description

Stressors originate from many sources, including life changes, daily hassles and workplace stressors. *Life changes* are occasional events incurring adjustments to lifestyle, like moving house. *Self-report scales* measure the impact of life events on health. Holmes & Rahe's (1967) *Social Readjustment Rating Scale (SRRS)* measured stressful life events as life change units (LCUs), to find a positive correlation between LCU score and the chances of becoming ill. *Daily hassles,* everyday irritations and annoyances, like traffic jams, have a greater negative effect due to the elevated, continual level of stress they produce. There are also *uplifts,* regular positive experiences, like socialising with

Fig 14.3 Being stuck in traffic jams on the way to work is an example of a stressful dai hassle

✔ SCR measurements are useful, as they can be used continuously throughout research without participants really noticing them and are easy to perform and are of low cost.

✔ Research illustrating the negative effects of workplace stressors has led to changes, like reducing workloads. This has lessened stress levels and therefore absenteeism, increasing profits for employers and better health for employees.

✔ Life changes and daily hassles have a mediating effect on each other, for example the life change of divorce leading to the daily hassle of increased housework. This suggests their cumulative effects can be considered.

friends, which can neutralise the negative effects of daily hassles. Self-report scales like Kanner's (1981) *Hassles and Uplifts Scales* demonstrate the harmful effects of daily hassles on health. *Workplace stressors* concern aspects of the work environment that exert a negative impact on health. *Workload* involves the number of tasks an individual has to complete within a set time, while *control* involves the degree of influence an individual has over their workload and job requirements. *Physiological measures of stress* concern objective, biological measurements of stress. For example, *skin conductance response* (SCR) measures electrical conductivity within the skin as a measure of psychological and physiological arousal.

✖ Negative evaluation

✖ The SRRS scale has pre-determined scores for life events. However, individuals experience events in dissimilar ways. The sudden death of a loved one is devastating for some, but if the loved one has been suffering for a long time, it may be a welcome release.

✖ It is difficult to isolate and test single workplace stressors and so therefore difficult to see which stressors have the most effect and what specific effects each has upon health.

✖ SCR measurements are negatively affected by external factors, like changes in temperature, leading to inconsistent readings. Internal factors, like medication levels, also negatively affect measurements, reducing the effectiveness of SCR readings.

Practical application

A practical application of research into life changes, daily hassles, workplace stressors and their measurements is that knowledge gained helps form effective therapies to counteract the negative effects of such stressors.

pp. 278–88

14 Stress

Individual differences in stress

Focal study

Friedman & Rosenman (1974) performed a longitudinal study over a 12-year period, assessing the personality types of more than 3,500 healthy, middle aged males. The participants answered questions relating to impatience, motivation towards success, competitiveness, emotions while under pressure and frustration at having their goals hindered. High scorers were categorised as Type A personality types, while low scorers were categorised as Type B personality types. Over twice as many Type A as Type B personalities developed cardiovascular disorders, which indicates that personality characteristics are linked to degrees of vulnerability to developing stress-related illnesses. It was also concluded that psychological factors can have physical effects, by the destructive physical effects of stressors being mediated via psychological personality factors, indicating that stressors are not destructive in themselves, but rather that it is how individuals perceive and respond to them that has a negative potential for health.

OTHER STUDIES

- Morris *et al.* (1981) found Type C women suppress emotions when stressed and are more vulnerable to developing cancer, due to emotional suppression leading to a weakening of the immune system and an increased risk of cancer.

- Temoshok (1987) found Type C personalities were cancer prone, with such individuals having difficulty expressing emotion and suppressed emotions, especially negative emotions like anger. This was supported by Weinman (1995), who found that such personality characteristics influenced the progression of cancer and a patient's survival time.

- Sarafino (1990) found that people who undertook hardiness training developed lower blood pressure and felt less stressed, suggesting hardiness reduces the negative effects of stress and can be taught to people as a stress management technique.

- Westman (2009) gave 326 Israeli Defence Force officer cadets a stress questionnaire at the start and finish of a training course and found that those displaying characteristics of hardiness experienced less perceived stress, supporting the idea that hardy personality type inoculates individuals against stress-related illnesses.

Description

Individual differences in the way people perceive and react to stressors are related to personality factors. Researchers have referred to *personality types,* general characterisations, where people share the same traits. *Type A Behaviour Pattern* (TABP) was suggested by Friedman & Rosenman (1959) when investigating non-physiological factors involved in coronary heart disease (CHD). TABP is characterised by *time urgency, excessive competitiveness* and *hostility* and correlates with greater vulnerability to CHD and high blood pressure. Recent research suggests hostility, characterised by non-specific dislike of others, the tendency to see the worst in others, anger, envy and a lack of compassion, is the best predictor

Fig 14.4 What some people see as stressful, those with a hardy personality perceive as a challenge to be mastered

- It may be considered unethical to perform research on Type C women suffering from cancer, as the additional stress of being studied could further negatively impact on health. However, through such research a greater understanding might be reached, leading to the formation of effective strategies that lessen the chances of Type C women developing cancer.

- Research into personality types and stress have led to an understanding that important differences exist in people's vulnerability to stress, which are dependent upon personality characteristics.

of CHD. *Type B* is a healthy personality type characterised by non-competitiveness, self-confidence and relaxation and is not associated with stress-related illness. *Type C* relates to vulnerability to cancer, with individuals having difficulties expressing emotions and tending to suppress or inhibit negative emotions, displaying instead 'pathological niceness', conflict avoidance and over compliance. *Hardiness* is characterised by *control* (individuals perceive themselves as having mastery over what they're doing), *commitment* (individuals have a sense of purpose in what they're doing) and *challenge* (individuals see stressors as enjoyable targets to reach) and is associated with low vulnerability to stress-related disorders.

❌ **Negative evaluation**

- Ragland & Brand (1988) found that 15 per cent of Friedman and Rosenman's original sample had died of CHD, with age, high blood pressure and smoking proving to be significant factors, but little evidence of Type A personality being a risk factor. This suggests the original conclusions are unsupported.

- There is no evidence that people divide easily into separate personality types. Individuals may have elements of several personality types. Indeed labelling people could lead to self-fulfilling prophecies, where individuals adopt the characteristics ascribed to the label put upon them.

- Funk (1992) believes a low hardiness score just means that a person is negative and it is this that results in the debilitating effects of stress.

Practical application

Research suggests that the components comprising hardiness, namely control, commitment and challenge, are learnable and therefore teaching individuals to develop these components helps to form an effective stress-management technique that lowers the risk of developing stress-related disorders.

pp. 289–93

14 Stress
Managing and coping with stress

Focal study

Kulik *et al.* (2013) assessed the effect of stress in mice being treated with drugs for prostate cancer. The first study used two types of male mice; ones implanted with human prostate cancer cells and ones genetically modified to develop prostate cancer. Both groups were given drugs used to treat prostate cancer. Half of each group were stressed, while half were kept stress free. The second study involved giving the mice a beta-blocker to reduce bodily functions. In study one it was found that in stress-free mice the drugs destroyed cancer cells and inhibited tumour growth. However, in the stressed mice cancer cells did not die and the drugs did not prevent tumour growth. In study two it was found that in all mice cancer cells were destroyed and tumour growth inhibited. It was concluded that stress reduces the effectiveness of anti-cancer drugs by stimulating adrenaline production, while beta-blockers inhibit adrenaline-controlled signalling pathways so that destruction of cancer cells can occur.

OTHER STUDIES

- Holcomb (1986) found that psychiatric patients responded better to SIT than drug treatments in reducing symptoms of anxiety, distress and depression. A 3-year follow-up study found that SIT treated patients required fewer hospital admissions for psychiatric episodes, suggesting that SIT is superior in long-term treatment of stress-disorders.

- Tamres *et al.* (2014) found that females use a wider selection of coping strategies and are more likely to seek social support to deal with stressors. Females were also more likely to engage in negative emotion-focused strategies, which explains why they perceive stressors as more severe than males did.

- Orth-Gomer (1993) found that the most common factors in males developing CVDs was smoking and lack of social support. Men with stressful lives who did not receive emotional social support were five times more likely to die than those who did receive such support. This illustrates the importance of social support.

Description

Drug therapy is a biological method of stress management. *Benzodiazepines* (BZs), such as Valium and Librium, are anti-anxiety drugs that dampen down the activity of the nervous system to create a sensation of calm and relaxation. *Beta-blockers* (BBs) are anti-anxiety drugs that block the transmission of nerve impulses, to reduce heart rate and alleviate the negative physical effects of stress.

Psychological methods of stress management include: (1) *Stress inoculation therapy* (SIT), a form of cognitive behavioural therapy that reduces stress by restructuring emotional and behavioural responses; (2) *Biofeedback*, a behaviourist treatment that involves training people to reduce stress levels by using physical signals from their bodies.

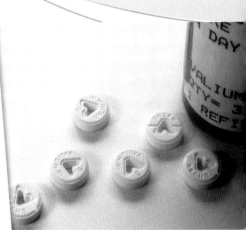

Fig 14.5 Used to reduce stress levels, the benzodiazepine Valium is the world's most prescribed drug, but can be addictive

✔ Both SIT and biofeedback are based on solid theoretical foundations of a cognitive and behaviourist nature and both have research backing from laboratory and real-life based backgrounds.

✔ BZs and BBs are easy to take, cost effective and popular with patients, as they are a known and trusted form of treatment.

✔ Gender differences in coping strategies may reflect gender differences in types of stressors encountered; females experience more emotional stressors and males more practically based ones.

✔ Different types of social support help in different situations, for example instrumental support in the form of babysitting is best for work commitment situations.

Stress generally produces the *flight-or-fight response* in males, but a *tend-and-befriend response* in females. Females tend to use social networks more when coping with stress and *emotion focused strategies,* which aim to make individuals feel more positive. Males use *problem focused strategies* more, where stressors are directly confronted. *Social support* involves the degree of resources and assistance available from others to help cope with stress. *Instrumental support* involves others providing practical assistance, while *emotional support* involves others showing support and sympathy and *esteem support* involves others showing they hold an individual in high regard.

✖ **Negative evaluation**

✖ BBs and BZs do not address causes of disorders; such medications only temporarily halt negative stress effects. When treatment ends symptoms may reappear.

✖ There are so many different components to SIT, such as relaxation, cognitive appraisal, life skills, etc., that it is difficult to assess which are the most effective ones.

✖ Findings of gender differences in coping strategies are generally based on self-reports, which are prone to bias and so may not be totally valid.

✖ If different types of social support are simultaneously given they can overwhelm and confuse an individual, making them less able to cope.

Practical application
Research into stress has not only led to the formation of stress management therapies, it has also shown the benefits and disadvantages of each, allowing more constructive use of such therapies in addressing the negative effects of stress.

AQA
AQA A-level
Psychology
2

Jean-Marc Lawton
Eleanor Willard

pp. 294–304

15 Aggression

Neural and hormonal mechanisms in aggression

Focal study

Brunner (1993) assessed the effect of a shortened version of the MAOA gene on aggression. 5 males from a Dutch family who possessed the shortened version variation of the MAOA gene gave urine samples for analysis. All 5 had a history of aggressive behaviour when they were under threat, frightened, angry or frustrated. They exhibited borderline mental retardation and displayed anti-social behaviours, such as impulsive aggression, arson, exhibitionism and rape. It was found that they all had excessive levels of *monoamines* (noradrenaline, serotonin and dopamine) in their bodies, which was caused by MAOA deficiency, a condition where individuals do not possess the ability to 'mop up' excess amounts of neurotransmitters. The findings suggest that the shortened version variation of the MAOA gene can negatively affect aggression levels of male members of families that possess the gene variation through its effect on the biochemistry of the body.

Description

The brain and biochemistry of the body can affect human aggression. The *limbic system* brain area, especially the *amygdala*, is involved in processing aggressive emotional responses by helping to mediate aggression levels by moderating amounts of testosterone in response to environmental triggers. Research has shown the neurotransmitter *serotonin* to be involved in aggression, possibly because individuals with low levels of serotonin cannot control aggressive emotional responses. However, some studies also indicate high levels of serotonin to be associated with aggression. Heightened levels of the male hormone *testosterone* are also associated with high levels of aggression. Testosterone plays a role in

OTHER STUDIES

- Raine et al. (1997) scanned the brains of 41 murderers and 41 non-murderers. He found, using PET scans, that some had abnormalities in the way that their limbic systems functioned. This suggests that the limbic system could be implicated in aggressive behaviour.

- Cherek et al. (1996) found that when men take drugs that increase their serotonin levels they display low levels of aggression. This suggests that there may be a causal link between serotonin and aggressive behaviour.

- Huber et al. (1997) found that increasing serotonin levels in animal species increased their aggression levels, casting uncertainty on to whether low or high levels of serotonin cause heightened aggression.

- Higley et al. (1996) found that testosterone affects how aggressive individuals feel, but not whether they will act on that feeling. It seems testosterone levels underpin emotional responses to situations, but that other factors, such as social learning, affect whether the aggression experienced influences the behaviour of individuals.

Fig 15.1 H.G. Brunner found evidence of a genetic link to aggression

Positive evaluation

✔ The MAOA gene may be present in a large number of individuals (about one-third of men in Western cultures possess it) because of the evolutionary advantage it bestows in giving individuals a competitive edge to compete for resources and access to females, which would bring reproductive success.

✔ There is a good degree of research evidence that suggests there are important neural and hormonal influences on aggression levels, especially via the limbic system brain area, the neurotransmitter serotonin, the hormone testosterone and individual genes, such as the MAOA gene – though environmental influences are important too.

moderating aggressive responses in the limbic system, but also affects the activity of serotonin in the brain, which affects aggression levels. No specific 'aggression' gene has been identified, but studies indicate a genetic influence upon aggression levels. It may be that certain genes moderate testosterone and serotonin production, which then affect aggression levels. The *monoamine oxidase A (MAOA) gene,* a gene which affects how neurotransmitters, including serotonin, are metabolised, has been dubbed the 'warrior gene' for its effect upon aggression. It is believed a variation of the gene affects aggression through its sensitivity to social experiences during early development, illustrating the interaction between genetics and environment.

Negative evaluation

✗ The role of the limbic system in aggressive behaviour is not clear cut. The limbic system is made up of many components so it is not altogether clear which parts are implicated. It could equally be that there is an interaction between components of the system.

✗ Much research into neural and hormonal mechanisms in aggression is performed on animals and as such presents problems of generalisation. Aggression appears linked to control of emotional responses, with emotional responses more dependent on cognitive factors in humans than in animals.

✗ Genes cannot account for aggression on their own as genes always need environmental factors to express themselves.

Practical application

If aggression is seen to be affected by biochemistry this creates the possibility of manufacturing drugs that alter the biochemistry of aggressive individuals to a more reduced and less hostile state.

pp. 308–15

15 Aggression
The ethological and evolutionary explanations for aggression

Focal study

Tinbergen (1952) assessed the role of fixed action patterns upon aggression in male sticklebacks. Tinbergen had observed that male sticklebacks turn red during the breeding season, which seemed to elicit aggressive behaviours among male fish. Under laboratory conditions models of different coloured fish were placed in a tank containing a male stickleback, but he only attacked those models coloured red. Also, when a mirror was placed in his tank, the sight of his red coloured image caused him to attack the image. From his findings Tinbergen concluded that an external triggering mechanism, in the form of a male's red belly, which is internally generated by hormone levels related to breeding behaviour, causes aggressive responses due to the presence of a fixed action pattern. Such behaviour is stereotyped, innate, universal to all members of a species, only used in one context and triggered by a specific stimulus.

Description

Ethology studies animal behaviour in their natural habitats. Lorenz believed animals have an innate mechanism for aggression that sees aggression levels building up until it is released as an aggressive act. This involves an *innate releasing mechanism,* an inborn device that prompts the release of aggression in response to a stimulus. This consists of the specific neural circuits hardwired into the brain which monitor the aggressive drive. *Fixed action patterns* involve the species-specific behaviours that are prompted by innate releasing mechanisms. Such behaviours occur as pre-set sequences to environmental stimuli. For instance, male sticklebacks will defend their nests by being prompted

OTHER STUDIES

- Sackett (1966) reared monkeys in isolation and provided them with pictures of monkeys playing, exploring and in threatening poses. As they matured they displayed reactions to the pictures of monkeys and threatening stimuli, suggesting that there is an innate mechanism to detect threat and then respond with aggressive behaviour.

- Daly & Wilson (1988) found that homicide rates are much higher when a man is about to be left, or has been left by his wife or partner, illustrating how the fear and jealousy involved in losing a partner can have aggressive consequences. This supports the evolutionary explanation that jealousy can lead to aggressive behaviour.

- Goetz et al. (2008) found that the main motivation for men's violence against partners was to punish them for perceived infidelity and/or to deter them from being unfaithful. This supports the evolutionary explanation that aggression will be used to maximise reproductive success by ensuring a male has fathered his partner's children.

Fig 15.2 Stags rutting is a way of displaying th attributes to potential mates

✔ Research into ethological explanations of aggression allowed aggressive behaviour to be studied in real-world scenarios, which gave insight into the biological nature of much of human aggressive behaviour.

✔ There is a wealth of research evidence to support evolutionary explanations of aggression in both humans as well as animals. As such similar patterns of aggressive behaviour are seen in many species, including animals, it gives support to the idea that aggression has evolved as an adaptive device to maximise reproductive opportunities and to gain valuable resources.

by the red bellies of other males to attack them. *Evolutionary explanations of aggression* see aggression as having being acted upon by natural selection to become more widespread in the population, as it has an adaptive survival value and increases reproductive fitness. Aggression in males helps them compete for females and resources. A common source of aggression here occurs through jealousy, where men fear the prospect of spending resources raising another man's genes if his partner has been unfaithful. This leads to aggressively guarding females and aggressively punishing females suspected of infidelity, even to the point of uxoricide, wife killing.

✘ **Negative evaluation**

✘ A key point of the ethological theory is that behaviour will be universal to a species. This does not seem to be true for humans, as there are large individual differences in response to the same situation. For example, some men behave aggressively in response to perceived jealousy and infidelity, while others in 'open' marriages would not mind.

✘ There are cultural differences in murder rates of unfaithful wives. If such uxoricide brought evolutionary explanations, the rates would be consistent globally.

✘ Much research support for ethological and evolutionary explanations comes from animal studies, presenting generalisation problems. It could be argued that humans have greater degrees of cognitive processing involved in aggressive behaviour that animals do not experience.

Practical application
Teaching people who respond aggressively to jealousy that it is a naturally occurring phenomenon is a tactic used by relationship counsellors to help such people gain an understanding of their behaviour, with a view to them then being able to better control it.

pp. 315–19

15 Aggression

Social psychological explanations for human aggression

Focal study

Zimbardo *et al.* (1973) investigated the role of deindividuation in a mock prison. 24 emotionally stable, non-criminal male participants were randomly assigned the roles of either guard or prisoner. Guards and prisoners were deindividuated within their groups by the use of uniforms and other procedures increasing anonymity; prisoners being referred to by numbers rather than names and guards wearing reflective sunglasses that made eye-contact impossible. The guards created a brutal atmosphere and as they stepped up their aggressive behaviour, the prisoners responded passively. Both groups demonstrated signs of deindividuation, leading to a loss of personal identity. The guards exhibited increased levels of disinhibited psychological and physical aggression and the study was cut short due to the levels and effects of their abuse.

OTHER STUDIES

- Bandura *et al.* (1961, 1963) found that children, who had been deliberately frustrated and who saw an adult model behave aggressively to a Bobo doll, were likely to imitate specific aggressive acts they had witnessed when allowed to play with the doll and increased aggressive acts if the aggressive model was reinforced. This supports the idea of aggression being learned via SLT.

- Pastore (1952) tested the frustration–aggression theory using scenarios where the frustration was brought about by 'justified' aggression, such as a bus not stopping to pick up passengers. He found that levels of aggression expressed in justified frustration settings were lower than in unjustified settings. This suggests the source of the frustration is key as to whether it leads to aggression or not.

- Guerra *et al.* (2003) looked at the effects exposure to models of violence had on children aged 5–12 in terms of aggression levels demonstrated. It was found that imitation of violence did occur, which gives support to the social learning theory.

Description

Dollard *et al.* (1939) created the *frustration–aggression hypothesis,* which argues that aggression is a consequence of frustration, which occurs from experiencing barriers to attaining goals. Aggression incurs relief from such frustration. The closer an individual is to attaining a goal, then the likelihood of frustration causing an aggressive response is heightened. If aggression is perceived as unlikely to remove a source of frustration, then aggression is unlikely to occur. *Social learning theory* (SLT) sees aggression as being learned via observation and imitation of vicariously reinforced aggressive models, where reinforcement is received indirectly by observing other people being rewarded for aggressive

Fig 15.3 Interactions with a Bobo doll

- ✔ Social learning is arguably a stronger force than biological influences, as there are whole societies that model and indulge in non-aggressive behaviour, such as the Amish communities in America.
- ✔ SLT can explain why people become aggressive only in certain situations and in certain ways. Aggression only occurs in situations and in ways that have been specifically reinforced and because mediating factors prevent aggression in certain circumstances. If aggression was biological, it would not be situation specific.
- ✔ Deindividuation can explain aggression occurring not just because of the anonymity of the aggressor, but also because of the anonymity of individuals being aggressed, for example where strangers are attacked.

behaviour. SLT therefore views the acquisition of aggression as occurring through environmental influences rather than innate or internal forces and therefore believes humans are not born aggressive, but acquire it like other social behaviours. *Deindividuation* involves the loss of individual identity and inhibitions when in a crowd, where the capacity for self-awareness and consideration of the consequences of aggressive behaviour is reduced. *Public* self-awareness, where individuals value the impressions they make on others, is reduced by the anonymity of crowds, along with a diffusion of responsibility for one's actions, while *private* self-awareness, where individuals consider their own thoughts and feelings, is also reduced.

- ✘ Deindividuation in crowds does not always lead to aggression, for example at music festivals and religious gatherings. This reduces support for the explanation.
- ✘ Research into SLT is criticised, as although it shows an immediate effect on the observer, it does not show whether this continues long term. This means that aggressive behaviour shown over a lifetime may not have been learned this way.
- ✘ Aggression is not always prompted by aggression. Many murders are planned and premeditated and not underpinned by frustration – additionally not everyone who experiences frustration reacts with aggression. This suggests that the frustration–aggression hypothesis cannot explain all aggressive behaviour.

Practical application

As deindividuation can occur in darkness, a practical application of the theory is to ensure areas are kept well lit at night time. CCTV has a similar effect, as it makes people believe their identification is likely, decreasing the likelihood of them being aggressive.

pp. 321–29

15 Aggression

Institutional aggression in the context of prisons

Description

Theories of *institutional aggression in prisons* focus on two explanations. (1) The *dispositional explanation* focuses on the personality characteristics of prisoners in order to explain the high aggression levels found in prisons. This explanation encompasses the *importation model*, which sees individuals as bringing their aggressive tendencies with them into prison, forming an aggressive sub-culture within the institution. (2) The *situational explanation* sees aggression as due to 3 specific types of factors found within a prison setting: (i) *organisational* – aggression being prompted by being forced to follow prison rules and norms, (ii) *physical* – aggression being prompted by poor social conditions and threatening

OTHER STUDIES

- Kane & Janus (1981) found that if a prisoner had previously had a low level of education, a serious criminal record and spent a lot of time unemployed, then they were more likely to be aggressive once in prison. This illustrates how violence can be imported due to the previous experience of offenders.

- Kane & Janus (1981) found that younger offenders and non-white prisoners were more likely to be aggressive while in prison. This may be due to the influence of gang culture and/or the marginalisation of ethnic groups. This supports the idea that outside influences affect aggression.

- Johnston (1991) found there is intense competition for resources available in prison. This competition elicits in-group/out-group aggressive conflicts between gangs formed explicitly to compete for such resources. This relates to deprivation of goods and services, therefore supporting a situational explanation for prison violence.

Fig 15.4 A person with aggressive tendencies will display them in prison as well as at home

✔ A strength of the dispositional model is that it looks at prisoners in a more idiographic way (sees prisoners as individuals who differ from each other rather than seeing them in a nomothetic way by perceiving them as all the same). This explains why some prisoners are aggressive and some are not.

✔ Riots in prison settings can give support to the situational model, as they tend to occur when there has been a withdrawal of privileges, or when the imposition of prison rules is tightened up. The resulting tensions and frustration often lead to an outburst of violence.

environments, and (iii) *staff characteristics* – clashes occurring due to attitudes and behaviour of prison officers. This explanation encompasses the *deprivation model*, which sees aggression as emanating from the injustices and deprivations of institutional life, like *deprivation of liberty*, *deprivation of autonomy* (independence), *deprivation of goods and services*, *deprivation of heterosexual relationships* and *deprivation of security*. Such deprivations lead to increased stress, with aggression being used in an attempt to reduce such stress and obtain deprived resources and therefore gain some control over the social constraints of institutional life. Both explanations are seen as valid theories of prison aggression.

✖ The importation model is accused of lacking recommendations of how to manage aggressive prisoners and reduce overall prison aggression levels. Theories that do not generate practical applications are generally seen as lacking validity.

✖ Although gang culture is a good predictor of violence levels in young offender institutions, it does not explain aggression in adult prisons very well. Poole & Regoli (1983) found levels of pre-institutional violence predicted inmate aggression in juvenile correction institutions, but not adult prisons, lowering support for the importation model.

✖ Although prison riots can occur due to deprivations within a prison setting, they can also sometimes flare up without any apparent reason, lowering support for the situational model.

Practical application
Research into aggression in prisons has led to the formation of strategies to reduce and manage aggression levels. Decreasing overcrowding, allowing more comforts and privileges, etc. have all been seen to help lower aggression levels in prisoners.

pp. 330–35

15 Aggression
Media influences on aggression

Focal study

Pinto da Mota Matos et al. (2011) assessed the impact of aggression in TV programmes on children's subsequent behaviour. The participants were 722 Portuguese school children aged 9–16 years. Age, school year and socioeconomic status were recorded and measures taken by questionnaire of how often they watched different types of aggressive TV programmes, how they would react physically and verbally to various aggressive scenarios in real life, how much they enjoyed violence on TV, how similar to real life they thought violent TV programmes were, and which TV character they would like to be. It was found that children's aggressive behaviour was related to degree of enjoyment of TV violence, how realistic programmes were and identification with violent characters. Children who watched the most violent TV showed more physical aggression. It was concluded that exposure to TV violence is linked to aggressive behaviour, with several factors involved.

Description

Media, such as TV and magazines, are sources of influence on aggression. *Computer games* desensitise players to the effects of aggression and provide positive reinforcements for violence, which are then re-enacted in real-world scenarios. Computer games could also be a source of catharsis, a safe release for aggressive tendencies. *Desensitisation* is the idea that if individuals watch lots of media forms of aggression, they will become so habituated (used to) such acts of violence that similar forms of aggressive behaviour may be enacted in real-world scenarios, as they have a reduced emotional reaction to such behaviour. *Disinhibition* occurs where people behave in uncharacteristically aggressive ways. Media sources, such

OTHER STUDIES

- Bushman (2009) found that when individuals who had been playing violent video games for 20 minutes saw someone injured in a fight, they took longer to help them than individuals who had been playing non-violent video games for 20 minutes. This suggests they were desensitised, as the injury did not affect them emotionally.

- Bandura et al. (1975) found that disinhibition (in the form of reduced responsibility) led to increased aggressive behaviour and the more disinhibited a person was, then the greater the aggressive behaviour. This suggests that disinhibition may be a factor in media sources of aggression.

- Josephson (1987) found that characteristically aggressive boys who watched a violent TV programme involving the use of walkie-talkies behaved aggressively when playing floor-hockey, which involved using walkie-talkies. However, characteristically non-aggressive boys were not similarly affected. This suggest cognitive priming only increases aggressive behaviour in aggressive individuals.

Fig 15.5 Violent video games can lead to desensitisation

- Research suggests that the negative effects of video games are short-lived, while positive effects can have a greater, longer-lasting impact, so that overall computer game playing can be regarded in a favourable light.
- Research has indicated that cognitive priming only has a negative effect on aggression levels of aggressively-inclined individuals. Only by conducting carefully executed research can such important findings come to light.
- It may be that disinhibition, in reducing the emotional impact to aggression, may reduce actual aggression levels in real-world scenarios, as aggressive responses usually require heightened emotion.

as computer games, can lead to such disinhibition where players demonstrate aggressive behaviours that they normally would not display. This occurs because of (i) *anonymity* – which reduces responsibility for aggressive behaviour, (ii) *solipsistic introjection* – becoming merged with a character in a media source, and (iii) *minimisation of authority* – the lack of legal consequences. The danger is that such disinhibition could lead to uncharacteristic acts of aggression in real-life scenarios. *Cognitive priming* is the idea that we are exposed to aggressive cues in media sources, which may trigger aggression when such cues occur in real life.

✖ Negative evaluation

- The correlation found between amount of aggressive/pro-social TV watched and degree of aggressive/pro-social behaviour exhibited may occur because aggressive/pro-social individuals choose to view more violent/helpful programmes.
- Prolonged use of computers can create disinhibition that makes users indifferent to the welfare of others, self-centred and lacking in real-life communication and social skills. This suggests that access to computer usage should have time limitations, especially for the young who are still developing their communication and sociability skills.
- The extent to which individuals become involved in the media they are experiencing varies. So, disinhibition only occurs in people who are fully engaged in playing and are not easily distracted by external stimuli (for example, introverts). This suggests disinhibition is not a universal effect.

Practical application

If watching and interacting with aggressive forms of media leads to increased aggression levels, then getting individuals to watch and interact with pro-social forms of media should have the opposite, positive effect of reducing aggression levels.

AQA A-level
Psychology 2

Jean-Marc Lawton
Eleanor Willard

pp. 335–41

16 Forensic psychology
Problems in defining crime

Focal study

Contemporary Statistics: The 14th Prisoner survey. For *male offenders* there was a decrease in drug use of 20 per cent. 45 per cent stated that they were drunk when committing their offence. This figure was higher for young offenders, with 68 per cent saying that they were drunk at the time. Young male offenders reported a high rate of alcoholism, with 90 per cent of them drinking more than 10 units a day when they were out of prison. One third of young male offenders were members of gangs and 67 per cent carried a knife. 44 per cent said they had witnessed violence in the home. For *female offenders*, 50 per cent reported being drunk when committing their offence. This was 5 per cent more than male offenders. 28 per cent reported that drinking alcohol affected their employment. 28 per cent were also worried that alcohol would be an issue for them when they were released.

OTHER STUDIES

- The Crime Survey for England and Wales (2014) estimated 7.3 million incidents of crime, a 14 per cent decrease from the year before, the lowest estimate since 1981 when the survey began. Despite overall figures decreasing shoplifting increased by 7 per cent and fraud by 17 per cent. Police recorded crime remained the same as the previous year. However, in previous years the amount of police reported crime had decreased year on year, which attracted criticism that the police were not recording crime accurately. If this was true, then the current figures show this decline has been addressed. It also seems that this change is in certain crime areas, such as violence and public order. Sexual offences recorded by the police increased by 20 per cent from the previous year. This is argued to be because of Operation Yewtree, which was investigating sexual abuse by celebrities. As the media coverage was widespread, more victims approached the police to report sexual offences.

Description

There are four issues that make crime difficult to define: (1) *culture* – definitions of crime vary across cultures; (2) *age* – the age of criminal responsibility varies from country to country; (3) *context* – changes to the legal system occur over time; and (4) *circumstance* – the situation in which an incident occurs can affect whether it is seen as a crime, for example a person's intentions.

There are several ways of measuring crime. *Official statistics* are collected by *The Office for National Statistics*, which monitors crime rates in England and Wales in several categories, though some types of crime, for example drug trafficking, are difficult to measure. Police recordings of crime are also used in the official statistics.

✔ The victim survey is updated annually to keep abreast of trends and the emergence of new crimes. This means that it attempts to include all possible crimes, even relatively new ones.

✔ Asking offenders about offences committed gives a good picture of the reasons behind offending behaviour, which helps deployment of resources to areas which might prevent further crime.

✔ The offender surveys give a fuller picture of the 'dark side of crime' because offenders have knowledge of exactly what crimes might be occurring when. It is an official channel through to the criminal 'underworld'.

Victim surveys involve *The Crime Survey for England and Wales,* which asks people about their crime experiences to identify trends in criminal activity. *Offender surveys* such as *The Offending Crime and Justice Survey* record self-reported criminal activity, including alcohol and drug use. It is a longitudinal survey and so can identify trends and patterns of criminal activity. As it also measures unreported crimes, it can sometimes give a more accurate picture of criminal activity than official statistics. In Scotland an annual survey of prisoners and young offenders is carried out, which offers insight into why they may have committed criminal acts.

❌ **Negative evaluation**

✘ Offender surveys are self-report measures and therefore have problems of reliability. It could be argued that offender surveys are even more liable to inaccuracy due to the legal implications of giving truthful answers.

✘ Figures from official statistics may be misleading, as some crime activity may be missing.

✘ Victim surveys are notoriously poor in reliability. Some people are reluctant to report crime, may forget they have been a victim of a crime or may lie. This means a lot of crime goes unreported. Unreported crime is known as the 'dark side' of crime and estimates of the amount this represents varies wildly, but is thought to be significant.

Practical application

Statistics relating to criminal activity can be useful in showing involved bodies where resources should be allocated and which criminal activities are becoming problematic and need more targeting and attention.

pp. 346–51

16 Forensic psychology
Offender profiling

Focal study

McCrary & Grant (1990) reported on the case study of Arthur Shawcross who, having served 15 years for murdering two children, murdered 11 prostitutes between 1988 and 1990. The profilers visited crime scenes and examined case files to decide the murderer was white, male, married, had a mental age of late 20s/early 30s, was a previous offender of violent crimes, was low paid, drove a cheap car, lived near the crime scenes and was a hunter. The profilers predicted the offender would return to a crime scene to mutilate a body, so a murdered body should be left in place under surveillance. This was done and the offender was arrested. The profile proved to be accurate and although Shawcross pleaded not guilty due to insanity, he was sentenced to a 250-year jail sentence.

OTHER STUDIES

- Pinizzoto (1984) identified that of 192 requests of criminal profiles, only 17 per cent were actually useful for identifying the suspects. However, the same research showed that 77 per cent of the respondents indicated that profiles had assisted them to focus on the investigations.

- Snook et al. (2008) reported that the number of cases using profiling to investigate a crime had increased, which suggests police officers are starting to recognise its credibility and usefulness.

- Shanahan (2008) found the responses to questionnaires sent out by the Criminal Investigation Department used to evaluate the effectiveness of the criminal profiling in the department were mainly negative. This was only when it had not worked effectively however, and Shanahan found that most police officers still expressed confidence in criminal profiling and its potential to help them.

Description

Profiling describes what type of person may have committed a crime. The key questions are: What happened at the crime scene? Who might have committed the crime? What kind of personality might they have? *Organised offenders* are intelligent and socially competent, with an orderly approach to life that is reflected in the way they commit crimes. *Disorganised offenders* are the opposite. The *top-down approach* uses crime scene analysis to create profiles and involves a 7-stage process:

1 *Murder type* – is it an isolated case or a serial killing?

2 *Primary intent* – was the crime premeditated or spontaneous?

3 *Victim risk* – how vulnerable was the victim?

4 *Offender risk* – how much risk did the offender take in committing the crime?

Fig 16.1 Arthur Shawcross: offender profiling helped to convict him of murder

✔ The top-down approach is best used for violent crimes, such as murder and rape, where it has proven to be reasonably effective in drawing up profiles of likely suspects.

✔ The bottom-up approach of investigative psychology is based upon research evidence and statistical likelihood, which makes it more scientific than the top-down approach. The use of statistics removes intuition (intelligent guess-work) from profiling, making it more reliable.

✔ Geographical profiling helps locate offenders of different crimes. It can be used to locate the likely home of burglars as they often concentrate their crimes not far from where they live. This means the method is applicable across many different types of crime.

Escalation – is the crime more serious than previous offences?

Time factors – what time of day did the crime occur?

Location factors – where did the crime occur?

he *bottom-up approach* builds profiles om data gained from similar crimes, like nvestigative psychology, based on five ssumptions: (i) *interpersonal coherence* – nat criminals exhibit consistent behaviour; i) *time and place* – where and when crimes e committed; (iii) *criminal characteristics* placing criminals into categories; (iv) riminal career – how experienced criminals e; (v) *forensic awareness* – to what xtent crime scenes have been tidied up. eographical profiling examines location nd timing aspects of crimes to discern ne living habits of offenders.

✖ Negative evaluation

✖ There is a lack of theoretical foundation to the top-down approach, which reduces its credibility. Indeed, it can be argued to rely more on guess-work than science, with the personal opinions and emotions of profilers clouding their judgement.

✖ Locations are important for the identification of offenders, but there are other considerations that need to be made, such as their psychological characteristics. Geographical profiling concentrates on location, which could miss important information if used in isolation.

✖ The bottom-up approach requires statistical information from previous similar crimes, which is not always easy to gather. Problems in measuring crime also reduce the effectiveness of the method.

Practical application

The main application of profiling is in helping the police to focus their inquiries when attempting to identify the perpetrators of crimes in a much more targeted way, so that they can be arrested before committing more offences.

AQA

AQA
A-level

Psychology
②

Jean-Marc Lawton
Eleanor Willard

pp. 351–58

16 Forensic psychology
Biological explanations for offending behaviour

Focal study

Farrington (1996) assessed the development of delinquency. 411 males living in London from nearly 400 families were monitored from age 8 to 32 through interviews, and from age 10 to 40 in crime records. Conviction rates of these men were compared to convictions of close family members. They found:

- 64 per cent of the families contained at least one convicted person
- 6 per cent of the families accounted for 50 per cent of all convictions
- convictions of one family member were strongly related to convictions of every other family member
- about 75 per cent of convicted fathers and convicted mothers had a convicted child
- approximately 75 per cent of families containing convicted daughters also contained convicted sons
- convictions of older siblings were more strongly related to convictions of the males than were convictions of younger siblings.

The conclusion was that offending is strongly concentrated in families, suggesting a genetic link.

OTHER STUDIES

- Hooton (1939) conducted a 12-year study comparing 13,873 male prisoners in 10 US states with a control group of 3,023 men to assess physical differences. He found criminals tended to possess a greater degree of sloping foreheads, protruding ears and narrow jaws, supporting the atavistic form explanation.
- Brunner (1993) examined the effects of the MAOA gene, which alters the levels of neurotransmitters of individuals with the shortened version of the gene. A link was found to heightened aggressive behaviour, which suggests a genetic and biochemical link to violent crime.
- Raine et al. (1997) assessed whether there were differences in brain activity of murderers and non-murderers. 41 violent murderers' brains were investigated using a PET scanner. Differences were found in activity in brain areas linked to aggression, such as the prefrontal cortex and the limbic system, which suggests brain physiology may be involved in murder.

Description

Atavistic form is a historical approach to explaining offending behaviour that saw criminals as having distinguishing physical features, such as a heavy brow and large ears. These were seen as reflecting an earlier, primitive state of development. The *genetic explanation*, although not arguing for a single 'criminal' gene, believes that criminality does have an inherited component to it, which is supported by research evidence from twin, family and adoption studies. It is probable that several genes are involved, with criminality more likely when an individual has more of these genes. The *neural explanation* sees offending behaviour as related to biochemistry, with high

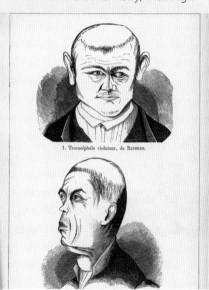

Fig 16.2 Atavistic features identified by Lombroso (1876)

levels of noradrenaline (associated with aggression) and dopamine (associated with pleasure) related to criminal behaviour, and low levels of serotonin (associated with impulsive behaviour). The *brain physiology* explanation argues that specific brain areas are involved with offending behaviour. The *limbic system*, where emotion is regulated, is especially linked, as criminals often feel little remorse or guilt about their offending behaviour. Research also suggests that low activity in the frontal lobes is associated with not having a conscience, which means that such people would have less restrictions on committing criminal offences.

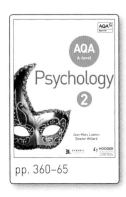

AQA
AQA A-level
Psychology
2

Jean-Marc Lawton
Eleanor Willard

pp. 360–65

16 Forensic psychology
Psychological explanations for offending behaviour

Focal study

Bowlby (1944) assessed a possible link between maternal deprivation and juvenile delinquency. 44 teenage thieves, caught stealing from a psychiatric facility, were compared with 44 controls who had not stolen from the facility. Mothers were interviewed separately. It was found that 14 of the thieves but none of the controls exhibited *affectionless psychopathy*, characterised by a lack of affection or empathy for others and lack of guilt for criminal behaviour. Bowlby also found that 12 of the affectionless psychopaths had been separated from their primary caregivers for more than 6 months before age 2. It was concluded that early separation from carers can lead to delinquency, with prolonged separation leading to affectionless psychopathy and an increased risk of vulnerability to criminality, due to reduced experiences of guilt and a lack of insight into the impact of their criminal actions upon others.

OTHER STUDIES

- Furnham (1984) found the best predictor of self-reported delinquency was high levels of psychotism, then high levels of neuroticism, low levels of moral guidance, high levels of extraversion and low levels of social skills, giving some support to Eysenck's theory of the criminal personality.

- Hollin *et al.* (2002) reported that offenders are in a less mature stage of morality than non-offenders, giving support to the cognitive explanation.

- Crick & Dodge (1994) found evidence to support a relationship between hostile attribution bias and aggression in children and adolescents. This was in hypothetical situations and actual situations, which suggests that the theoretical explanation can be applied to everyday behaviour, as well as research scenarios.

- Alarid *et al.* (2000) found that differential association theory was applicable to the offending behaviour of 1,153 newly convicted criminals, especially for male offenders. This suggests it is a good general theory of crime, with a high degree of validity in explaining criminal behaviour.

Description

Eysenck's (1963) personality theory has been applied to offending behaviour. High levels of extraversion are associated with the thrill seeking element of criminality, while high levels of neuroticism are associated with the strong degrees of emotionality evident in some criminal behaviour. High levels of psychotism are associated with criminality, as such people lack a conscience to act as a brake upon offending behaviour. *Cognitive explanations* focus on the idea of criminals having developed lower levels of moral reasoning, with *cognitive distortions* (misperceptions of reality) seen as generating negative emotional states, such as *hostile attribution bias*, where others' behaviour is misperceived as intimidating, leading to aggressive

Fig 16.3 When do we understand the difference between right and wrong?

✔ Moral reasoning can largely account for individual differences in offending behaviour, for example, why one individual, but not another would commit a particular crime.

✔ There is such a large body of research evidence to support a link between hostile attribution bias and offending behaviour that it has become seen as a general precursor of aggressive behaviour in children, adolescents and adults, which can lead to violent criminal actions.

✔ Research indicates a relationship between the amount of minimalisation and level of offending behaviour in criminals, which suggests minimalisation is a valid explanation of offending behaviour.

responses, and *minimalisation* where offenders self-deceive themselves to rationalise their criminality as excusable. Alternatively, *differential association theory* is a behaviourist explanation that sees criminality as learned from environmental experiences. There are also three *psychodynamic explanations*: (1) *superego* – where a conscience does not develop properly, making criminal behaviour more likely; (2) *maternal deprivation hypothesis* – delinquent behaviour is seen as arising from disruption to attachment bonds; and (3) *defence mechanisms* – offenders justify criminal behaviour to reduce anxiety levels created by guilt, as well as using criminal acts to express their unconscious desires.

✖ Eysenck is criticised for the limited sample he used to develop his theory, which entailed certain personality types wrongly appearing dominant, which implies that the results cannot be generalised to the general population.

✖ Hostile attribution bias cannot explain all instances of violent offending behaviour. It does appear linked to impulsive acts of aggression, but not to acts of pre-meditated, planned aggression; this lowers its validity as a general explanation of criminality.

✖ Psychodynamic explanations, like defence mechanisms, are based upon the untestable notion of an unconscious mind. The general lack of research support means such explanations are not well considered.

Practical application

Psychological explanations lend themselves to psychological interventions for offending behaviour. Psychodynamic explanations suggest a role for psychotherapy in reducing criminality, while differential association theory suggests using reinforcements to condition non-criminal behaviour. Cognitive explanations also suggest a role for cognitive therapies that replace irrational thought processes with rational ones.

pp. 366–76

16 Forensic psychology
Dealing with offending behaviour

Focal study

Ireland (2000) assessed the effectiveness of anger management programmes in reducing anger levels in offenders. In the research, 50 prisoners were assessed on two measures of anger both before and after completion of an anger management programme, which involved 12 hours' worth of intervention spread out into one hour intervals over a period of three days. The measures were a self-report questionnaire and a checklist of 29 problematic behaviours. There was also a control group of 37 prisoners (matched for offending behaviour profile) who did not receive any anger management and completed the same measures as those that did. The results from the two groups were compared and it was found that there was a 92 per cent reduction in anger levels for the intervention group on at least one of the two measures. This suggests that anger management programmes are effective in reducing anger levels in offenders.

OTHER STUDIES

- Hollin (1992) found evidence to suggest that prison became 'home' to some prisoners. The fact that they received three meals a day, together with a bed and companionship, was preferable to them than what they had to deal with outside of prison, illustrating the effect of institutionalisation upon recidivism levels.

- Cartier et al. (2006) found a strong relationship between substance abuse and reoffending rates, although interestingly this was not linked to violent offences. This suggests addiction, if not treated within the prison system, can lead to prisoners reoffending upon release.

- Hobbs & Tyllon (1976) found that introduction of a behaviour modification programme in three young offenders' institutions reduced the amount of undesirable behaviour within the institution when compared with an institution with no such programme. This demonstrates the short-term benefits of behaviour modification, though there is no guarantee the modified behaviour will continue outside of prison.

Description

Custodial sentencing involves convicted offenders being sent to prison, which serves four functions; *deterrence* (to stop people reoffending), *retribution* (punishment for the offending behaviour), *confinement* (to prevent further offences) and *rehabilitation* (the teaching of skills to prevent reoffending). There are psychological effects of custodial sentencing, such as *institutionalisation,* where inmates become unable to live independently outside of prison, and negative effects on mental health, like increased levels of depression. *Recidivism* involves individuals who reoffend after serving a custodial sentence for earlier criminal actions. About 26 per cent of sentenced offenders reoffend within 1 year of

Fig 16.4 Custodial sentencing serves several functions

✔ Restorative justice is considerably cheaper than custodial sentencing, so is a popular sentencing option. It also has the advantage of being psychologically helpful to individuals who have been the victims of crime.

✔ Behaviour modification takes little training or expense. This makes it a cost-effective technique, which is easy to introduce, as there are few problems with staff being skilled enough to administer it, unlike other interventions such as anger management.

✔ Anger management gives offenders insight into how they think and can help them gain an understanding of problems in their thinking, which have led them to offend in the past.

release from prison, which may occur due to institutionalisation, poor levels of mental health and addiction problems. To reduce reoffending levels, *behaviour modification programmes* are used where reinforcements, in the form of 'tokens', are given for demonstrating desired behaviour. These can then be exchanged for desirable goods and luxuries. *Anger management* is a cognitive intervention, which trains individuals to recognise what makes them angry, teaches skills to reduce anger and offers opportunities to practice such skills. *Restorative justice programmes* attempt to get offenders to realise the impact of their criminality by getting them to meet the victims of their offending behaviour in a controlled environment.

❌ **Negative evaluation**

✘ It appears, from recidivism rates, that the aims of deterrence and rehabilitation are not fulfilled by custodial sentencing, as reoffending rates are high The idea that rehabilitation is effective is also questionable, as it may actually serve to teach criminals how to offend more skilfully.

✘ It is difficult to assess whether prisoners' mental health issues are due to being incarcerated in prison or were imported into prison by offenders.

✘ Although behaviour modification programmes work well in the short term, there is little evidence to suggest they work once the offender has left the institution. This means they have limited rehabilitative effect.

Practical application
The main practical application of research into dealing with offending behaviour is the establishment of practices and techniques to reduce high levels of recidivism, such as anger management programmes, behaviour modification and restorative justice programmes.

pp. 378–88

17 Addiction

Describing addiction and risk factors in the development of addiction

Focal study

Wan-Sen Yan et al. (2013) investigated the relationship between stress levels, personality characteristics and family functioning in internet addiction. 892 Chinese students were assessed on five constructs that measured *demographic variables* (age, gender, education, etc.) *family functioning* (how cohesive families were), *addiction level* (measured from a 26-item scale), *personality* (from measurements of extraversion, neuroticism and psychoticism) and *stress* (measured from self-ratings of life changes in the last 12 months). It was found that 10 per cent of the sample had severe internet addiction and a further 11 per cent had mild internet addiction. No link was found between demographic variables and level of addiction, but individuals with severe addiction had low family functioning levels and high levels of neuroticism and psychotism and low levels of extraversion and higher levels of life change related stress. Milder addicted individuals had higher stress levels than non-addicted individuals. It was concluded that there is a relationship between family functioning, personality type, stress and internet addiction.

OTHER STUDIES

- Marks et al. (1997) found that alcoholics were more likely to have a higher nicotine dependence, as they smoked more heavily. As a result, alcoholics often experience greater discomfort from nicotine withdrawal when attempting to give up smoking, demonstrating the effects of withdrawal syndrome.

- Tsuang et al. (1996) evaluated the genetic influence on addiction by examining the records of 3000 male twins, with addiction defined as at least weekly use of an illegal drug. The data showed that MZ twins (100 per cent genetically similar) had a higher concordance rate for addiction than DZ twins (50 per cent genetically similar), supporting the genetic explanation.

- Akers & Lee (1996) looked at smoking levels of young adults aged 12–17, finding that social influences, like family and peer influences, affected the smoking behaviours of these participants, to either try smoking, continue smoking or quit smoking, illustrating the effects of family and peer influences as risk factors in addiction.

Description

Diagnostic manuals describe the symptoms involved in *psychological and physiological dependence*, with gambling listed as the only behavioural addiction. *Tolerance* involves the need to take higher levels of a substance to get the same physical and psychological effects, while *withdrawal* involves the psychological and physiological reactions of individuals abstaining from dependence behaviour. There are several risk factors in the development of addiction. *Genetic vulnerability* involves several genes being associated with risk of addiction; the more of these an individual has, the more at risk they are. High levels of *stress* are also associated with increased vulnerability to addiction, though addiction itself

Fig 17.1 Wan-Sen Yan *et al.* studied cyber addiction in university students

✔ Research evidence indicates a genetic vulnerability to addiction, though no twin study concordance rates of 100 per cent have ever been found, meaning environmental influences play an important role too.

✔ Research evidence also suggests that personality traits are involved in determining an individual's level of vulnerability to addiction, though little support has been found for the more extreme idea of an addictive personality type.

✔ Peer influence appears to get stronger with age; Rich-Harris (1998) found that peer influence especially increases in adolescence, often a time when addictive behaviours are established, illustrating the importance of peers in establishing dependency behaviours.

can be stressful. There is also the view that possession of certain *personality* characteristics increases vulnerability to addiction, especially high levels of neuroticism and psychotism. *Family influences* can also influence addictive behaviour through social learning theory, where family members role model addictive behaviour to be observed and imitated, as well as helping to create positive expectancies of indulging in addictive behaviour. *Peers* are an additional source of social learning for dependency behaviours, as well as being able to provide access to substance abuse and encourage relapse from attempted withdrawal from addictive behaviours.

❌ Negative evaluation

✗ Stress research is often conducted on animals because of ethical issues in using humans. This means that there are problems generalising findings to humans, which lowers the validity of such research in explaining addiction.

✗ Peer group influences are just one of many social context effects that should be considered when assessing vulnerability to addiction, such as economic and social deprivation – these effects should be considered collectively, as addiction is rarely due to one factor.

✗ Although there is a genetic link to addiction, it varies across dependency behaviours, which means that genetic vulnerability to specific dependencies is difficult to ascertain.

Practical application

Research into stress and vulnerability suggests the possibility of a vulnerability measure that could predict an individual's level of risk to addiction, or indeed their risk of relapsing after withdrawal from dependency behaviours.

pp. 393–406

17 Addiction

Explanations for nicotine addiction

Focal study

Goldberg *et al.* (1981) performed a laboratory experiment that assessed the role of operant conditioning in addictive behaviour in squirrel monkeys. The monkeys were trained to press a lever in order to receive a positive reinforcement of a nicotine injection and their response rate was compared to the response rate exhibited by a group of similar squirrel monkeys who had been trained to press a lever to receive a positive reinforcement of an injection of cocaine. It was found that both groups of monkeys produced similar levels of response when pressing the lever. This illustrates the important role that operant conditioning plays in the maintenance of addictive behaviour and demonstrates that addictive behaviours are indulged in, due to their positively reinforcing effects.

OTHER STUDIES

- Chiara (2000) reported that dopamine is one of the main causes for the addictive nature of nicotine. The rewarding aspect of the drug, such as the feeling of pleasure, is released through dopaminergic activity and so is responsible for the addictive nature of the drug. If pleasure was not felt then the smoker would not continue to smoke over time. This illustrates the important role of brain neurochemistry in smoking behaviour.

- Watkins *et al.* (2000) reviewed the research into the neurobiology of nicotine addiction. They found that dopamine release was reduced following chronic exposure to nicotine. This means that tolerance of the drug occurs due to the level of reward felt decreasing. This illustrates how nicotine consumption increases to the point of addiction due to brain neurochemistry.

- Calvert (2009) found that smokers, when shown cigarette packets, experienced strong activation in the ventral striatum and nucleus accumbens brain areas, suggesting a biological explanation of craving behaviour. However, this also supports the idea of cue reactivity and therefore the brain activation produced may show the neural basis for classical conditioning.

Description

An explanation based on *brain neurochemistry* centres on the role of the neurotransmitter dopamine in boosting the brain's reward system, due to smoking behaviour creating pleasant sensations. The stimulation of dopamine neurons triggers activation in the limbic system, which in turn boosts activity in the pre-frontal cortex creating a euphoric 'high'. Through repeated usage the level of nicotine needed to produce the high becomes greater, with cravings created that result in addiction. With *learning theory* smoking behaviour is explained as a two-stage process involving *social learning theory* and *operant conditioning*. An individual is seen as initiating smoking

Fig 17.2 Are certain personalities more predisposed to addiction?

behaviour through the observation and imitation of smoking role models via the use of *vicarious reinforcement* (seeing the model being positively reinforced for their smoking behaviour). Continuation of smoking behaviour then occurs by the positive reinforcement that consuming nicotine incurs in the form of pleasurable sensations and the reduction of anxiety. *Cue reactivity* involves associations that are made through *classical conditioning*, such as smoking when having a drink in the pub beer garden, with the drink/location acting as a conditioned stimulus, creating a strong desire to smoke (conditioned response) in such situations.

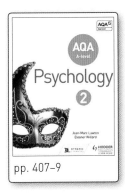

pp. 407–9

17 Addiction

Explanations for gambling addiction

Focal study

Griffiths (1994) tested the idea that gamblers think differently to non-gamblers due to cognitive bias. 30 regular and 30 occasional gamblers were given 30 ten-pence bets on a fruit machine with the target being to stay on the machine for 60 gambles and win back the initial £3. If successful, they kept the money and could carry on playing if they wanted. Participants spoke their thoughts out aloud as they played. Comments from regular gamblers indicated they thought they were more skilful than they actually were. Regular gamblers also had irrational beliefs, like believing the machine had moods that influenced pay-outs. They also saw losses as 'near wins'. 44 per cent of regular gamblers achieved 60 gambles, with one-third continuing until all money was lost. 22 per cent of the occasional gamblers achieved 60 plays; only two continued until all money was lost. It was concluded until that regular gamblers misperceive their gambling skills and are affected by cognitive bias.

OTHER STUDIES

- Parke & Griffiths (2004) found that gambling is positively reinforcing due to the money, thrill and excitement it produces, but the sensation of 'near misses' produced by losing is also reinforcing. This means that gambling is reinforced whether winning or losing, making it highly addictive.

- Blaszczynski & Nower (2002) found that that gamblers fell into three categories: behaviourally conditioned gamblers, emotionally vulnerable gamblers and antisocial impulsivist gamblers. The first group became addicted due to conditioning experiences, giving supporting to learning theory. However, as not all gamblers are classed this way, it may only serve as an explanation for some addicts.

- Rogers (1998) found there was cognitive bias in the reasoning behind individuals regularly buying lottery tickets, such as a belief in luck, an illusion of control and unreasonable optimism. This illustrates that cognitive biases are a key feature in the maintenance of gambling behaviour into addiction.

Description

Learning theory, as applied to gambling addiction, focuses on the role of operant conditioning. Gambling behaviour is positively reinforced through the winning of bets, but there are more subtle reinforcements too, such as the pleasurable thrill experienced at the possibility of a win. With *partial* and *variable reinforcement*, gambling behaviour is reinforced only some of the time, such as: *fixed ratio reinforcement* (reinforcement comes after a set number of responses), *variable ratio reinforcement* (reinforcement comes after a set number of responses on average), *fixed interval reinforcement* (reinforcement comes after a set amount of time), and variable *interval reinforcement* (reinforcement comes after a set amount of time on

Fig 17.3 How can we best explain gambling behaviour?

✓ The best way to apply learning theory to an understanding of gambling addiction, is to see initiation of gambling behaviour as explicable through social learning theory, through observation and imitation of role models, and maintenance of behaviour through operant conditioning via reinforcements.

✓ Also well supported by research evidence, the cognitive explanation is improved if social aspects of gambling are considered alongside it. For example, someone may be initially attracted to gambling because they have financial problems which a quick win would solve. The maladaptive thinking that might then occur would fit the cognitive explanation.

average). These produce different response rates, with variable ratio reinforcement producing gambling behaviour the most resistant to extinction. *Classical conditioning* can have an influence through positive associations being made to gambling behaviour and social learning theory explains the initiation of gambling through observation and imitation of role models. *Cognitive theory* sees addiction occurring through maladaptive thought processes, with *cognitive bias* playing an important role through gamblers focusing on the positive aspects of gambling, like winning, and downplaying the negative aspects, like losing. Cognitive biases often produce an 'illusion of control' that gamblers can positively influence the outcomes of betting.

✘ **Negative evaluation**

✗ Use of self-reported introspection (like Griffiths getting participants to say their thoughts out loud) is difficult to test in an empirical way, and as such lowers the validity of explanations based on cognitive bias.

✗ Learning theory cannot explain why one person may have a big win and not become addicted to gambling, whereas another individual might. If learning theory was correct then all individuals would be affected equally. This reduces support for the explanation.

✗ Explaining gambling addiction through operant conditioning alone is an example of stimulus–response reductionism. Research suggests many other factors are also involved.

Practical application

Cognitive therapies centre on the idea of distorted thinking being responsible for gambling addiction. Making addicts aware of their irrational cognitive biases is an important first step in addressing gambling addictions.

AQA
A-level
Psychology
2

Jean-Marc Lawton
Eleanor Willard

pp. 409–15

17 Addiction
Reducing addiction

Curtiss *et al.* (1976) assessed the effectiveness of aversion therapy in treating nicotine addiction. The participants were all nicotine addicts who had expressed a desire to quit their smoking behaviour. The experiment had two conditions: one condition involved being part of a discussion group and rapid and continual smoking (in order to induce nausea and vomiting) and the second condition, which only involved participation in the discussion group. Five months after the treatment finished, the researchers measured the degree of smoking behaviour of the participants in both conditions. It was found that both groups had decreased the amount they smoked, but there was no significant difference in the effectiveness of the treatment for participants who had additionally received the aversion therapy. It was concluded that aversion therapy as a treatment for nicotine addiction is not effective as a treatment that produces long-term smoking cessation.

Description

Drug therapy is a biological method of reducing addiction. *Methadone* is used to treat heroin addiction by reducing cravings while constantly lowering the amount taken. Smoking addiction is treated with *nicotine replacement products*, like patches and gums. Sedatives like *benzodiazepines* are used to reduce cravings in alcoholics and *Antabuse* is given to induce nausea when alcohol is drunk. Antabuse is also a behavioural intervention, used as part of aversion therapy to break down positive associations of drinking alcohol and replace them with negative associations (feeling sick when drinking). This operates on the principles of classical conditioning with alcohol acting as a conditioned stimulus to produce

OTHER STUDIES

- McLellan *et al.* (1993) found that 69 per cent of participants receiving treatment of methadone only had to be withdrawn from the study, as they had eight consecutive positive urine samples indicating they were taking heroin again. Other treatment groups who received methadone plus other interventions, such as psychotherapy, responded far better, which suggests combination treatments are more effective.

- Ashem & Donner (1968) looked at the efficacy of covert sensitisation, finding that 40 per cent of patients receiving covert sensitisation for alcohol addiction, were still abstinent 6 months after treatment, whereas none of the control group remained alcohol free in that time. This suggests that covert sensitisation is an effective treatment for alcoholism.

- Young (2007) used self-report measures on 114 participants to assess the effectiveness of cognitive behavioural therapy in treating addiction to the internet. Over 6 months, 12 sessions of CBT were given, with most clients maintaining reductions in addictive behaviour 6 months later, demonstrating the effectiveness of the therapy.

Practical application

Research into treatments of addiction allows clinicians to learn which treatments are most effective for dealing with different sorts of individuals, who are suffering different types and degrees of addiction. This allows treatments to be more specifically targeted.

a conditioned response of vomiting. Another behavioural intervention is *covert sensitisation,* where, in a relaxed state, an alcoholic has to imagine feeling ill while drinking, then to imagine actually being sick in public. The greater the negative emotion produced, the greater chance the therapy has of working. *Cognitive behavioural therapy* on the other hand aims to alter the irrational thought processes associated with addiction. Addicts learn to recognise and challenge their irrational thinking and are taught substance-refusal and relapse-prevention skills, such as how to deal with everyday problems that could act as a gateway back into addiction.

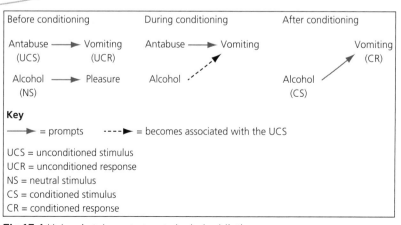

Before conditioning	During conditioning	After conditioning
Antabuse ⟶ Vomiting (UCS) (UCR)	Antabuse ⟶ Vomiting	Vomiting (CR)
Alcohol ⟶ Pleasure (NS)	Alcohol ⤏	Alcohol (CS)

Key

⟶ = prompts   ⤏ = becomes associated with the UCS

UCS = unconditioned stimulus
UCR = unconditioned response
NS = neutral stimulus
CS = conditioned stimulus
CR = conditioned response

Fig 17.4 Using Antabuse to treat alcohol addiction

pp. 417–25

17 Addiction

The application of theories of behaviour change to addictive behaviour

Focal study

Velicer *et al.* (2007) assessed the effectiveness of Prochaska's six-stage model of behaviour change to addictive behaviour. A meta-analysis of 5 studies involving 58,454 participants was conducted that investigated the success levels of smoking cessation programmes that were based upon Prochaska's model. It was found that there was a 22–26 per cent success rate in participants having maintained cessation of smoking behaviour 6 months after first withdrawing from smoking behaviour. The researchers found no demographic differences in success rates, such as gender or age related factors, which suggests the programme is widely applicable to all types of people. It was discovered though that success was generally dependent on how frequent smoking behaviour had originally been. As the success levels compare favourably with other types of intervention in addressing nicotine addiction, it suggests Prochaska's model can be regarded as being effective.

OTHER STUDIES

- Oh & Hsu (2001) used a questionnaire to assess gamblers' previous gambling behaviour, their social norms, attitudes, perceived behavioural control (such as perceived gambling skills and levels of self-control), along with behavioural intentions. A positive correlation was found between attitudes and behavioural intentions and actual behaviour, supporting the TPB.

- Walker *et al.* (2006) used interviews to assess whether theory of planned behaviour could explain gambling behaviour. It was found that behavioural beliefs and normative beliefs were important but that perceived behavioural control was not. Intention was, however, found to be a good predictor of behavioural change. This supports some elements of the TPB but not others.

- Aveyard *et al.* (2009) assessed the effectiveness of Prochaska's model, finding that there was no increase in effectiveness of cessation from smoking behaviour if an intervention was tailored to the stages of change an individual was in. This contradicts the findings of Velicer.

Description

The *Theory of Planned Behaviour* (TPB) sees attempts to abstain from dependency behaviours as due to factors supporting decision making, rather than predisposing factors, but with an added component where addicts need confidence in their abilities and available resources to quit. TPB has three components: *behavioural beliefs,* involving the subjective probability that behaviour will produce abstention; *normative beliefs,* involving the degree of perceived social pressure to quit; *control beliefs,* involving individual beliefs about the ability to abstain. TPB assesses an individual's motives for continuing dependency and their resolve to abstain. The higher their level of perceived behavioural control, the more likely

Practical application

Both models have applications as therapies to address addiction. Prochaska's model allows intervention to be tailored to which stage of change an individual is in, while the TPB is used to decide whether an intervention may be effective, which means money, time and effort can be saved if it will not be effective.

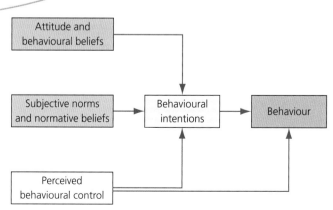

✓ Positive evaluation

✔ The TPB is used widely in health psychology and health economics (which examines the cost effectiveness of treatments). This suggests that practitioners acknowledge its validity and deem its predictive power as useful.

✔ A strength of the TPB is its acknowledgement of the role of peers in influencing behaviour. This influence does not stop once an addiction is developed and therefore needs to be considered in predicting outcomes of behaviour change programmes.

✔ Looking at change as a series of stages means that interventions can be designed to match the stage of Prochaska's model that an individual is currently in, with some evidence to support the effectiveness of this.

they'll quit. *Prochaska's six-stage model of behaviour change* details the process of changing from unhealthy to healthy behaviours. (1) *Pre-contemplation* involves recognition of unhealthy behaviour, but with no compulsion to address it. (2) *Contemplation* involves an admission that action is needed. (3) *Preparation* involves planning for how such action will occur. (4) *Action* involves putting the plan into action, which usually involves cutting down or withdrawing from the dependency behaviour. (5) *Maintenance* involves using strategies to prevent relapse, such as focusing on the benefits of withdrawal. (6) *Termination* involves reaching a state where temptation is no longer experienced.

✗ Negative evaluation

✗ There is no consideration of emotion within the TPB, which can influence the likelihood of behavioural change. This is especially the case with addiction, which is a vulnerable state influenced by mood.

✗ Both models rely on self-report measures to assess their effectiveness, which could be problematic, as addicts are often not in a state to honestly appraise their own behaviour and frame of mind.

✗ Research support for Prochaska's model is mixed, lowering support for the explanation. It may be that wide individual differences mean the model suits some, but not all cases of addiction.

Fig 17.5 Theory of Planned Behaviour (Ajzen, 1991)

pp. 425–29

221

18 Revision and exam skills
Revision

HOW TO REVISE EXAM QUESTIONS

When first practising exam questions you will need all learning materials to hand, such as notes and handouts. Ensure you fully understand the requirements of the question from the *command words* and know how much to write by referring to the number of *marks* on offer. Make a plan in numbered or bullet point form, and then have a go at writing your answer, giving yourself the same amount of time as in the real exam (about 1 minute and 15 seconds per mark). You will probably have to refer to learning materials when writing your answer, but as you become familiar with this method, you will increasingly be able to write answers without them. A good way to achieve this is to read through relevant materials first, then put them away before writing your answer.

Revision strategies

Many students incorrectly see revision as something done immediately before examinations. Although pre-examination revision is important, revision is something that you should incorporate into your studies regularly throughout the course and indeed is an integral part of the learning process. At the end of studying each element of a topic, revise the material to develop a deeper understanding and to check that you have covered everything and that you fully understand it. The best way to achieve this is to engage with the material, for example by reading through notes/worksheets etc. and highlighting the main points. Make use of available textbooks to further elaborate your

PRE-EXAMINATION REVISION

All topics need to be revised, including ones you find difficult, as they have an equal chance of being on the exam paper. Ensure you have listed all the topics on the specification and have all materials necessary for revising each topic. Find somewhere comfortable to revise away from distractions. Make sure that everything you need for revising, like tidying up your desk, is done before revision starts. It is easy to spend all the designated revision time on distraction activities, like sorting out books and sharpening pencils. About 90 minutes a session will be best, using the revision method you have practised all year – namely, reading through necessary materials, highlighting important points, using previous exam questions to construct answers. Give yourself a planned reward for completing revision sessions, be it chocolate or a favourite TV programme. Revising in a constant, organised way like this is the best route to maximising exam performance.

knowledge; better candidates will be making use of more than just one source of information. After this, attempt an exam-type question to assess your level of knowledge and understanding and also to familiarise yourself with the kind of questions you may be asked in the exam. Such questions can be accessed on the AQA website, where you will find sample questions. These also include (in the mark schemes) advice on what types of things to include in your answer. Over time, make sure that you include all types of possible questions in your revision, not just those concerning outlining and describing, but also those requiring explanations and evaluations.

MAKING A REVISION TIMETABLE

Before starting pre-exam revision you will need a revision timetable. This is best achieved by having morning, afternoon and evening sessions for each day (though there is no reason why you can't divide your days up differently, for example just morning and afternoon sessions, or even hour by hour). You can then use this as a template for each separate week of revision.

For each of your subjects, make a list of the topics you need to revise. Then, using a pencil at first, slot in the topics, making sure that you first block out any sessions that are not available due to other commitments. It is probably best initially to revise subjects and topics that will be examined first. A revision programme has to be achievable, so ensure that there are a few spare slots each week to use if any planned revision sessions do not occur. When you have finally got all the topics entered, colour them in using a different colour for each subject.

Put your revision timetable up on a wall and tick off sessions as you go. You might even give a copy to a parent so they can police you and make sure sessions get done. Having a revision timetable like this increases confidence that revision can be completed, which in turn increases motivation to revise.

Time	Monday	Tuesday	Wednesday	Thursday	Friday	Saturday	Sunday
9am-11am	Social influence		Memory			Attachment	
11am-1pm	BREAK	BREAK	BREAK	BREAK	BREAK	BREAK	BREAK
1pm-3pm		Psychopathology			Research methods		
3pm-5pm	BREAK	BREAK	BREAK	BREAK	BREAK	BREAK	BREAK
5pm-7pm				Approaches			Biopsychology
7pm-9pm		Research methods					

Fig 18.1 Revision timetable

18 Revision and exam skills
Exam skills

The exams

For the A-level qualification, students sit three papers:
- **Paper 1** is called *Introductory topics* and consists of four sections: the social psychology topic of *social influence*, the cognitive psychology topic of *memory*, the developmental psychology topic of *attachment* and the individual differences topic of *psychopathology*. Each of these sections is worth 24 marks, for a total of 96 marks. Research methods questions may be incorporated into all four of these sections. Paper 1 accounts for one-third of the overall marks for the A-level. You will have 2 hours to sit this paper, with all questions being compulsory for all candidates.
- **Paper 2** is called *Psychology in context* and consists of three sections: *approaches*, *biopsychology* and *research methods*. Approaches and biopsychology are worth 24 marks each, with research methods worth 48 marks, for a total of 96 marks (and thus an overall total for both papers of 192 marks). Research methods questions can again occur in all sections. Paper 2 accounts for one-third of the overall marks for the A-level. You will have 2 hours to sit this paper, with all questions being compulsory for all candidates.
- **Paper 3** is called *Issues and options in psychology* and consists of four sections: (a) the compulsory topic of *issues and debates,* worth 24 marks, then three optional sections: (b) *relationships, gender, cognition and development*, (c) *schizophrenia, eating behaviour, stress*, and (d) *aggression, forensic psychology, addiction*. Each of these is worth 24 marks and candidates answer questions on one topic from each section. Paper 3 accounts for one-third of the overall marks for the A-level. You will have 2 hours to sit this paper, with a total of 96 marks available.

The exam process
You may have attended all lessons, completed all work, revised hard and be extremely motivated to succeed. However, unless you perform well in your examinations you won't get what you deserve. Therefore, it is essential that you fully understand the exam process in order to achieve and get that grade you want.

TYPES OF MARKS

There are three types of marks that can be gained in the examination.
- **AO1 marks** – these are awarded for relevant *description* of psychological knowledge. For example, describing the multi-store model of memory. The availability of these marks in a question can be identified by the use of certain *exam injunctions* ('command words' – the words in a question that inform you what kind of answer is required) within the question (see oppostite for a list and explanation of exam injunctions).
- **AO2 marks** – these are awarded for relevant *application* of psychological knowledge to scenarios that are provided. For example, applying your knowledge of normative social influence to a scenario that illustrates its usage. The availability of these marks in a question can again be identified by the use of certain *exam injunctions*.
- **AO3 marks** – these are awarded for relevant *evaluation* of psychological knowledge. For example, assessing the degree of research support for the learning theory explanation of attachment formation. The availability of these marks in a question once again can be identified by the use of certain *exam injunctions*.

Exam injunctions are the 'command words' in a question, the words that tell you what kind of answer is required in terms of description, application and evaluation. Some questions may involve creating answers that focus on only one of these injunctions, for example a 'description only' answer, while other questions may involve creating answers that focus on two exam injunctions, for example a 'description and evaluation' question. There is even the possibility of an 'application essay', which would require creating an answer that focuses on all three of the injunctions.

In order to fully understand what type of answer you should be writing, familiarise yourself with the following different exam injunctions. This should help you to avoid the trap of writing answers that contain irrelevant material in terms of what a question requires.

AO1 injunctions

- *Identify* means simply to name, no other description is required
- *Define* involves explaining what is meant by
- *Outline* means give brief details without explanation
- *Describe* means give a detailed account without explanation
- *Correctly complete* means to fill in the missing information
- *Select* means to choose the correct option

AO2 injunctions

- *Refer* means to include information from a certain source

AO3 injunctions

- *Give* means to show awareness of
- *Explain* means to give a clear account of why and how something is so
- *Evaluate* means to assess the value or effectiveness of
- *Discuss* means to give a reasoned balanced account (including descriptive and evaluative material)
- *Assess* means to judge the quality/importance of

Different question types

There are, broadly speaking, six main types of question and students should ensure that they have had regular experience, under exam conditions, of each of them. Remember that all topics can be examined by each of the question types, so ideally students should be familiar with all question types for all the topics listed in the specification.

Each question type is quite different from other question types and has a certain way in which it must be answered to maximise marks. Therefore it is worthwhile having a look at some common mistakes that students make with each question type and learning some strategies that will help to increase the marks you gain in the actual examination. The differences between one grade and another in the examination can be just a few marks, so by learning and practising strategies that maximise your marks you could easily improve by one or two grades. Let's have a look at the question types now. Sample question answers are on **pages 227, 229, 231, 234–37, 239–41, 243–45**.

18 Revision and exam skills
Question practice: selection questions

With this type of question students are given information from which they select appropriate choices. There will often be a spare option left over at the end. This is so that a choice always has to be made between options when answering the question.

Questions

1 Match the following descriptions to the types of LTM listed in the table below. One description will be left over. [3 marks]

A Knowing that a telephone is for communicating with people

B Knowing how to ice-skate properly

C Being able to recall someone's phone number you've just been given by repeating it sub-vocally

D Knowing that your sister is younger than you

Type of LTM	Description
Semantic	
Episodic	
Procedural	

2 Select from the following descriptions to complete the table below concerning sex and gender. One statement will be left over. [4 marks]

A Low masculinity, low femininity

B High masculinity, low femininity

C Moderate masculinity, moderate femininity

D High masculinity, high femininity

E High femininity, low masculinity

Category of person	Description
Masculine	
Feminine	
Androgynous	
Undifferentiated	

Strategies for improvement

✔ Ensure you have regular experience of this question type.

✔ Attempt selection questions for all topic areas.

✔ Create your own selection questions, swap them with other students and then mark their answers.

✔ Identify the command words (the words that inform what specific information/skill is required) in questions before attempting them. First though you will need to understand what the types of command words used in questions mean (see **page 225**).

✔ Use the marks in brackets that appear after a question as an indication of how many selections are required.

Common pitfalls

✘ Unfamiliarity with such questions

✘ Not understanding the requirements of the question

✘ Not making sufficient selections

Answer 1

Type of LTM	Description
Semantic	A
Episodic	C
Procedural	B

Exam tip

1 mark is earned for each correct selection, up to a maximum of 3 marks.

Feedback

2/3 marks. 1 mark for selecting statement A as being an example of semantic memory and 1 mark for selecting statement B as an example of procedural memory, but no marks for selecting statement C as an example of episodic memory – the correct selection there should have been statement D.

Answer 2

Category of person	Description
Masculine	B
Feminine	E
Androgynous	D
Undifferentiated	A

Exam tip

1 mark is earned for each correct selection, up to a maximum of 4 marks.

Feedback

4/4 marks. All four correct selections have been made – option C has correctly not been used as it does not fit any of the categories featured in the table.

18 Revision and exam skills
Question practice: short-answer questions

With this type of question, very specific brief answers are generally required, with a need for elaboration (detail) to gain any additional marks available.

Short-answer questions can require description-only type answers (AO1) (such as questions 1 and 3 below) or evaluation-only type answers (AO3) (such as questions 2 and 4 below).

Questions

1 Outline the deviation from social norms definition of abnormality.   [3 marks]
2 Explain one strength of the deviation from social norms definition of abnormality.   [2 marks]
3 Outline one explanation for success in dieting.   [3 marks]
4 Explain one limitation of the genetic explanation for obesity.   [2 marks]

Strategies for improvement

✔ Identify the command word(s) before attempting the question (as with selection questions).

✔ Use the marks in brackets as a guide as to how much to write. In an exam you would have about 1 minute 15 seconds per mark available, so a 2-mark short-answer question should take you about 2 minutes 30 seconds to answer, while a 3-mark question should take about 3 minutes 45 seconds. As the average student writes about 20 words a minute, that works out at 50 words for a 2-mark question and 75 words for a 3-mark question.

✔ Use the partial mark technique. This can be used for short-answer questions worth up to 3 marks, as such questions are assessed by examiners referring to mark descriptors, which guide examiners as to what an answer should contain to earn different amounts of marks.

✔ If, for example, a question is worth 3 marks, create an answer worth 1 mark and then add sufficient elaboration (detail) to earn 2 marks and then again to create an answer worth 3 marks. So for the question 'Outline one explanation for failure in dieting [3 marks]', first produce an answer worth 1 mark, such as, '**One explanation for failure in dieting is creating an unsustainable form of dieting.**' Then give sufficient elaboration to gain the second available mark, such as adding '**such as by restricting themselves to far too few calories a day so that the diet cannot be sustained.**' Finally, give further elaboration to gain access to the third mark available, such as then adding '**An extremely low-calorie diet brings unpleasant side-effects, such as dizziness and stress, which leads to loss of motivation and abandonment of the diet.**' Create examples for all topics on the specification. You could even match up with another student and answer and mark each other's efforts.

✔ Practise short-answer questions regularly under exam-type conditions.

Common pitfalls

✘ Not addressing the requirements of the question, for example outlining a definition of abnormality when the question asks for a strength or limitation

✘ Giving an accurate, relevant answer but not providing any/enough elaboration

✘ Writing too much – reducing time available for other questions and gaining no extra marks

Answer 1

The definition sees abnormality as behaviour that violates social rules, such as by being naked in public.

Answer 2

One strength of the definition would be that it helps protect society.

Answer 3

Success in dieting can occur through creating incentives for weight loss. Positive reinforcements could be used to reward meeting weight-loss targets.

Answer 4

One limitation of the genetic explanation for obesity is that genes cannot explain the recent upsurge in obesity levels. Genes haven't changed, but environmental factors, like the availability of food, have, which suggests environment plays a larger role.

Feedback

Answer 1: 2/3 marks. 1 mark is earned for stating that the definition sees abnormality as behaviour violating social rules, with the example sufficient to earn an additional mark. Additional elaboration would be needed to gain the third mark, such as by explaining that 'social norms are unwritten rules for acceptable behaviour'.

Answer 2: 1/2 marks. A relevant strength is identified, so a mark is gained, but there is no elaboration to show understanding of the point made, such as that the definition helps protect society by allowing the state to intervene in abnormal people's lives.

Answer 3: 2/3 marks. 1 mark is earned for presenting an accurate and relevant answer, involving the use of incentives for weight loss, with an additional mark earned for elaboration concerning the use of positive reinforcements for meeting weight-loss targets. Additional elaboration would be needed to gain the third mark, such as by providing a relevant example of a positive reinforcement, e.g. the purchasing of new clothes to fit their new body shape, to show an understanding of how such positive reinforcements work.

Answer 4: 2/2 marks. 1 mark is earned for presenting an accurate and relevant answer, involving the recent upsurge in obesity levels, with an additional mark earned for the elaboration concerning the contribution of environmental factors.

Exam tip

Answers 1 and 3: 1 mark would be earned for a relevant point, with up to 2 further marks for sufficient elaboration (detail).

Exam tip

Answers 2 and 4: 1 mark would be earned for a relevant point, with an additional mark for sufficient elaboration.

Question practice: application questions

With this type of question answers require relevant psychological knowledge to be combined with information drawn from a given scenario. The key is to provide the necessary psychological knowledge (e.g. explaining what unanimity is and its effect on conformity), while simultaneously using information drawn from the scenario as evidence to support the explanation. Generally speaking, if only psychological knowledge is provided (however good the description is) and there is no application to the scenario, then only half marks can be awarded.

Questions

1 When a group of Trevor's friends said they all thought that the tea in the college cafeteria tasted like coffee, Trevor found himself publicly agreeing with them, even though privately he thought it did taste like tea. However, a few days later when his friends agreed again that the tea tasted like coffee but one friend stated that she thought it tasted like drinking chocolate, Trevor felt able to truthfully state that it tasted like tea.

   Refer to the scenario above to explain how unanimity affects conformity rates.   [4 marks]

2 Betty has been diagnosed as suffering from schizophrenia. She began hearing voices that criticised her behaviour and became convinced that she had been chosen by God to save the human race. Her family found it increasingly hard to understand her speech and she would only answer questions with very brief answers. It was also noticeable how Betty, who usually dressed very smartly, had become scruffy in her appearance and unenthusiastic about life in general, though she would spend hours walking backwards and forwards in her room.

   Refer to the scenario above to identify negative and positive symptoms of schizophrenia.

[4 marks]

Strategies for improvement

✓ Use the marks in brackets at the end of the question as an indication of how much to write.
✓ Use the PEA rule: (P) make a critical point, (E) explain it, (A) apply it.
✓ Use two highlighter pens, one colour to highlight psychological knowledge and another colour to highlight the application in your answer. That way you can easily see whether you are getting the 'balance' right between the amount of psychological knowledge and application to the scenario.
✓ Practise answers in pairs – one of you does the theory part, the other one does the application part.
✓ Regularly practise strategies that get you to apply your psychological knowledge to a specific scenario until it becomes an automatic process to do so.
✓ Make sure you have attempted application type questions for all topic areas.

Common pitfalls

✗ Giving the correct psychological knowledge but not linking it to the scenario
✗ Commenting about the scenario without linking it to relevant knowledge
✗ Not writing sufficient information to gain access to all the marks available

Answer 1

Unanimity concerns how much agreement there is within a majority group. The greater the level of agreement, the more likely it is that an individual would conform. In a variation of Asch's experiment, one dissenter gave the correct answer when the rest of the confederates all gave the same wrong answer and conformity fell from the 32 per cent that occurred when all confederates gave the wrong answer to just 5.5 per cent. Indeed, when a dissenter gave a different wrong answer, conformity still fell sharply to 9 per cent. This shows that dissenters model that disagreement with a majority is possible.

Feedback

2/4 marks. A really good, informative and coherent explanation of what unanimity is and how a lack of it reduces conformity. Well backed up with relevant research evidence too. Unfortunately, as too many students do with this type of question, there is no engagement with the scenario. The candidate here could easily have talked about how Trevor felt pressured to conform when all his friends said the tea tasted like coffee, but less pressured when a dissenter gave a different answer to the majority, even though their opinion was different again to Trevor's.

Exam tip

However good the quality of the psychological knowledge concerning how unanimity affects conformity rates, no more than 2 marks would be earned unless there was sufficient reference to the scenario to back up the points made.

Answer 2

Betty is experiencing delusions and hallucinations which suggest a lack of reality. For example, she is hearing critical voices and she is convinced that she has been chosen by God to save the human race. Such behaviours are known as positive symptoms.

Negative symptoms interfere with normal functioning and in the case of Betty these include her answering questions with only brief answers and being unenthusiastic about life and becoming scruffy in her appearance.

Feedback

4/4 marks. Both negative and positive symptoms are identified within the scenario and are clearly explained in a way that suggests understanding of the terms. The answer is applied to the information given within the scenario to such an extent that full marks can be awarded.

Exam tip

However good the quality of the psychological knowledge concerning positive and negative symptoms of schizophrenia, no more than 2 marks would be earned unless there was sufficient reference to the scenario to back up the points made.

18 Revision and exam skills
Question practice: research methods questions

This type of question requires answers centred on aspects of research methods, often focused on questions formed around specific topic areas. Sometimes such questions are orientated at a general research methods topic area, for example, Question 1.

Such questions therefore require an answer focused only on the general topic area specified, in this case the strengths of peer review. However, this type of question can also be more specific in its requirements, for example, Question 2 concerning Asch's conformity study.

Research methods questions can often involve mathematical skills. They may require calculations, such as in Question 3, drawn from the attachment topic.

Such questions can also merely require knowledge of mathematical skills to be exhibited, such as in Question 4.

Questions

1. Explain one limitation of the role of peer review in the scientific process. [2 marks]

2. Asch (1955) performed a famous laboratory experiment investigating normative social influence. Explain one strength of the design used in this study. [2 marks]

3. A researcher wished to know whether infants have formed their first attachment by 7 months of age by using measurements of separation distress and stranger anxiety with 10 babies. The findings from the study can be seen in the table below showing number of 7-month-old babies who had formed an attachment.

Infant	Attachment or no attachment
1	Yes
2	No
3	Yes
4	No
5	Yes
6	Yes
7	Yes
8	Yes
9	Yes
10	Yes

Using the data from the table on infant attachment, calculate a sign test to assess whether the number of infants with an attachment is significant at the 0.05 significance level for a one-tailed (directional) hypothesis. You will need to make reference to the critical value table below to achieve this. Show your calculations.   [3 marks]

The table below shows the critical values for the sign test.

Level of significance for a two-tailed test				
	0.05	0.025	0.01	0.005
Level of significance for a one-tailed test				
N	0.01	0.05	0.02	0.01
5	0	–	–	–
6	0	0	–	–
7	0	0	0	–
8	1	0	0	0
9	1	1	0	0
10	1	1	0	0
11	2	1	1	0
12	2	2	1	1
13	3	2	1	1
14	3	2	2	1
15	3	3	2	2
16	4	3	2	2
17	4	4	3	2
18	5	4	3	3
19	5	4	4	3
20	5	5	4	3

4   Explain what is meant by ordinal level data.   [1 mark]

5   (After description of a research study) The study uses a repeated measures design. Explain one strength of the repeated measures design.   [2 marks]

6   A researcher tested the effect of sleep deprivation by getting two groups of participants, one who had 8 hours sleep the previous night and one who had none, to do an IQ test. One group of participants did the test in one room while the other group did it in a different room.

Identify a possible extraneous variable in the above study and explain what its effect could be on the findings if it was uncontrolled.   [3 marks]

7   A group of female participants and a group of male participants read some information about the meanings of various words and 1 week later were given a test of recall to assess their semantic LTM ability. The scores gained in the test can be seen in the table below.

Participant	Male scores on test of semantic LTM (out of 20)	Female scores on test of semantic LTM (out of 20)
1	10	11
2	11	10
3	14	16
4	8	9
5	16	15
6	8	9
7	12	11
8	9	11

Calculate the mean score for semantic LTM for male participants. Show your calculations.   [2 marks]

8   What type of graph should be used to plot data from a correlational analysis?   [1 mark]

Strategies for improvement

✔   Identify command words before attempting an answer.

✔   Use marks in brackets as a guide to how much to write/how much elaboration is required.

✔   Practise these types of questions for all topic areas regularly.

✔   Use the partial answer technique.

Common pitfalls

✘   Not addressing the requirements of the question (for example, providing evaluation in a question that only needs description or providing description in a question that only requires evaluation)

✘   Not writing/elaborating enough to gain access to all of the marks available

✘   Using relevant knowledge but not applying it to the specific circumstances, for example when the question says 'in this study' but only giving a general answer

Answer 1

One limitation of the role of peer review is that it is not always unbiased and objective.

Feedback

1/2 marks. Correct, but no elaboration of the point, so only 1 mark. The candidate could have gone on to explain why it can be biased, for example that a reviewer may have a negative social relationship with a study's author.

Exam tip

1 mark would be earned by making a relevant point, with an additional mark available for sufficient elaboration.

Answer 2

Asch's study used an independent measures design and one strength of this is that there were no order effects, as participants only did one of the two conditions of the study.

Feedback

2/2 marks. 1 mark for correct identification of a strength and the additional mark for explaining sufficiently why it is a strength.

Exam tip

To gain the first mark a relevant strength must be identified, with the second mark being gained by providing elaboration that shows an understanding of why this is a strength.

Answer 3

S = 2 and the critical value is 1. This is not significant.

Feedback

2/3 marks. The calculation of the test is correct, as is stating it to be significant. However, the calculations made are not provided.

Exam tip

1 mark for correct calculation of the sign test, with an additional mark for stating whether this is significant or not. The other available mark would be gained by providing the calculations made.

Answer 4

Ordinal level data means that the data can be put into rank order, such as 1st, 2nd, 3rd and so forth.

Feedback
1/1 mark. A clear and correct answer.

Exam tip
1 mark for explaining what ordinal data is in a way that differentiates it from other forms of data, such as nominal or interval/ratio data.

Answer 5

One strength of a repeated measures design is that there are no participant variables.

Feedback
1/2 marks. Correct, but no elaboration of the point, so only 1 mark. The candidate could have gone on to explain why there are no participant variables, for example because each participant is compared against themselves.

Exam tip
1 mark would be earned by making a relevant point, with an additional mark available for sufficient elaboration.

Answer 6

One extraneous variable could be the fact that the participants did the test in different rooms. This could make the results invalid.

Feedback
2/3 marks. 1 mark for correct identification of a possible extraneous variable and 1 additional mark for the comments on the validity of the results. Elaboration would be required to gain the other mark, possibly by explaining how the extraneous variable could become a confounding one.

Exam tip
To gain the first mark on offer an extraneous variable needs to be identified, but this must be drawn from the scenario. The other 2 marks would be for explaining its possible effect in confounding the results. Sufficient elaboration would be necessary to get the second mark here.

Answer 7
The mean is 11.
Working out:
10 + 11 + 14 + 8 + 16 + 8 + 12 + 9 = 88
88 divided by 8 = 11

Feedback
2/2 marks. Correct and the calculations are shown, so full marks.

Exam tip
1 mark for correct calculation of the mean, with an additional mark for showing the calculations to achieve this.

Answer 8
A scattergram would be used.

Feedback
1/1 mark. Correct.

Exam tip
1 mark for each correct identification of a scattergram (or scattergraph).

Question practice: research study questions

This type of question requires answers that focus on description and/or evaluation of research studies. Descriptive content will need to be focused on aims, procedure and conclusions of research studies, while evaluation could centre on methodological and ethical considerations, as well as what conclusions can be drawn, for example the degree of support for an explanation. There are some studies that are explicitly listed in the specification, such as Ainsworth's 'Strange Situation' or Pavlov's research into classical conditioning, so these could form the basis of such questions, for example Questions 1 and 3, which are drawn from the Attachment and Approaches topics. Questions could also be asked that allow a choice of research study, for example Questions 2 and 4.

Questions

1   Outline the aims and findings of Ainsworth's 'Strange Situation' study of attachment.

[6 marks]

2   Outline and evaluate one research study of memory. [6 marks]

3   Outline Pavlov's research into classical conditioning. [6 marks]

4   Outline and evaluate one research study of the biological treatment of OCD. [6 marks]

Strategies for improvement

✔ Identify command words before attempting an answer.

✔ Use marks in brackets as a guide to how much to write/how much elaboration is required.

✔ Make sure you have studied a research study in sufficient detail (aims, procedure, findings, conclusions and evaluative points) for all topic areas.

✔ Make sure you have studied in sufficient detail all studies that are explicitly listed in the specification.

✔ Practise these types of questions for all topic areas regularly.

Common pitfalls

✘ Providing a lack of necessary detail

✘ Focusing on the wrong elements of a study (for example, giving findings and conclusion when the question explicitly asks for the aims and procedure)

✘ Using studies solely as a form of evaluation rather than describing the necessary features

Answer 1

The aim of Ainsworth's 'Strange Situation' study was to test how infants behaved under conditions of mild stress and novelty and to assess differences in mother and infant pairs in terms of the quality of their attachments. Ainsworth found three main types of attachment: Type A – insecure-avoidant, Type B – securely attached and Type C – insecure-resistant. However, although the 'Strange Situation' is regarded as a reliable measurement of attachment type, as it produces consistent results, it is not seen as a valid measurement, as it does not measure an infant's general attachment type but its attachment type to one specific person.

Feedback

3/6 marks. Two relevant aims of Ainsworth's study are clearly stated and the findings quoted about types of attachment are accurate. However, the findings lack detail – a brief description of the behaviours associated with the different attachment types would have easily gained the other marks available. Also, unfortunately the final comments about the reliability and validity of the study, although accurate, are not relevant to the question, as they are a form of evaluation.

Exam tip

Marks would only be awarded for description of Ainsworth's aims and findings, so any outlining of procedure or evaluation of the study would not earn credit and would waste valuable time. The actual mark gained would depend on the level of accurate detail provided.

Answer 2

One research study of memory was Peterson & Peterson's (1959) study of the duration of short-term memories. Participants were presented briefly with nonsense trigrams, words of three letters that did not make sense, and then asked to count backwards in 3s from 100 (to stop rehearsal of the presented trigram) for varying amounts of time. About 90 per cent of participants correctly recalled trigrams after 3 seconds, but only 5 per cent after 18 seconds, which suggests that the duration of short-term memories is quite short.

The task performed in this laboratory experiment, recalling trigrams, is not an everyday task and so can be said to lack ecological validity and so may not reflect the duration of short-term memories in real-life scenarios.

Feedback

5/6 marks. A relevant study is selected and is detailed in a fashion that shows a thorough knowledge of the study in terms of its aims, procedure and findings. A brief conclusion is given, as well as a fair point concerning the study's lack of ecological validity, which is done in such a way as to suggest the candidate understands what the term means. However, the answer probably needs a little more in terms of evaluation to deserve being awarded all the marks available. For example, there could be some comment about whether the short duration of memory was due to the information decaying over time or whether displacement of the letters in a trigram was occurring by the numbers that were being said aloud because the capacity of short-term memory is limited to a maximum of about 9 items.

Exam tip

The answer calls for both description and evaluation of a relevant research study, which could be achieved by detailing the aims, procedure and findings. The evaluation could focus on relevant methodological and ethical points, as well as what conclusions could be drawn about the results.

Answer 3

Pavlov was the pioneer researcher into classical conditioning. He became interested while researching the role of salivation in digestion in dogs as to how dogs learned through association to predict the arrival of their food. Using the reflex action of salivation, Pavlov found that if a bell was rung 7 times when food was presented to a dog, it would subsequently salivate just to the bell. Originally the dog would only have salivated to the presentation of food. It was concluded that the dog had learned to associate the sound of the bell to being fed, hence the salivation in anticipation of food.

Feedback

4/6 marks. A 'solid' description of Pavlov's research is evident. It is accurate, relevant and coherent. However, there is a lack of detail and specialist terminology, which prevents the answer being placed in the top level of marks. This could have been achieved by using specialist terms such as unconditioned stimulus, conditioned stimulus and conditioned response when describing Pavlov's research to show a higher level of detail and understanding.

Exam tip

Marks would only be awarded for description of Pavlov's research, so any evaluation would not earn credit and would waste valuable time. The actual mark gained would depend on the level of accurate detail provided.

Answer 4

One research study into the effectiveness of anti-depressants in treating OCD was a study by Koran et al. (2000). They aimed to see how effective Olanzapine was when combined with the SRI drug Fluoxetine in treating non-responsive forms of OCD. There were 10 participants, all of whom had had OCD for at least a year. They were being treated with Fluoxetine and increased levels of Olanzapine were then added to their treatment for 8 weeks. The findings showed that the combined treatment was superior in reducing symptoms than by treatments with just Fluoxetine alone. Some participants did suffer the side-effect of significant weight increase.

Feedback

4/6 marks. A good answer in terms of description. There is accurate and somewhat detailed reference to the aim, procedure and findings of the study. However, the answer is unbalanced as only the final sentence can be classed as evaluation.

Exam tip

The answer calls for both description and evaluation of a relevant research study, which could be achieved by detailing the aims, procedure and findings. The evaluation could focus on relevant methodological and ethical points, as well as what conclusions could be drawn about the effectiveness of the treatment.

18 Revision and exam skills

Question practice: essays and longer-answer questions

This type of question will generally require both descriptive and evaluative material (but could be just description or evaluation), with a maximum of 16 marks at A-level. Such questions can include application essays requiring description and/or evaluation with, additionally, use of information drawn from a scenario provided.

Questions

1 Discuss the nature–nurture debate.   [16 marks]

2 '5-year-old Breagha has always liked sweet-tasting foods, such as honey and cakes, but has also always shown a dislike for bitter and sour-tasting foods, like broccoli and lemons.'

   Outline and evaluate evolutionary explanations for food preferences. In your answer make reference to the experience of Breagha.   [16 marks]

Strategies for improvement

✔ Identify command words before starting an answer.

✔ Practise writing to the mark allocation – remember it is about 1 minute 15 seconds per mark (that is 7½ minutes of description and 7½ minutes of evaluation in a 12-mark question) or alternatively about 20 words per minute.

✔ Structure answers so that they have a common 'theme' running through them.

✔ Shape material to specifically meet the requirements of a question.

✔ Use methodological material only where it specifically fits the needs of a question.

✔ Practise dividing answers into separate paragraphs.

✔ Create (and practise using) lists of specialist terms that go with each topic area.

✔ Practise building your evaluative material into elaborated commentaries that use several types of evaluation built upon each other.

✔ Shape material as evaluation by signalling its usage as such – for example, by using phrases such as 'research support comes from...' and 'these findings suggest that....'.

✔ Practise assessments under exam conditions regularly.

Common pitfalls

✘ Failure to address command words

✘ Not writing to the mark allocation – often by producing too much description

✘ Wandering off the question

✘ Irrelevant use of methodological points

✘ Lack of organisation into paragraphs

✘ Lack of specialist terminology

✘ Lack of elaboration/commentary

✘ Not 'shaping' material as evaluation – material intended as evaluation can often be phrased as descriptive material

✘ Use of generic content (material that is not specifically focused on the question)

Answer 1

Psychologists who adopt a nativist perspective believe that the cause of behaviour is the result of nature in the form of innate factors, such as genes and hormones; on the other hand, psychologists who adopt an empirical perspective believe that behaviour is the result of the environment and develops through experience (nurture).

What is noticeable here from the start is the accurate use of specialist terminology, such as 'nativist', 'innate' and 'empirical'. This helps to show the candidate's level of understanding, as well as summarising the debate.

Research into the debate has often focused on twin studies in which MZ twins who are 100 per cent identical are studied. The rationale behind such research is that if their behaviour is identical then nature/genetics could be concluded to be the cause; however, if their behaviour is not identical then the cause must be nurture and a result of the environment/experiences. Such an approach has been used to investigate schizophrenia and criminality; however, caution is required, as MZ twins are often raised in identical environments, being treated in identical ways, and therefore cause and effect is hard to establish as it could equally be concluded that the environment and nurture were the cause of behaviour, therefore it is hard to isolate nature/nurture factors.

The material on the rationale of studies (the thinking behind them) counts as AO1 description, though the final comment about cause and effect relationships is an evaluatory AO3 comment.

Geneticists suggest that they have developed a mathematical equation which can be used to calculate the influence of genetics and the environment on behaviour. This is known as the heritability equation and can be used to calculate the contribution of each factor on behaviour. This equation was used by Shakeshaft, who stated that IQ is influenced 64 per cent by genetics. However, caution again is needed in the interpretation of such findings, as again it is hard to isolate purely nature influences – for example, in the Shakeshaft study it was suggested that the figure of 64 per cent genetic influence on IQ was only relevant to middle-class children; for children from poorer backgrounds the influence was closer to 10 per cent, therefore suggesting socio-economic and environmental factors may be affecting educational achievement.

The first sentence is AO1 description, with after that some good evidence of combining evaluatory points into a structured 'commentary', always a good route to gaining higher-level marks.

Perhaps a more suitable approach to explain behaviour would be to adopt an interactionist approach. This approach suggests that to obtain a true understanding of behaviour it is vital to understand the role of both nature and nurture. This would suggest that our genes may make us predisposed to behave in a certain way, but environmental circumstances must exist for it to do so. Therefore recent research has tended to acknowledge the potential influence of both nature and nurture by adopting an interactionist and less reductionist approach.

The material here on interactionism has been shaped as evaluation, that is to say commenting on its suitability as an explanation as opposed to both the nature and nurture points of view. There are more marks available for evaluation (10) than description (6), so it is a sensible strategy.

243

Feedback

12/16 marks. The descriptive material is accurate and has clarity, while the evaluative content is well shaped to the question. However, there is probably a need for more evaluation in the form of research evidence and for more detailed development of evaluative material to show a higher level of understanding.

Exam tip

Only 6 marks are available for the description, in this particular instance the nature–nurture debate, so don't over-describe it, as the majority of the marks, 10 of them, are available for the evaluation. In terms of time that is about 7½ minutes to describe the debate and 12½ minutes to evaluate it. Also, effective evaluation will be created by forming evaluative points together into a structured commentary rather than being a series of unconnected evaluative points.

Answer 2

In the Environment of Evolutionary Adaptiveness (EEA), food was often only periodically available, so it made sense for humans to evolve, through natural selection, the ability to not only find food, but to identify which foods were highly nutritious and energy-rich and which ones were potentially harmful and toxic and so should be avoided. Evolutionary explanations see a preference for sweet-tasting foodstuffs becoming widespread in the population because sweetness in a foodstuff suggests that it is energy-rich and also non-poisonous. Breagha therefore has a preference for sugary foods like honey and cakes because she has inherited the evolutionary ability to prefer sweet-tasting foods.

An accurate description of the evolutionary explanation for sweet-taste preferences is provided that shows a good level of understanding. This is then well linked to the experience of Breagha.

Desor et al. (1973) and Steiner (1977), using choice preferences and facial expressions, found neonates prefer sweet foods to bitter ones, which implies the preference to be innate. This was backed up by Meiselman (1977), who found people of all ages prefer sweet foods to other tastes, and further supported by Capaldi et al. (1989), who found this was also true for other species, such as horses, bears and ants. However, some doubt is thrown onto the idea of a universal preference for sweet tastes, as Stefansson (1960) reported that Copper Eskimos were disgusted by the first ever taste of sugar, which lowers the validity of the evolutionary explanation, as if it was valid, then the preference should have been universal. A practical application of a sweet-tasting preference is the idea of placing a tax on sugar, to reduce consumption, as over-indulgence is associated with becoming obese.

The candidate moves on to providing research support for an evolved sweet-taste preference, joining several pieces of research into a reasonable commentary. Especially good is the inclusion of content that throws doubt on the explanations, which brings a good sense of balance to the answer. The inclusion of a valid practical application is also commendable.

Breagha also demonstrates a dislike of bitter-tasting foods, and evolutionary theory would explain this as being sensible, as bitter and sour tastes are often indicative of the presence of toxins. This means Breagha not eating bitter and sour foods might help her not to get ill, or even die, from food poisoning. Plants often produce toxins, which taste bitter, to discourage people and animals from eating them. Herbaceous animals, like cows, will eat bitter plants, as they have evolved high tolerance levels to toxins contained in plant foods.

The candidate here successfully joins the experience of Breagha into outlining the evolutionary explanation concerning bitter and sour tastes. This is done in an informative, relevant and accurate fashion.

Go et al. (2005) looked at the prevalence of the bitter-taste receptor genes TR2 in humans and 12 other primate species and found humans have accumulated more pseudo-genes (dead genes) than other primates. This suggests that humans' bitter-tasting abilities have deteriorated more rapidly. Perhaps natural selection is now acting to reduce humans' ability to detect bitter tastes. Additionally, Merrit et al. (2008) found that people with the PTC bitter-taste gene have an ability to detect and reject a wider range of bitter, toxic compounds than those without the gene, which gives them an evolutionary survival advantage.

Research evidence concerning bitter tastes is given, but the studies quoted do not really join together to form any sort of commentary. This takes away from any sense of deeper understanding being conveyed.

The fact that there are only two taste receptors for sweet tastes but 27 for bitter tastes suggests that the need to detect potentially bitter tastes is more important than the need to detect sweet tastes. A practical application is to sweeten children's bitter-tasting medicines so they can swallow it.

The answer concludes with a couple of relevant evaluative points, but again they seem a little disjointed, which takes away somewhat from their effectiveness.

Feedback

14/16 marks. Focus is on the two food preferences mentioned in the question, which for the time available, 20 minutes, is probably a sensible decision. There is a good balance between the degree of descriptive and evaluative material, though the evaluation is not always used completely effectively. An attempt is also made, as the question requires, to include reference to the experience of Breagha.

Exam tip

6 marks would be available here for descriptive content and 6 marks for evaluative content, with a further 4 marks for the application of Breagha's experience to the answer. Therefore care should be taken to generate sufficient material, and no more, that permits access to all of the different types of marks available.